CONTEMPORARY KOREAN SHAMANISM

CONTEMPORARY KOREAN SHAMANISM

FROM RITUAL TO DIGITAL

LIORA SARFATI

INDIANA UNIVERSITY PRESS

This book is a publication of

Indiana University Press
Office of Scholarly Publishing
Herman B Wells Library 350
1320 East 10th Street
Bloomington, Indiana 47405 USA

iupress.org

© 2021 by Liora Sarfati

All rights reserved
No part of this book may be reproduced or utilized in any form or by any means, electronic or mechanical, including photocopying and recording, or by any information storage and retrieval system, without permission in writing from the publisher. The paper used in this publication meets the minimum requirements of the American National Standard for Information Sciences—Permanence of Paper for Printed Library Materials, ANSI Z39.48-1992.

Manufactured in the United States of America

First printing 2021

Library of Congress Cataloging-in-Publication Data

Names: Sarfati, Liora, author.
Title: Contemporary Korean shamanism : from ritual to digital / Liora Sarfati.
Description: Bloomington, Indiana : Indiana University Press, [2021] | Includes bibliographical references and index.
Identifiers: LCCN 2020057370 (print) | LCCN 2020057371 (ebook) | ISBN 9780253057167 (hardback) | ISBN 9780253057174 (paperback) | ISBN 9780253057181 (ebook)
Subjects: LCSH: Shamanism—Korea (South) | Religion and sociology—Korea (South)—History—21st century.
Classification: LCC BL2236.S5 S27 2021 (print) | LCC BL2236.S5 (ebook) | DDC 299.5/7—dc23
LC record available at https://lccn.loc.gov/2020057370
LC ebook record available at https://lccn.loc.gov/2020057371

CONTENTS

Accessing Audiovisual Materials   vii

Acknowledgments   ix

Note on Transliteration   xiii

Introduction   1
1. Gods on Stage: A Mediated Performance   20
2. The Changing Image of Musok in Films   59
3. Agendas, Power, and Ideology in Museum Displays of Korean Shamanism   94
4. Getting to Know a Korean Shaman through Television Representations   128
5. Shamans Online: Internet Promotion of Musok Practitioners   156
   Conclusion: From Ritual to the World Wide Web and Back   176

References   181

Index   201

ACCESSING AUDIOVISUAL MATERIALS

AUDIOVISUAL MATERIALS ARE AVAILABLE FOR this volume and can be viewed online at https://purl.dlib.indiana.edu/iudl/media/n59q08c02r. Information for each individual entry follows.

Item 1. Korean Shaman (무당). "Possession by the Spirit of Changgun," performed by Kim Nam-sun and Sŏ Kyŏng-uk. Seoul, 2007. Credit: Author and Shai Sarfati.

Item 2. Korean Shaman (Mudang 무당). "Objects of Worship: Material Culture in Korean Shamanism," performed by Kim Nam-sun, Sŏ Kyŏng-uk, and Kang Ok-hui. Seoul, 2007. Credit: Author and Shai Sarfati.

Item 3. Korean Shaman (Mudang 무당). "Writing Charms for Protection," performed by Sin Myŏng-gi. June 2007. Credit: Author and Shai Sarfati.

Item 4. Mansin Kim Nam-sun performing a tari-kut ritual to appease the dead. Seoul, August 2015. Credit: Author.

Item 5. Paksu Yi Sŏng-jae standing atop a sharp chaktu blade with a pig mounted on his back. Seoul, July 2014. Credit: Author.

ACKNOWLEDGMENTS

WRITING THIS MONOGRAPH WAS FAR from the familiar imaginary scenario of a lone scholar sitting in a dark attic, typing frantically while surrounded by scattered papers and books. It required long stays in Korea, meeting various individuals, and participating in religious events and performances. Many people and organizations contributed to the process of researching, writing, and publishing this book. Without their kind help, this project would not have been possible. I was fortunate to encounter and benefit from many inspiring scholars and teachers throughout the process. A few influenced my academic interests and perspectives in particular. In Israel, Prof. Atay Citron offered my first mediated encounter with the worlds of shamanism, rituals, and performance studies and has been a constant source of support during my research and writing. Prof. Yaacov Raz, who introduced me to Buddhism, also shifted my dissertation fieldwork plans when he suggested many years ago that Korea would be a worthwhile location for the research of contemporary shamanism. Prof. Irit Averbuch's classes and her exciting stories about her own research experiences stimulated my initial interest in Asian folk religion, and her constant encouragement has steadily supported me in the shaky path of academic progress. Prof. Haim Hazan enhanced my understanding about the interlinks between culture and society. Prof. Yoram Bilu taught me about the subtle aspects of ecstatic religion, and Prof. Asaf Goldschmidt has been a kind and knowledgeable adviser throughout my academic path and a tireless source of support. His comments on parts of this book were extremely valuable. My colleagues in the Department of East Asian Studies at Tel Aviv University offered attentive ears to absorb my laments on the long process of manuscript publication, which is full of ups and downs.

During my years at Indiana University, Bloomington, many people in the departments of Folklore and East Asian Languages and Cultures provided me with indispensable training, advice, and inspiration. Prof. Richard Bauman's thought-provoking comments and ideas always challenged my thinking and pushed my analysis further. The late Prof. Roger L. Janelli's professionalism, preciseness, and knowledge helped me cross several narrow bridges that I faced in the research process. Prof. Yun Kyoim has been a great teacher of Korean and a colleague in studying Korean shamanism. Prof. Michael Robinson instructed me in using critical perspectives while exploring East Asian cultures and histories. Prof. Thomas Keirstead supported me in my studies of Japanese history. Prof. Henry Glassie's ideas about artifacts were a formative influence, and I learned much from his virtuosity with words. Prof. Pravina Shukla's insights about museums and objects inspired my interest in a new discipline. Prof. Beverly Stoeltje's clear thinking enriched my ideas about performance and nationalism. Prof. Jason Baird Jackson's extensive knowledge of material culture theories and his constant faith in the importance of this research have been a true blessing. The late Prof. Nancy Abelmann of the University of Illinois, Urbana-Champaign, provided invaluable guidance before and after my dissertation fieldwork. Prof. Clark Sorensen of the University of Washington, Seattle, read and commented on the initial manuscript and provided me with lots of food for thought. Profs. John Lie and Theodore Yun Yoo taught me how to publish my first academic book in a junior faculty workshop sponsored by the Korea Foundation and the SSRC. Their clear thinking and sharp comments changed the manner in which I pursue my academic writing. Gilly Nadal refined the language and style of the book, and several anonymous readers took the time to read the manuscript and write detailed reviews that are greatly appreciated. Their efforts significantly helped shape the final manuscript. I deeply thank all these people for their kind hearts and their willingness to help this research project come to light.

During my fieldwork in Seoul, many people showed genuine hospitality and friendship by hosting me and sharing their knowledge. I am deeply indebted to all of them. Dr. Yang Jongsung (Chong-sŭng), who took me to my first shamanic rituals, has continued to acquaint me with the marvelous world of *musok* throughout my stays in Korea. Leading figures in the world of Korean shamanism were central to this project: Mansin Kim Nam-sun, Sŏ Kyŏng-uk, Chŏng Hak-pong, Sin Myŏng-gi, Yi Hae-gyŏng, and Yi Sŏng-jae. They invited and allowed me to join them in religious performances, pilgrimages, and daily life activities, which I enjoyed greatly and learned from tremendously. Their knowledge of Korea's traditions became my main sources of data for understanding musok and analyzing its various representations. Their advice and comments on my initial observations have been crucial for this book's conclusions. Several owners of religious goods stores provided me with advice about musok artifacts and practices. Among them, I especially thank Mrs. Yi Yŏng-nam, who always offered hospitality, knowledge, and a chair in front of her stove during cold winters. Mr. Kim Yong, a photographer and media specialist, shared with me indispensable information about the internet industry of musok. I also thank the community of Korean scholars whose work and insights enriched my observations of Korean culture, especially Prof. Yim Dawnhee (Im Ton-hŭi), who kindly shared her extensive knowledge of Korean shamanism and governmental culture-preservation policies. Although these people were my main sources of information, support, and inspiration, any mistake or misunderstanding that might appear in this text are my fault alone.

The research and writing of this book were made possible thanks to generous support from two Korea Foundation field research fellowships, the Richard Dorson dissertation grant, the Frieberg Center postdoctoral fellowship, and funding from Tel Aviv University. This book was published with the support of the Israel Science Foundation.

Finally, I wish to thank my family and friends for being there throughout the long and difficult process of my research, offering love, support, and even a few good laughs. I thank my parents Sara and Isidoro Donskoy for teaching me to believe in the goodness of this world, and my brothers Eran and Yuval for expecting and even requiring me to be quick and brave. Prof. Sharon Andrews offered help and showed me kindness when I needed them the most. My husband, Shai Sarfati, has been a wonderful companion in our joint adventures, and his support, encouragement, and dedication have been a deeply appreciated anchor in my life. Our beloved children—Sinai, Yahav, Halleli, Harel, and Tevel—shared my excitement at living in various places and cultures, adapted beautifully to every situation, and were a great team during several *kut* that we observed together. They fill my life with light.

NOTE ON TRANSLITERATION

I USE THE TERM *South Korea* or *Korea* to refer to the Republic of South Korea. Korean words are transliterated using the McCune-Reischauer system. Textual translations from Korean to English are mine. Please note that in spoken Korean, the McCune-Reischauer transliteration "sin" should be iterated as "shin."

CONTEMPORARY KOREAN SHAMANISM

Introduction

IT IS A WARM DAY in September 2009. A male Korean shaman (*paksu*) bows with his hands clasped together while chanting the names of Korean gods and spirits. He is wearing a traditional silk outfit of many colors, with a bright red vest, a skirt, and a wide sash embroidered with intricate, traditional patterns of a dragon, cranes, and pine trees. The observers recognize that this costume represents the spirit of a premodern Chosŏn Korea warrior. The traditionally attired shaman calls Yi Ŭn-jŏng to stand and come closer—she is a twenty-seven-year-old woman in a gray T-shirt who says she has been suffering recently from headaches and general bad health. She wants the paksu to check whether her illness might have a supernatural cause. He shakes a cluster of brass bells and recites several chants in ancient Korean to begin examining her. Then he steps onto two sharp blades that are standing on the floor. His feet are bare—and the knives' sharpness was tested a short while before, as he cut pieces of cloth by merely placing them on the edges—but he does not get hurt. The observers understand that he is protected by the supernatural powers with which he is communicating. He asserts that a spirit has just descended into his body, and he asks this supernatural entity to help solve the young woman's problem. Speaking in what some believe to be the voice of the spirit, he tells Miss Yi that she must become a *mansin*,[1] a practitioner of spiritual mediation. She puts her hands over her ears, refusing to hear it, and runs out of the room. Suddenly, she stops and collapses on the floor.[2]

It is well documented in Korea's tradition of shamanic initiation that practitioners of spirit-descending rituals (*sin-naerim kut*) usually fight this religious calling. Many are reluctant to become a mansin and carry the liminal status of this line of work. Miss Yi fleeing from the room is an expected response to the news that the experienced practitioner has just delivered. What might be less expected is the setting of this event. Rather than a mountain shrine, the practitioner's home, or Yi's own room, this event was filmed in a television studio in Seoul as part of a program called *Eksosisŭt'ŭ* (Exorcist). The practitioner was a real spiritual mediator, and the next televised episode followed the process of religious initiation through which Miss Yi would eventually become a devout adviser and diviner who can tell people what the spirits and gods wish to convey to them. Indeed, over the past decade, such televised reperformances of ancient folk practices have become widespread. Many Koreans, even those who do not believe in this creed and view it as artistic folklore at best, have encountered mediatized representations of mansin and paksu. Does that mean that the religious tradition has become fully commercialized? Has Korea's vernacular religion (*musok*) ceased to be a tradition performed in face-to-face encounters?

In this book, I discuss precisely these points. What are the boundaries between the folk religious ritual and its representation and reperformance in various commercialized, consumption-related contexts? Do practitioners still perform religious rituals per se, as they used to in many decades of documented folklore? Have representations of musok in national, commercialized, and screen-mediated settings altered the religious message passed on by the mansin? How have producers of representations affected the transmission of this tradition to Korean audiences? How have the material aspects of musok evolved to fit the new forms of representation? I examine the relationships between folklore and its contemporary representations in mass culture—particularly, in staged rituals, museums, films, television programs, and the internet. I discuss how technology is used and emphasized in representations of musok and how the public image of this vernacular religion has changed in different kinds of cultural products over the past half century. I consider how the politics of cultural exclusion and inclusion are manifested through the production process of such representations and reperformances. These complex relationships have increased the availability of mass-media representations, which are central to this indigenous tradition continuing to thrive in the hypertechnologized, urban society of Korea.

The contemporary mansin continues to communicate with the dead, pray on sacred mountains, heal, divine the future, prepare elaborate offering altars, tell of possession by various gods, and stand on sharp blades to please spirits of ancestors and the powers of nature (fig. 0.1). Daily folk rituals, such as regular offerings to the house gods, have declined in an urban reality of nuclear family or single residences; however, the more professional aspects of the vernacular belief in gods and spirits, mediated by a mansin, have been increasingly sought.

Fig. 0.1 A sumptuous *kut* offering altar, 2015, with Mansin Kim Nam-sun. Credit: Author.

Most urban Koreans have not practiced folk rituals since their early years, and when they fear supernatural interventions or in times of life-threatening crises, they look to professionals for help. The continuous presence of the mansin as a mediator is closely related to the constant exposure of Koreans to depictions of possession and supernatural interventions and solutions in public venues and the media. The numbers of mansin are not diminishing, and they engage in daily veneration in a hypertechnologized society within the huge metropolis of Seoul. Their long rituals, called *kut,* are colorful performances that combine various kinds of folklore, including traditional music, recitation of ancient myths, beautiful crafts and foods, theatrical stanzas, and ecstatic dance.

The stirring experience of the kut ritual might not be possible for readers of this book, and even in Korea, more people read about it or watch it on a screen than actually participate. Before the 1980s, Korean village life allowed many people to attend every ritual held in the area, whereas today's urban Koreans have to initiate a meeting with a mansin to experience kut firsthand (V. Brandt 1971; Janelli and Janelli 1982). Full rituals are performed in the outskirts of cities, mainly at rented shrines, and are not attended by large crowds; rather, the contemporary kut is usually a private matter, observed by only one or a few clients. Despite growing acceptance, this religious practice is still stigmatized as superstitious and menacing.

Although contemporary Koreans may lack opportunities for direct experience with musok, they can observe kut rituals that they do not attend in person. They can even participate in kut to various degrees through representations and reperformances in staged rituals, museums, films, television programs, and new media. Most Koreans I met who were not avid aficionados of musok still had many mediated encounters with this religious practice. Typically they had watched a famous film about a diviner, and many were well versed in the plot details of a television drama about a young woman who, to her dismay, discovers that she is bound to become a mansin. Even Koreans who have never met a mansin in person usually know how a ritual looks based on media representations of it. In fact, many of the religious, material aspects of this practice, such as offerings and paintings of gods, have maintained their premodern symbolism and form, even in short, mediated kut.

Mediation has been addressed often in late-modern societies. Appadurai theorized, based on observations in India, that "the idea of the mediant allows us to foreground the sociological point of view through specific materialities, such as housing, without ignoring other actants, and without insisting on the priority of whole human 'individuals,' of the classic variety" (2015, 228). Appadurai adopts the term *actant* instead of *actor* to draw attention to the fact that objects and other agency-exerting entities can be significant in producing meaning. Such actants, including the media, are discussed in this book as central to the recent changes in musok's image in Korea. If mediation is "a practice, assemblage, or site, as clearly distinguished from *media*, which is the specific historical technology of this mediation" (233), then separating the analysis of human and medium agency becomes unnecessary and superficial. This theory, which Appadurai calls "mediation assemblage theory" (235), is still developing but is useful for interpreting my holistic findings on contemporary musok representation. Consequently, this book moves from the behavior of human individuals to material representations and then back.

By addressing historical and contemporary musok in the context of the evolution of Korean society, I discuss the significant role of public representation in preserving Korean folklore and transforming it into national heritage. Moreover, I assert that for the practitioners and many of their clients, the religious efficacy of the ritual is still the most central concern, even when it is reperformed in short mediatized versions. Questions related to the survival of this old folk tradition and its ability to thrive are not new to the twenty-first century. They were discussed extensively during the fast modernization of Korea. However, previous research that focused on the transition of musok from premodern to modern times (e.g., Choi 1987; Kendall 1985, 1988) could not analyze the new mediums, such as television and the internet, that are now available in Korea—the internet did not exist, and television content was not as broad and diverse. More recent writings (e.g., S. Kim 2003; Kendall 2015) began to address how mansin handle new media and internet settings, but there has been no thorough analysis of the manners in which musok has been represented in different kinds of cultural productions. In this book, I look at various forms of reperformance, some screen mediated and some materially tangible, because each cultural and technological form offers a unique potential for creating and manipulating the public image of musok.

I begin by analyzing staged rituals and then focus chronologically on modes of representation—film, museums, television, and the internet—that mediate between the mansin and the public. I use *mediated* in the sense that the ritual is not a direct encounter between mansin and audience—technological means help communicate the performance's text and visuals to the audience. These technologies can involve the tangible presence of a mansin, as in the case of a staged ritual being amplified electronically and shown on a large screen simultaneously with the actual, on-stage occurrences. In other cases, mediation occurs through screens and the media more broadly.

Several processes have brought about this mediated presence of the practice. In the colonial period and shortly after independence, a national search began for a Korean identity that was unique within Asia and independent of foreign influences (Pai 2000). Many Korean scholars of the early twentieth century began to search for their origins in vernacular religion and nationalistic interpretation of archeological findings. In the 1970s, South Korea's rapid modernization and westernization led the government to revise its national identity based on rationalism and scientific logic, which seemed requisite for economic success. Unfortunately for musok, this New Community Movement (*saemaŭl undong*) included a campaign to eliminate vernacular practices of possession. Nevertheless, by the 1980s, people took new interest in their traditional practices through the *minjung* movement. Musok was again promoted as an ancient, well-preserved, and indigenous Korean system and became a part of the government's Intangible National Heritage program (Choi 1987; Yang 1994, 2004b; K. Yun 2013). That system of preserving tradition is also a response to the colonial period and the portrayal by Japanese scholars of Korea's culture—and musok, in particular—as inferior to its Japanese counterpart (Chŏn 2012; K. Howard 2006; K. Kim 2013; Maliangkaij 2013; Pai 2000, 2013; H. Sorensen 1993). Extensive documentation by the colonial anthropologists shows that the costumes used by mansin to attract spirits to the ritual place and the painted depictions of the various gods resemble early modern ones photographed in the nineteenth and early twentieth centuries (Sarfati 2010). Many religious, textual, and material qualities of musok have been preserved not only thanks to the government's acknowledgement but also because many people view it as their valued folklore.

At the same time, religious practitioners sought increased cultural visibility in the new social structures that emerged. Earlier generations selected mansin based on the artistry of their performance, their ability to elicit emotions, and especially their knowledge of the ritual style of a particular province (Choi 2003). Today's potential clients know little more than what they see in the media about the conventions of kut performance. Instead, they seek out mansin who have earned government designation as cultural assets or appeared in the media. Increased cultural visibility has improved the social image of mansin and mitigated their historic geographical and cultural marginalization. Moreover, mansin have been portrayed as politicized emblems of the Korean people who fought for democracy in the minjung movement since the 1970s (Abelmann 1993; K. Kim 1994; Tangherlini 1998). Since the Asian economic crisis in 1997, Koreans have been globalizing their cultural identity, focusing on national pride that relates to international forms of cultural participation, such as sports and pop culture (Campbell 2016). International events held in Korea, like the Olympic Games in 1988, the World Cup in 2002, and the Winter Olympic Games in 2018, required South Koreans to exhibit performative traditions, and musok was chosen as one of these forms (K. Yun 2006). In some respects, this trend led to increased nostalgia for imagined traditions and a glorious rural past, in which musok was perceived a cultural heritage to preserve (Kendall 2009). On more personal levels, the crisis resulted in cultural processes that drive young Koreans to frame their personal identities "based on new ties such as gender, sexuality, and class rather than on the ties of national units and nations" (Campbell 2016, 20). Such tendencies allow practitioners and clients to move away from considering musok as part of a national identity and to frame it within their personal choices related to well-being and self-fulfillment. Such trends have become increasingly central to the depiction of musok by scholars and the media.

Many mansin willingly accept these new kinds of encounters with scholars and media professionals as an integral part of the heterogeneous cultural arena of spirit communication, performance events, individually tailored cosmologies, and elaborate material manifestations. Echoing Richard Schechner (1981, 1985) and other performance theory scholars, my definition of musok includes certain practices and activities beyond the ritual itself, such as their depiction in the media. However, for many aficionados of Korean folklore, such practices seem destructive to the "authenticity" of musok traditions. An ongoing task of many Korean folklore scholars is the examination of a particular practitioner's level of fidelity to documented historic kut performances in order to ratify what is perceived as "original" musok (K. Kim 2000, 63). Such perceived authenticity might be lost in shortened versions of staged kut and filmed sequences. I discuss these debates in chapter 1.

Questions about new representational venues for musok have received little or no attention in existing scholarship. In the Korean language, most scholars have engaged in formulating norms for evaluating the authenticity of musok rituals (K. Kim 2000). Their books try to preserve specific regional styles or specific ritual characteristics through detailed description (e.g., H. Cho 1983; Hong 2006; T. Kim 1966; M. Pak 1996; Yang 2003). Most English-language scholars have focused on microlevel ethnography, for example, discussing networking and relationships within groups of mansin who perform together (e.g., Bruno 2002; Grim 1984; Kendall 1985), the commercialization of urban rituals (Kendall 1996), the life histories of particular performers (Harvey 1979; Kendall 1988; C. Kim 2003), and the particularities of change in ritual materiality and its wider spread (Kendall 2008; Kendall and Yang 2014). The theoretical approaches informing such scholars are mainly gender hierarchy reversal (Harvey 1979; Kendall 1985, 1988), ritual process and performance (Bruno 2002; Kister 1996; Seo 2002; Walraven 1994), and the effects of capitalism and urbanization (Bruno 2007b; Kendall 2009; D. Kim 2015; T. Yi 1996). Few, if any, have looked at musok from the perspective of the ethnography of communication and mass representation, as I do in this book.

KOREAN SHAMANS, POSSESSION, AND MATERIAL INNOVATION

Korean shamans are often denoted by the term *mudang*, which encompasses a variety of folk religion practitioners, including mansin and other kinds of spiritual consultants. While most Korean scholars, mass media, and public discourse apply *mudang* to both trance and nontrance practitioners, the terms *mansin* or *kangsin-mu* (god-descended mediators) more narrowly denote possessed practitioners such as the ones I discuss in most of this book. *Sesŭp-mu* are hereditary practitioners; they do not assert that gods descend into them and were not ordained after *sinbyŏng* (spirit possession sickness) (Yim et al. 1987, 369). This kind of initial possession serves as a demonstration that the practitioner was chosen by supernatural entities to be their mediators with people.[3]

The term *mudang* can be applied to both kinds of practitioners because before modern urbanization, regional traditions primarily determined which kind of mudang would be common in each place. Although hereditary shamans are not possessed, they still engage with and talk to spirits. Sometimes they harness the help of a spirit medium who can deliver messages from spirits and gods, although she cannot perform the kut ritual on her own. Furthermore, the dances and songs of this received cultural tradition are significant in terms of artistry because they are learned for many years, sometimes from a very young age. The artistry of the hereditary mudang tradition has been acknowledged by the government designation program. Such programs also designated several possessed practitioners, or mansin. *Mansin* means "ten thousand spirits" and refers to the polytheistic nature of this possession-based folk religion (Bruno 2002; K. Ch'oe 1978, 1981; Harvey 1979; Kendall 1985, 2009; T. Kim 1966, 1998, 1999; Seo 2002). All of my informants prefer this term over the derogatory *mudang*. Using the term *mansin* is more respectful and demonstrates knowledge of the various kinds of mudang.

Despite the clear scholarly identification of the two main kinds of mudang, the line between god-descended mansin and hereditary sesŭp-mu is blurry. When talking with mansin about their family heritage, I found that many had several mansin relatives, often a grandmother or aunt (see Kendall 2009, 106). Likewise, in hereditary shamanism, families lacking descendants who could continue the family's traditional occupation often adopted sons or daughters and taught them musok performance secrets (Mills 2007, 15, 99; M. Yi 2004). Korean media often overlook these distinctions and refer to both kinds of practitioners as *musogĭn* (people who practice musok professionally). It is worth noting that the term *musok* originated during the colonial period to describe shamanistic activities that the Japanese Government-General defined as nonreligious and primitive. Consequently, even this common term, which I use extensively in the book, is laden with value judgment.

Many publications in English dispense with local terms altogether in favor of the more global term *shamanism*. This term is also used in Korean academic discourse. For example, the private museum opened by Dr. Yang Chong-sŭng in 2013 to showcase his extensive collection of musok artifacts (discussed in chapter 3) is called *Shiamanijum Myujium* ("Museum of Shamanism"). By using Western terminology, many Korean scholars and government offices have created semiotic distance from the local, religious meaning of *musok* and have added a global dimension to this tradition. The term *shaman* derives from *saman*, used in Siberia to indicate a person who can talk to the spirits while in a state of trance. It has been extant in English since the seventeenth century and was applied to Korean mudang since the late nineteenth century (Bishop 1897/1970; Clark 1932/1981; Coulson 1910, 79; Laufer 1917; Lowie 1924). Ch'oe Nam-sŏn (N. Ch'oe 1927) introduced the term *salman'gyo* (shamanism) to Koreans following Torii Ryūzō and Czaplicka in 1927, and Akamatsu and Akiba (1938) took to using *shamanizumu* after World War I (Allen 1990). However, mansin do not practice the famous Siberian shamanic flight, in which the shaman's soul is believed to leave his body and travel to the sky or the underworld (Eliade 1964/2004, 5). Moreover, diagnostic physiological features of trance (e.g., rolled-back eyes, trembling; see Lewis 1971) are often absent in Korea's musok. Therefore, even the term *trance* has been debated in the Korean context (Hogarth 1998; Kendall 2009, 207n3). Ch'oe Kil-sŏng (K. Ch'oe 1999) concludes that trance cannot be the main characteristic of shamanism. Nevertheless, mansin clearly state that they embody the deities, and the moment of a god's entry is clearly marked in dance with a specific outfit that symbolizes that particular deity (D. Lee 1990).

Many Korean scholars through to the present (e.g., An and Yi 2014; Chŏn 2012) have been provoked to examine Eliade's statement that the Korean case "may be the result either of deterioration in traditional shamanism or influences from the south" (1964/2004, 462). This view by a world-acclaimed scholar was added to the "national embarrassment" caused by the typical derogative colonial perception of musok in comparison to Japanese folklore, as expressed by colonial ethnographers in the early 20th century (Akamatsu and Akiba 1938; Akiba 1957; Cruikshank 2005). To avoid the controversial nature of the term *shaman*, I apply the Korean terms *musok* for the practice, *mansin* for female possessed practitioners, and *paksu* for male ones.

It is difficult to assess authoritatively how many people practice musok in Korea. As discussed earlier, the definitions of *mansin* and *mudang* are themselves somewhat vague. I agree with estimates that more than 200,000 people provide this kind of religious service (K. Lee 2003, 222). Many thousands live and work in Seoul, as attested by my recent observations and interviews in the numerous shops that specialize in providing musok artifacts to practitioners.

The increased urbanization and impersonal commercialization of this mystical practice has come to include the ability to manipulate various promotional media venues and to be a "star" (Choi 1987, 2003). Some mansin have been accused of being too media-oriented or derogatively called "superstar shamans," implying that they have neglected their religious quest to some extent. Practitioners themselves rarely make such observations. One very famous mansin, who has been featured in newspaper articles and films, told me, "I view my media depictions as integral to my religious vocation. I feel that I can help more people in need when I appear in front of so many viewers and reveal the options that musok avails for solving personal problems." This, she said, is the core of her vocation as a *posal* (bodhisattva; a kind of Buddhist saint). She favors the title *posal* over *mudang* or *mansin*, because it references the Buddhist values of compassion and selflessness, which she says are encapsulated in being a mansin (fig. 0.2). These values, for her, do not conflict with her affluence, newly constructed home shrine, and televised performances. The various channels of mass media are viewed by the mansin as important venues through which to share her worldview, which is not necessarily accepted by all Koreans (Choe 2007).

It would be naïve to assume that before modernity, all participants in kut were religiously ardent. Indeed, historical data suggest that, since antiquity, musok has been a debated practice scorned by many. Some Confucian scholars viewed it as harmful, whereas some aficionados of court culture looked down at the folk performances. Detailed accounts of it were rarely written in premodern times. Korean Christians have mostly disdained spiritual practices that ignored the monotheistic god and objected to the role of mansin as healers and diviners. However, Christian missionaries wrote extensive descriptions of kut and musok cosmology in order to understand the people they wished to convert. Such contrasting views are also evident in the reaction to contemporary rituals, which marks them as continuous with Korea's premodern culture (O. Kim 1993). In my fieldwork I met many Koreans who, although they were self-proclaimed Christians, professed fear of avenging spirits, framing them in the newer religious terminology as "demons" or "agents of Satan" (see also in Guillemoz 1992, 117). Their expression of belief in the power of vernacular cosmologies demonstrates the deep influence of musok in Korea and the ongoing disparate responses to it. Some Christians even expressed fear of objects related to musok (Kendall et al. 2015, 126–127). Negative attitudes toward musok were especially manifest during the 1970s, when the dictatorship launched a campaign to eradicate superstition from Korea (Kendall 1988).

To sustain their tradition of communicating with the supernatural in an unsupportive cultural sphere, urban mansin increasingly participated in representations of their cult outside ritual grounds. Such innovative mediations of ritual experience have become widely practiced and call for academic attention. My purpose in this book is to explore these representations, the agendas and intentions behind them, and their evolution over time and in response to social change. The particular context in which mansin operate—as practitioners of an ancient, ecstatic religion and as active participants in a hypertechnologized, urban society—is fertile ground for exploring several enduring social questions. I investigate the adaptations and innovations of ancient tradition to fit within

Fig. 0.2 A field of Buddha statues, 2017, in Manshin Sŏ Kyŏng-uk's home shrine. Credit: Author.

Fig. 0.3 A catalogue of commercialized gods' painting, in a *musok* goods store. Credit: Author.

technologically enhanced performance venues, the purpose that each medium of mass communication serves in its representation of such practices, and the promoters and sponsors of contemporary spiritual practices.

As I will show in this book, the objects used by mansin exert agency through affective presence (as discussed by Armstrong 1981 and D. Morgan 2012). Accordingly, I also examine how commercialization—by which such artifacts are manufactured and marketed through impersonalized systems—has contributed to processes of adaptation and created new kinds of networks between people and materiality, as discussed by Latour (2005) (fig. 0.3).

Answering these questions contributes to a deeper understanding of the intricate ways in which the ancient is intertwined with the contemporary. Each kind of representation tracked in this book unveils a different kind of engagement among society, mansin, and technology. The representations reflect the influence of power structures and cultural norms constructed at the grassroots level. Governmental support has allowed mansin to perform in public, on respectable stages, and to be the subject of exhibits in educational museum displays. The public's willingness to accept this new recognition has allowed further proliferation into screen-mediated representations, created within the free market and private domain. Given the broad technological changes in musok performance in recent years, it would be easy to assume that essential content has been lost, or at least transformed. However, I argue the contrary—that the core religious message of musok ceremonies endures through technological innovation and reperformance in the media.

Reperformance is used here to distinguish between face-to-face religious practice, which is still performed in contemporary Korea, and its mediated appearances. In mediated representations, the mansin and other content producers pick and choose among the wealth of songs, dances, and prayers of the kut to make musok appealing to the public (Van Zile 1998). In the case of musok, reperformance does not necessarily mean a "an artistic result far removed from its claims to authenticity and presence" (D. Taylor 2016, 149). Rather, it serves other religiously understood purposes, mainly to make musok available to people who otherwise would not have access to it and to attract future clients who will eventually participate in private rituals.

As I will demonstrate, some aspects of the ritual that might be perceived as offensive by the general public are missing from museum displays and representations in films. Notably, animal sacrifice is rarely seen in such representations, although it exists in almost every kut ritual, especially those of possessed mansin. In contrast, the ritual sequence in which a mansin dances over sharp blades has become an expected, entertaining, circus-like part of most staged rituals or cinematic depictions.

For these reasons, I discuss such mediated, shortened, tempered rituals as reperformance of the quintessential long kut, which is still perceived as a local vernacular tradition, even when performed in Seoul (for shamans in other cities around the world, see Humphrey 1999; Van Deusen 2004). The mediation includes not only the technological means to put together ritual fragments into a screened version but also the content editing done in the process. The tradition undergoes adaptations based on several agents: the government or other official sponsoring institution, the interpreter or scholar who attests to the ritual's value, and the performing team led by the senior mansin. The agenda and expectations of each agent in the process determine the form of intervention in the ritual and its final, mediated representation. My main goal is unraveling these complex processes of producing representations.

FIELDWORK SITES AND RESEARCH DIRECTIONS

My fieldwork in Korea began in 2005. I looked into the world of contemporary musok, hoping to find out how practitioners maintained significant continuity in their performance and in what aspects they allowed changes and innovations to be introduced into their work. I planned to live in a rural area, where I thought traditional Korean life would be readily available. After visiting several villages to choose my location, I realized that musok was practiced more extensively in Seoul, and several rural mansin suggested that I would learn more about musok if I lived in the city. My initial plan for an "authentic" setting changed quickly, and I embarked on an urban ethnography. As often happens in ethnographic fieldwork, the field dictated how it needed to be investigated (Bilu 1997). I returned for more extensive fieldwork in 2007 and spent a year in Seoul. Since then, I have met my informants during summer fieldwork sessions and have followed their online activities and media representations throughout the years.

During my initial research into this intriguing world of meaning and performance, I was concerned mainly with the perceptions of practitioners and clients. It turned out that the clientele of mansin in the city was much broader than I expected. Highly educated Korean men and women in their thirties and forties were reluctant at first to speak of their own consultations with mansin and acknowledged these only once we developed better acquaintance. One friend had her marriage date fixed by a mansin. Others met a mansin before giving birth, opening a new business, or sending a child to university entrance examinations. Still others sought out a mansin after the death of a parent or spouse.

During my research, I established close contacts with five mansin teams and followed their performances and daily practices in Seoul and during their travels across the country for mountain pilgrimage, folk performance festivals, and sponsored rituals. As I observed rituals and walked through sacred mountain paths and shrines, I came to see the scope and liveliness of this folk tradition. I conducted multiple, in-depth recorded interviews with ten mansin and informally interviewed thirty more. I also interviewed thirty musok clients and conducted numerous informal interviews with Koreans between twenty and sixty years of age about their perceptions of media representations of musok. To learn how mansin organize to create their public image, I visited the offices of a large mansin association, participated in several of its events, read its newsletter, and followed its internet portal. Conversations with the officials of this mansin organization and with various media people who take part in the musok internet arena contributed to my understanding of mediated processes in the musok world.

All my mansin informants asked to have their proper names cited within the ethnography; none chose to use a pseudonym. This reveals the evolution of mansin's social acceptance and their awareness of scholarly writing as a means to achieve public and international visibility. In past research, many mansin preferred to maintain their anonymity through the use of nicknames or false names (Harvey 1979; Kendall 1985; Choi 1987; C. Kim 2003). Mansin–client relationships used to exist in a local community context rather than an urban, mass-populated environment. A mansin was unlikely to become famous, known by name in various places and walks of society.

Research into cultural spheres such as television and the internet has increasingly become inseparable from anthropological, sociological, and psychological analysis of various societies (R. Howard 2005, 2006, 2011; Shields 1996; Miller and Slater 2000; Turkle 1995). Media research often shows the instrumentality of media in informing the public about the world, particularly those areas in which audiences do not possess direct knowledge or experience (Gamson and Modigliani 1989; Happer and Philo 2013). The ways in which audiences actively interpret media representations have also attracted research efforts (Morley 1986; Lull 1990). I chose to analyze media representations after noticing that, through them, contemporary mansin have more ample opportunities to control and shape their public image than their premodern counterparts did.

WHY REPRESENTATION MATTERS

In my first visit to a large-scale kut in the summer of 2005, I was stunned by the overwhelming sensuality of the experience. The offering altar was laden with fruit, sweets, incense, meat, fish, rice, and paper flowers in all colors. Colorful paintings depicted gods and spirits (Yun and Cho 2004; Zo 1973, 1978, 1980). The music of gongs, drums, pipes, and cymbals played constantly (P. Yi 1982). I had read descriptions of kut and seen them in documentary films before visiting Korea, but these representations did not prepare me to see the carcasses of a cow and a pig in the shrine's front yard or to watch them cut to pieces and placed on plastic sheets three feet away from me on the floor of the shrine room. The day-long event felt not only like the material manifestation of a polytheistic belief system but also like a fantastical set from a melodramatic film. For a vegetarian like me, the sight and smell of piles of raw meat in the small, crammed shrine room were hard to bear, especially in the humid heat of August. I have gotten used to such scenes but still find the sumptuous kut performance a sensually overwhelming experience that would be difficult to replicate without a face-to-face encounter.

It is not surprising that film producers take on the challenge of transferring these performances into screened depictions. The colorful and aesthetically rich audiovisual qualities of kut make it worth filming; however, not all the sensual aspects can be encapsulated in such portrayals. The screened reperformances hint that the actual ritual would be worth watching, and many viewers of screen representations look for actual performances to observe—combining both mediated and first-hand experience of musok. Some also venture into a personal encounter with a mansin and a face-to-face, private consultation. Several interviewees described such a path from a random, screen-mediated encounter to becoming regular clients of a mansin or, in some cases, mansin apprentices.

Screen culture can interact with off-screen life. Mediated depictions of musok exist within an extensively practiced, living tradition. This case is different from mediated depictions of other traditions, such as straw sandals or the preparation of thatch roofs, that are no longer practiced for the same ancient purposes. In the case of musok, a person who is exposed to screen representations is reasonably likely to find a real mansin close by. Because of their extensive internet marketing, a short online search leads the interested observer to a one-on-one meeting with a mansin. If the mansin can advertise herself as an officially designated performer, her chances of obtaining new clients increase significantly. In all cases, having their representations circulate in public increases the visibility of practitioners and their folk traditions.

Most mansin believe that a ritual is pleasing to the spirits, regardless of its context and the clients' beliefs. As the ones who negotiate with the supernatural, the mansin care primarily about the practice and its effects. Within the audience, we can see diverse attitudes toward the performances' religious aspects. Some believe wholeheartedly that spirits can help after being appeased through dance, music, and offerings. Others merely enjoy the virtuosity of the performance and its entertaining aspects. This diversity in reactions is a traditional trait of musok. As Henry Glassie states, "tradition is the creation of the future out of the past," and relates to the "many ways people convert the old into the new" (1995, 395). In musok, new technology is embraced, but its cosmology, mythology, and symbolic forms remain the same. Each practitioner chooses how to move into various new media environments.

The main changes in the staged and mediated representations are that the audience is more diverse and less able to interact with the representations and with each other. These changes are significant, but they do not alter what the mansin deem crucial—that people communicate with the afterworld and the supernatural realm to decrease suffering and create a more harmonious life. This was their mission in premodern times, and it is still what they undertake to do. In my work with Korean spiritual practitioners, I found that—far from changing their message in response to mediation—mansin adopted media specifically in order to extend the proliferation of existing musok messages. Korea's national identity, Korean-ness, and social hierarchies have changed significantly over the years, and thus the roles of mansin with respect to these macrolevel concerns have changed. However, it is not material innovation but rather general social and cultural processes that have determined the changes that musok has undergone in the past century. These processes determine the aspects of musok textual, artistic, and ideological content that are included in the public culture, which are excluded, and how. In this book, I describe these patterns in detail.

This book is not strictly an anthropological study of how mansin have adapted their traditions to urban contemporary settings, nor is it entirely an analysis of mass media renderings of reperformed ancient rituals. Rather, it connects individual behaviors with broader cultural production and image-making processes to understand the contemporary thriving of a performative, textual, and material religious tradition—one that has been significantly affected by social and cultural debates. This interdisciplinary approach is particularly appropriate in analyzing not only textual dimensions and institutions but also various social groups' interests in these different representations of musok. In the twenty-first century, Koreans have moved to mostly urban settings and increasingly formulate their worldviews through interactions with various forms of mass media. New lenses are needed to understand how mansin and other Koreans perceive this ancient tradition. Without understanding the representation of musok in these technologically innovative platforms, one might be led to believe that mansin still live in small communities, unaware of global and local cultural changes.

BOOK STRUCTURE

My major goal in this book is to demonstrate that the liveliness of musok has been maintained and its social acceptance increased thanks to its intensive representation in nonreligious settings. The five chapters discuss mediation, mediatization, and representation in relation to five mass culture venues, showing the potential of each for cultural production.

Each representation works differently in this respect. Staged rituals, discussed in detail in chapter 1, are prepared for large audiences but are a one-time event. Such public events are the result of governmental and regional preservation efforts that have created a new kind of kut. In these shortened reperformances, audience members often come to observe rather than participate, and the mansin can communicate with them only to a limited extent. However, through artifact manipulation, song, dance, and prayer, mansin strive to maintain a form that has been transmitted orally for generations.

The change of attitude among the ruling and intellectual elites, from considering musok a dangerous superstition to a valuable cultural asset, led to more favorable inclusion in recent films. Filmed reperformances are more enduring than live performance and extend the audience but are devoid of the sensuous elements of the actual ritual. In chapter 2, feature films, documentaries, and experimental films are discussed to demonstrate the evolving image of musok in this mass media venue.

Museums, discussed in the third chapter, offer a three-dimensional depiction of musok objects, but they are mostly static and do not allow audience engagement. In addition, without real mansin to add their perspectives, the exhibit's effect depends heavily on the curator's stance toward musok. I discuss how and why musok has been given a central role in some museum exhibits but not in others.

Increased public interest in the personalities and lifestyles of individual mansin led to the creation of television programs about them, and these are discussed in chapter 4. Television programs grant mansin the possibility of shaping their public image by participating in reality shows or appearing as guests on talk shows. For television audiences, such representations create the opportunity to learn what mansin do, think, and feel and how their services can be of use in various contexts.

In the mid-1990s, when the internet became an efficient channel for business promotion, many mansin established their own websites. This was the natural result of urbanization, increased competition, decreased neighborliness, and the digitization of Korean society in general, as demonstrated in chapter 5. The internet is different from other representation forms discussed in the book because it combines the longevity and broad audience of other screened representations with options for communication between audience and mansin and increased agency for practitioners. While watching television, audience members can imagine that they are viewing a mansin in her daily routine and actual practice, but they have to content themselves with a passive stance. Internet platforms allow both observation of and interaction with practitioners.

This book elaborates how a prosperous, contemporary mansin works with clients seeking good health, financial success, or communication with their deceased loved ones and also with film directors, scholars, television producers, museum curators, and internet website designers. The new representation platforms grant the female mansin, traditionally marginalized for both profession and gender, more ways to exert agency. Paksu, the male practitioners traditionally stigmatized in multiple ways, seem to be represented significantly more in the media than in real life. In all the media discussed, the mode of culture production affects the level of personal engagement of both mansin and audience with the materials presented. However, it does not change the religious message of musok or diminish the significance of ritual efficacy and communication with the supernatural. By looking at both the micro and macro levels of such cultural meaning production, readers can grasp how deeply and broadly musok is embedded in contemporary Korea and how new social and technological developments have ensured the continuity and cultural centrality of this folk religion and art form.

NOTES

1. The majority of mansin are women, but around a fifth of all such practitioners in Korea are men. Male mansin are often addressed with the specifically gendered term *paksu*. In Korean, mansin and paksu are used both as single and plural forms.

2. The terms *South Korea* or *Korea* refer to the Republic of South Korea. Korean words are transliterated using the McCune-Reischauer system. Please note that the transliteration *si* is pronounced in spoken language as *shi*. Several terms, such as *mansin* and *kut* are used as both singular and plural, following the Korean language rules. Textual translations from Korean to English are mine.

3. *Sinbyŏng* is constructed from the words *sin* (gods and spirits) and *byŏng* (illness or sickness). Although the term's translation as "traumatic possession sickness" by Laurel Kendall (1985, 27) has been used in research about musok, I prefer "spirit possession sickness" because not all the practitioners that I know view sinbyŏng as trauma. Some consider it a hardship that was necessary in a process of personal growth. Not all the symptoms of sinbyŏng involve possession, and several scholars have argued that *possession* is a term that generalizes a plethora of local contexts and practices (Boddy 1994). For most mansin, sinbyŏng is related to possession, and they clearly differentiate between two types of godly grasps of their bodies. In the sinbyŏng type, symptoms of possession are uncontrollable, whereas *sin-naerim* (descending of the spirits) includes the alternative states practitioners experience after initiation, with mostly controlled and functional behaviors. Therefore, I prefer using the term with its emic meaning, as a sickness created by gods and spirits, with a process that involves all kinds of behaviors that are viewed as out of the ordinary, painful, and related to spirit possession. To retain this specific meaning, I chose to use the nontranslated Korean term *sinbyŏng*.

ONE

Gods on Stage

A Mediated Performance

SEPTEMBER 20, 2007—IT IS NOON on a cloudy autumn day in Seoul's World Cup Stadium Park. This urban green space lies beside a huge stadium built for the 2002 World Cup games. Loudspeakers play traditional Korean music at full volume in the park, and a pond at the far end of a paved yard reflects the gray sky. A folklore performance of *musok* (Korean shamanism) will take place here this evening. Spirits and gods will deliver their divinations and blessings to the gathered audience through a human agent, the *mansin* (a Korean practitioner of possession trance rituals). She will mediate between the human world and other realms of existence.

Communication with the supernatural will be achieved not only through the skillful performance of the mansin but also through various intermediaries. Some are other professionals, such as a professor who will interpret the traditions shown onstage for the audience. Other mediating agents are material and technological. The spirits will be represented and appeased using various artifacts. Their presence and acceptance of ritual offerings will be mediated through the manipulation of objects. The voice of the mansin will be heard through a sound amplification system, and her dancing figure will be seen in the dark night thanks to electric lights. The whole event will be broadcast online for audiences who cannot come to the arena for the performance. These technologies mediate between the performer and audience in ways that augment the unassisted, private, traditional practice. The space inhabited by the supernatural entities, the mansin, and the audience will be filled with these objects, mediating the performance in many respects.

Near the ritual space, three cargo vans come to a stop. Five men jump out and begin unloading boxes, trays, metal and wooden poles, rolls of cloth, bundles of goods wrapped in pink handkerchiefs. Several women supervise the operation and give orders about where to put what. Within half an hour, the area is full of goods, and the vans leave. The men begin setting up a metal frame, about fifteen feet high and thirty feet long, close to the waterfront. They seem to be trained in erecting it, as they proceed in an orderly and synchronized way. The frame's parts have been prepared to fit together smoothly; it takes less than an hour to put up this impressive metal structure.

After discussing whether the structure is stable enough, the constructors begin opening green plastic tubes and taking out rolled polyester sheets, about two feet in width. The workers climb tall ladders and hang these rolls on the frame. They let go of the edges and then, with a crisp sound, the polyester sheets unfold, revealing colorful paintings of gods and spirits. Each sheet has four different paintings, organized vertically, that are large and can be seen from a distance (fig. 1.1). They are copies of paper paintings used in Korean shamanic rituals (*kut*) as representations of the various spirits. These supernatural entities will soon be invited to the event, which has been well advertised and will be covered by the media. This evening's performance will be a public *Ch'oe Yŏng changgun tang* kut ritual by the famous mansin Sŏ Kyŏng-uk, who was lately given the official designation of preserver of this ritual. The illustrious performer has not yet arrived at the scene. She trusts that her helpers are knowledgeable enough to mount the background set for her staged kut.

The event organizers have scheduled the ceremony to begin at 7:00 p.m., and there is much to accomplish before then. From the top center of the metal frame, where painted gods and spirits begin to rule the scene with menacing eyes, the men tie colorful cloth strings in red, green, blue, yellow, and white. The strings are spread out and attached to metal poles some three hundred feet away. They form a sort of circus tent over the performance area and the audience's seats. The men arrange thick ropes from the edges of the frame to the sides of the ritual arena, and tie paper decorations onto them. These decorations mainly consist of a metal circle covered with colorful, patterned paper, from which paper streamers with god paintings hang down to create beautiful mobiles about two feet in diameter and four feet in height. Their edges flare in the windy afternoon, just above people's heads. These objects do not have a specific religious significance, but they line the boundaries of the religious space with representations of supernatural entities. Other banners with musok symbols and texts, such as "State Mansin Sŏ Kyŏng-uk," are hung along the ropes, adding an official appearance to the scene. This ritual is sponsored by the Ministry of Culture, and the artifacts deliver two messages: one based on a religious worldview and the other a construct of national identity (Brennan

Fig. 1.1 God's paintings printed on polyester sheets, 2007, World Cup Stadium, Seoul. Credit: Author.

1990). These messages communicate to the audience that the mansin is endorsed by the state and thus mediate a separate social story of identity politics and hierarchies related to musok practice (to be discussed in chapters 2 and 3). These objects mark the mansin's importance and emphasize the value of the coming performance.

Each mansin's ritual artifacts reveal her agency and power. Over the years, Mansin Sŏ has developed elaborate musok props suitable for outdoor venues, contributing a unique ingenuity to her kut staging. The polyester painting imprints were prepared to be rolled and carried conveniently, and they are rain and tear resistant. Most other practitioners have not adopted new materials in lieu of traditional paper paintings, even in rainy outdoor conditions, for fear that "fake pictures" might be perceived as a corruption of the traditional staging norms. However, in this ritual, no audience members or attending scholars remarked negatively about this innovation. One reason for accepting the printed images is that the mansin owns the original hand-painted paper versions and displays them in her home shrine. The most outstanding spirit among the thirty-three hanging paintings is that of General Ch'oe Yŏng (1316–1388), of the late-Koryŏ historic period, copied from a specially ordered centerpiece painting in Mansin Sŏ's home shrine. He is painted with full armor, helmet, and sword. Colorful and awe-inspiring, General Ch'oe will preside over the event. He will also possess the mansin during the ritual and be the main provider of blessings for the audience, as he has been for Mansin Sŏ since her initiation. He is perceived as a very strong spirit-guardian in musok.

Mansin Sŏ owes the central position that she has achieved in the world of musok not only to her powerful supernatural protector but also to her own outstanding personal charm and abilities, which have resulted in a powerful and wealthy clientele. She regularly conducts consultations and rituals for politicians and businesspeople, and the large, official, black cars used by such figures can be seen daily in her front yard. Other mansin often state that she has earned her fame and fortune thanks merely to her indisputable physical beauty. However, her serious work and professional performances attest to more than that. She owns an impressive collection of musok goods of the Hwanghae-do style that she practices, and she conducts rituals mainly in her home shrine in Yangju-si, a twenty-five-minute car ride from Seoul's city center. She maintains a personal web page to promote her public rituals and has been the topic of several newspaper articles (K. Kim 2008; Chŏng 1999).

Mansin Sŏ's absence from the stage setup before the important World Cup Stadium performance is no coincidence. It is the deliberate choice of a conscious performer in a society characterized by theatrical commercialization. In preindustrial Korea, spiritual practitioners closely supervised the preparation of ritual altars in villages—as they continue to do in private contemporary rituals. Their main responsibility was to appease gods and spirits. Accordingly, they had to make sure that the offerings and decorations were prepared in accordance with custom. They worked in teams of initiated practitioners, apprentices, musicians, cooks, butchers, and general assistants. Producing a contemporary, urban, staged ritual also includes many other professionals. Positive evaluations of today's urban mansin depend not only on her spiritual abilities but also on her production skills. These include prop management, voice amplification, lighting, media coverage, scholarly legitimization, and public relations. The success of today's performance will rest in part on Mansin Sŏ's ability to enable direct communication between humans and supernatural powers and in part on professional staging, including her makeup and meticulously cropped hair. Consequently, while her stage crew prepares the place where gods, spirits, and humans will meet within a few hours, another team of hair and makeup artists perfects the mansin's appearance for this large-scale ritual.

The venues of public rituals have changed from village squares and palace halls to open-air stages, museum performance halls, and festivals. The production has increasingly incorporated technological innovation and mass media. The mansin no longer negotiates her performance directly with her client but through the mediation of academic referrals and festivals, at least in the case of staged performances such as the one discussed here. She no longer faces just a small audience with a few assistants and musicians; she reaches a large audience, many members of which she will never meet in person, using stage mics, camera angles, lighting, and makeup. Nevertheless, the sincerity with which performers treat the supernatural remains intact. Attention to detail, careful planning, and ritual expertise are still the driving forces of the mansin team, and for many viewers, ritual efficacy is still the main concern. In these respects, new performance venues have not changed the kut ritual's cultural and personal message—that people and supernatural entities can and should interact in a controlled cultural performance, supervised by possessed practitioners who are well versed in the traditional scripts of the rite.

MEDIATING BETWEEN KOREANS AND THEIR HERITAGE: THE KOREA TRADITIONAL PERFORMING ARTS FESTIVAL

The Korea Traditional Performing Arts Festival reveals how mediation by the government and academia affects choices of the particular rituals to be presented, selection of the mansin performers, and criteria for authenticity. I observed the first such festival at the World Cup Stadium Park on September 20–23, 2007. The location was central, easy to reach by public transportation, and spacious enough to allow a large ritual stage to be constructed. The second festival also took place at that location, and the third took place in the National Museum of Korea in 2009.[1] In the 2007 festival brochure, the Minister of Culture and Tourism, Kim Chong-min, introduced the festival by relating it to broader political issues: "Among our splendid traditional arts, traditional performing arts are the most eminent treasures. . . . They can be developed as a cultural tourism product if their presentation is modernized. . . . Regrettably, however, such precious performance arts have been eliminated from people's lives as a result of Japanese colonization and rapid industrialization. . . . The festival is the first attempt of its kind, organized and supported by the government to promote traditional arts, aiming to reach broader audiences nationally and internationally" (Traditional Performing Arts Festival 2007, 3). The text reveals the important role of politicians in financing and legitimizing large-scale ritual displays such as the one discussed here. This kut ritual, and other kut rituals that were performed in the two subsequent nights of the festival, was paid for by the Ministry of Culture and Tourism. Along with other music and dance performances, the festival offered the Korean public a free opportunity to experience staged reperformances of their folklore and heritage. The mansin acknowledged this event as a reperformance, because she viewed it as continuous in form and content with previous rituals, albeit shortened to a mere few hours for this event. For the festival organizers, the reperformed aspect was articulated in the title "Traditional Folk Art Festival," which assumed that presenting various folklore activities required archiving them as folk arts by curators and experts. In this respect, bundling kut with secular folk arts allowed the minister to overlook the ritual's religious aspect, and the mansin could publicly call the gods that she venerates to a sumptuous feast.

Her dispensation to do so derived from her performative rather than spiritual abilities, but her personal interest in participating included religious intentions. The festival was a venue in which to celebrate with the supernatural, as Mansin Sŏ expressed before the event: "In such a respectable event, the gods like to come and promise blessings to the country, Seoul, and the people. In the past, the queen used to sponsor such events, but now there is no queen to support out tradition, and the government has to supply the means." Sŏ referred to the common assumption that in the nineteenth century, Queen Min (the last queen of Korea before the Japanese occupation) was a sponsor of musok (Simbirtseva 1996; Walraven 1998, 57–59). Sŏ's dedication to the religious symbols of the event, the meticulous preparation of the offerings, and the elaborate costumes and props brought in several trucks from her home shrine demonstrate that she took the event's efficacy seriously. However, such a religious agenda was not reflected in the words of the Minister of Culture and Tourism. Each person expressed a different meaning of the same phenomenon because of the inherent quality of such a symbolic practice: it can be interpreted in various manners and encapsulates the differential meanings simultaneously (Turner 1967/1972, 1969/1977, 1982/1992).

For Minister Kim, economic and diplomatic interests in tourism and international acknowledgment intertwined with national pride related to the dark period of Japanese colonization and to more recent Western influence. This combination of needs is why the kut ritual, a controversial religious activity, could be included in a formal government event as a demonstration of artistic ability and cultural uniqueness. This presentation was seen not as a religious ritual per se but rather as an artistic reperformance of ancient heritage, with new patriotic intentions. This stance was also professed when the performing mansin hung banners that endorsed her as a national shaman (narat mudang).

In Western contexts, reperformance has been questioned as a legitimate means of exhibiting art, and some critics have disputed the benefits of a direct experience over a screened version of past performances (R. Morgan 2010). In contrast, the official, public, and religious discourse around Korea's traditional arts has been widely appreciative of such staged reperformances as a viable means of preserving and promoting national heritage. Banned and ridiculed in the past, kut was presented in 2007 with monetary sponsorship from the state and academic approval from the festival's advisers.

Each evening of the festival featured a kut ritual representing a different region. Dr. Yang Chong-sŭng, a government employee who served at that time as a senior curator at the National Folk Museum, was in charge of the arrangements for these three kut performances. Since the beginning of my fieldwork in Korea in 2005, I have worked closely with Dr. Yang, who introduced me to various mansin and showed me his extensive collection of musok art. Thanks to our research collaboration and friendship, I was able to observe the festival's planning process. My observations convinced me that, in this case at least, the fact that the ritual was to be performed onstage mattered. In private rituals, a client meets a mansin for a specific purpose, and the mansin selects the ritual based on her skill set and her diagnosis of the client's problem. Illness requires help from certain, mostly Buddhist spirits to whom dance and vegetarian oblations are offered, whereas business problems often call for the intervention of the spirits of generals such as the aforementioned Ch'oe Yŏng.

In contrast, in the festival setting, the interposition of the government and academia occasioned different choices. The most elaborate staging was expected, and the most colorful practices, such as dancing on sharp blades, had to be performed. There was no specific problem to solve for a client, and the main purpose of the performance organizers was to manifest onstage the richness and virtuosity of Korean folklore. Although the mansin perceived this performance as religious, she was well aware of how a staged ritual is expected to be performed. She met these expectations wholeheartedly because it was an opportunity to extend her clientele and potentially inform more people of her spiritual skills in case they need them in the future. Every mansin invited to participate in the festival accepted this opportunity.

It was not easy for Dr. Yang to choose only three performers among the many that he knew. He chose Sŏ Kyŏng-uk in part for her veneration of General Ch'oe Yŏng, a historic warrior who died as a national hero in 1388. His fabled strong character and bravery assured his status as a powerful spirit in the musok pantheon. He is also widely perceived as the protector of Korea; therefore, his ritual opened the festival with supernatural favor. Many mansin venerate this mythical figure, but Dr. Yang had to choose only one to participate in the festival. He chose this particular performer mainly for her attested knowledge of old ritual texts and protocols. For a regular client, this aspect of the mansin's performance is far less important than her reputation for solving her clients' problems. Still, being acknowledged by scholars certainly has its effect on the popularity of mansin, as discussed by Laurel Kendall (2009) and Chongho Kim (2003). The festival brochure noted that the ritual's purpose was "national prosperity and the welfare of the people" (Traditional Performing Arts Festival 2007, 12). Staged kut are often dedicated to such general causes. An ancient tradition of village- and court-sponsored rituals for prosperity and health has been transformed into a new form of government-sponsored rituals that serve both a religious purpose and the national need for indigenous cultural icons that can be presented as entertaining performances.

The Ministry of Culture and Tourism sponsored the kut described here as part of a festive celebration of Korea's uniqueness and affluence. A large-scale outdoor ritual costs more than ten million Korean won (equivalent to approximately $10,000), so it is crucial to find the proper ritual to sponsor. The need to choose among the thousands of performance teams that practice in Korea calls for evaluation criteria and professional evaluators. The government wishes to sponsor kut only if they are proven to be "carrying great historic, artistic or academic values" (CHA 2012).

Terminology such as "authentic shamanic rituals" has been used by many scholars of musok; however, it must be treated prudently (Kendall 2009; D. Kim 2012; K. Yun 2007). Authenticity is judged according to different criteria depending on context and participants, and contradictory meanings and usages are produced (M. Anderson 1982). Paradoxes and conflicts arise when some members of a community look for sincerity and ritual efficacy, whereas others are concerned with "historic accuracy" (Shea and Citron 1982). Rituals and performances that have no antecedents in history have often been called "invented tradition" (Hobsbawm and Ranger 1983), "folklorism" (Šmidchens1999), or "fakelore" (Dorson 1973, 199–200). These labels suggest that some traditions are genuine and properly performed, whereas others are fake or contemporary inventions with little value. Hobsbawm and Ranger's book *Invented Tradition* treats technological innovation as contradictory to performance authenticity. However, invented tradition as a value judgment has been challenged by many who prefer the term "living tradition" (Handler and Linnekin 1984; Vlastos 1998).

Still, contemporary musok events in Korea might well be labeled with these derogatory terms by some critics, given all the technological innovations noted.

Even musok practices that could be labeled "genuine old ways" (following a continuous line of transmission), according to Hobsbawm and Ranger's (1983) terminology, have often been restructured to fit new contexts and interests. An undisrupted line of transmission does not necessarily mean that contemporary performers are mere bearers of ancient traditions. Just as with Sponsler's observation regarding European rituals, kut are produced in our times as "creative shaping to meet new ends" (2004, 98).

Nevertheless, in the Korean context, the ends remain religious. The mansin that I have observed performing officially sanctioned, staged kut invariably espoused deep sincerity and considered such short public performances part and parcel of their religious beliefs. They made sure that the rules and customs were strictly followed for the religious success of the ritual and used most of the ritual fee to purchase the best offerings and hire the most accomplished musicians. The audience also treated staged kut seriously by donating money for personal blessings and waiting eagerly to receive the special ritual foods and lucky charms that were distributed at the end. Moreover, most mansin have undergone the same initiation process used in premodern musok practices.

Mansin Sŏ was initiated in her late thirties, although other mansin had been telling her since she was a child that she had been chosen by the spirits to be their servant and to facilitate communication between people and the supernatural. Old men with long, white beards used to appear in her dreams and visions, asking for food and water. However, she refused to accept her destiny several times, despite scary near-death experiences. A common belief in Korea is that refusing to serve the spirits leads to misfortune and even death. However, the life of a mansin tends to be so heavily stigmatized and full of uncertainties that most mansin tell a similar narrative about their efforts to avoid this calling. Mansin Sŏ knew that being a mansin would probably hamper her marriage prospects and, later on, those of her daughters. She changed her mind only when her young daughter began to hear strange voices and have dreams of old men with beards. Mansin Sŏ understood these events as a sign that the spirits had given up on her and decided to go after her daughter. With the intervention of an experienced mansin, she bargained with supernatural entities to become a mansin herself in order to release her daughter from the grip of this profession. Her story resembles those of many mansin that I met and those represented in the media, where mansin tell about fearful encounters with spirits before their initiation as spiritual healers (as this book will show).

Mansin are believed to interact regularly with the dead, whose hands are said to be "thorny." This means that spirits might harm people even unintentionally—for example, when hugging their living descendants. Mansin are supposed to know how to control their negotiation with the supernatural, but ordinary people are afraid of becoming afflicted. Once she finally accepted her destiny as a spiritual practitioner, Mansin Sŏ was not afraid that the spirits might harm her. Her personal identity narrative is the expected one for a practitioner of musok, part of a long line of such historical and folkloristic reports. In terms of religious belief and initiation process, musok has mostly maintained its traditional structure.

Changes in ritual protocol should not be taken as evidence that kut is an inauthentic or invented tradition, because tradition is a constant process of adaptation and change in social and cultural norms. Moreover, in contemporary musok practice, abundant evidence shows continuity in ritual artifacts and text alongside many changes and deviations from older recorded ritual processes (Sarfati 2014). While the word *tradition*, in everyday speech, often refers to the petrified remnants of a glorious cultural past, contemporary research in folklore and culture requires a more precise approach. The term *tradition* is better understood as signifying ways of using the past to create a future and the means to incorporate various interpretations of the past into present social conditions (Glassie 1995; Handler and Linnekin 1984).

As a part of the adaptation process, and in accordance with contemporary lifestyles, the Korea Traditional Performing Arts Festival's staged kut was shortened to fit the festival's schedule, enhanced by microphones and light projectors, interpreted by a well-known Korean folklore researcher, and filmed for future reference by various parties, including me, the visiting anthropologist. The festival created a connection between people and their heritage, vernacular religion, and traditional arts.

MATERIAL MEDIATION BETWEEN PEOPLE AND THE SUPERNATURAL: MOUNTING THE RITUAL SET

Not only do musok practitioners consider their mediated festival performances authentic, if brief, interactions with the gods, but onlookers also perceive these performances as authentic religious rituals. This perception is achieved through the effect of material performances with and of objects. Bruno Latour's (2005) actor-network theory accounts for the complex ways in which nonhumans—including objects—can have agency and efficacy that are revealed in their interactions with people. According to Latour, such interactions include interpretation and manipulation that mark the role of each human and object in the creation and consumption of culture. This idea can help us understand how musok ritual sets affect both practitioners and audiences.

By manipulating objects in the ritual space, the mansin and their helpers produce and direct specific interactions between objects and people. The success of the performance is determined, in part, by the objects and their arrangement. An attractive setting will result in more interest by the audience and in beautiful documentation products; a large audience will promote the chances of future invitations to perform such sponsored events. Folklore scholars will appreciate adherence to traditional norms of musok, and pleasing the spirits will enhance the supernatural abilities of the mansin. Therefore, the material aspects of the ritual should not be taken as background but as a significant performance in their own right. Images of gods and spirits, which are hung on the metal frame, affect the audience members' internal ideas about the supernatural (D. Morgan 2012). Korean gods appear in human shape in their material depictions, which helps ritual participants understand why the gods require food and drink as offerings and why they enjoy song and dance. The bells, fans, and costumes used by practitioners produce a sensual, emotional impact through music and dance. The offerings on the altar create a festive atmosphere and indicate reverence for the supernatural entities. Consequently, preparing the stage and decorating the ritual set are meaningful parts of the ritual process. Likewise, during the performance, people in the audience donate money to thank the mansin and the spirits for their service and thus shows appreciation for musok through material means.

Following Latour's emphasis on the agency of objects, Robert Oppenheim (2007, 481) suggests focusing on spatiality. The place where people and spirits interact during kut is arranged in a plan that begins affecting the audience's feelings even before the mansin steps onstage. When audience members approach the stage, they are surrounded by symbols that are not seen in other cultural contexts. These local emblems of the Hwanghae-do ritual style are understood by the observers as their own heritage, as opposed to global products. The canopy that the stage crew set above the audience joins performers and observers together in this material experience. Most of the dancing is conducted onstage, but the colorful strips of cloth extended above the audience members connect them symbolically and sensually to the artifacts on the stage. The spatiality of ritual props offers an especially elaborate display of spirit representations in paintings and an abundance of offerings. Such material, nonverbal layers of the kut transmit extensive musok knowledge, compared with other regional styles in which few paraphernalia are used. A small home or rental shrine provides the proper cozy setting for a private kut, whereas outdoor stages of public rituals require different spatiality to enables the audience to feel a personal connection to the staged event (C. Yi 1983).

Most audience members that I interviewed during the World Cup Stadium kut understood that this ritual was a *representation* of musok in a public festival context. They all knew that a kut is usually held privately and for a specific reason, such as healing, whereas the festival used the religious reperformance for its artistic value rather than as an efficacious ceremony. Still, when asked whether they thought that the mansin really spoke with spirits, most interviewees stated that she probably could. One elderly woman recalled her past experience with such rituals: "When I was a child, my neighbors held kut for three days. Their grandmother had just died and they wanted to send her spirit off peacefully. Back then I knew the mansin who lived at the edge of the village. She knew how to talk to the spirits but did not dance as beautifully as this one. I think that kut now are much more beautiful and elaborate. Look at all these paintings!"

With these considerations in mind, we can go back to observing Mansin Sŏ at work. We can appreciate the complex mediation of her performance while acknowledging that this mediation does not rob her performance of religious content, for either herself or her audience. The next steps taken to arrange the material aspects of the ritual demonstrate how the visual dimension of the performance maintains traditional symbolism.

Back at the pond, people are busy. The female supervisors hurry toward the elevated main stage, at the other end of the yard. There, Mansin Sŏ has just arrived and is preparing for a sound rehearsal. She wears a simple, traditional *hanbok* (formal Korean dress) with a light yellow skirt and white top. A young stage technician attaches a wireless microphone to her chin and waist. She is clearly accustomed to this kind of equipment and gracefully collaborates with the technician's instructions while checking that all the technology works. She holds a fan, brass bells, and a scarf of green, yellow, and red cloth. These are the bare essentials of a musok rite (Yang 2001). On the stage beside her, an elderly woman beats an hourglass drum (*changgu*), a ten-year-old apprentice beats a large brass gong, and a pipe player puts much effort into blowing his Korean pipe (*p'iri*). Everyone has microphones set before them; during the ritual, they will be heard shouting encouragements, speaking, echoing the mansin's words, and singing. Unlike the pond-side stage, this main stage has not been set for a kut. The background is decorated with large silver curls and a screen with the festival's logo. The kut sequence will be only one part of an extensive presentation of various folk performances in the opening ceremony. After that, the kut will move to the altar at the other end of the yard.

The sound rehearsal is also the first part of the religious ritual. The space is purified of evil spirits, and the purpose of the ritual—peace and harmony for the nation—is chanted. With a playful smile, clearly enjoying the loudspeakers, Mansin Sŏ adds a brief performance of the popular folk song *Arirang*, widely considered a national emblem. Stage workers and passersby stop and listen to her clear voice. She likes being center stage as she gets ready for her public performance, collecting compliments and preparing for the audience to come.

When the rehearsal is over, the female helpers rush to the pond-side stage. They begin unwrapping cloth bundles and setting the offerings on altars. The team includes various roles and statuses. Mansin are distinguishable from their helpers by their traditional bun (Tchokchin mŏri) hairdo and are perceived as authoritative figures in determining the stage setting and the order of offerings on the altars. Female cooks and other helpers usually wear their hair in a permanently curled, short hairdo, like most middle-aged Koreans, and are treated with much less respect by the festival employees. A cook's request to move a loudspeaker away from where the fruit should be set receives little attention, but when a mansin helper requests the same adjustment, it is granted. Even young festival staff members would not risk enraging a spirit or her embodying agent. The top decision-maker is Mansin Sŏ, but she has just retired into a small plastic tent to refresh after the rehearsal.

The altar-mounting team takes a long piece of white cloth and covers wooden shelves that were placed below the metal frame—the task is difficult because the wind is blowing hard. Trays with fruit, fried eggs, rice cakes, and sweets are set along the shelves beside brassware holding paper flowers of various sorts. Alas, the clouds that have hovered all day begin to open, and the helpers run in the drizzle to cover the offerings with large, clear, nylon sheets. Luckily, the paintings on the frame are waterproof. The festival management has prepared two white plastic sheds nearby, and some offerings and goods are carried to safety. Mansin Sŏ has joined to supervise the scene and looks worried. As it rains harder, her helpers urge her to stay under cover, so as not to smear her makeup. After all, her professional appearance is crucial to the success of the event. The men are still busy draping a red cloth over a wooden staircase connected to a six-foot-tall platform. This platform will hold the *chaktu* knives on which Mansin Sŏ will stand and dance during the ritual's climax. She will use the staircase to reach the high posts on which the knives will be waiting.

As the rain fades back to a thin drizzle, the assistants remove the plastic covers and resume their work. Everyone says, "God bless clear plastic covers." Modern technology and products helped beat the weather and kept the offerings fresh and presentable. The women finalize the altar preparation. Silk flags in red, green, yellow, white, and blue are rolled together and stuck into a brass bowl of uncooked rice. During the ritual, they will be used to divine the future for audience members. Bouquets of paper flowers are brought back from the sheds and placed symmetrically along the top shelf: pink flowers for the general, multicolored for the ancestors, and white for vegetarian Buddhist gods such as the *samsin* spirit of child conception. Other offerings, including three-fold paper hats, rice cakes, rice wine, and liquor, are arranged to please the various spirits that are invited.

Two women slowly stretch a long piece of white paper lace behind the offerings, as a kind of a screen, and behind several smaller altars. These are set around the performance arena for any wandering spirit that might be attracted to the place by the noisy kut music. One of the small offering tables is carefully carried to the main stage, away from the metal frame and large altar. The *madang* (outdoor performance space) is ready. Passersby gaze at the colorful array of decorations and ask when the performance will begin. They seem to know what this setting represents and show interest in attending.

Hanbok, wooden hourglass drums, brass gongs, bamboo pipes, paper lace, and piles of fruit and sweets all mark this setting as a traditional one. The decorated hairdos, chaktu platform, and paintings of various entities mark it as a musok event. These elements are part of the visual dimension of this performance, which has maintained its traditional symbolism. It can be recognized even by those who do not know this performer. Yes, there are microphones, plastic covers, and vehicles, but do they mark a deviation from the message of the village kut? Most of my interviewees at this festival were interested in the performance both as entertainment and as a nonharmful, traditional divination. Unlike private rituals, which are concerned with a specific problem, this event is for general blessing—similar to premodern, public, village rituals held during festivals. It is safe to assume that the premodern audience believed in the ritual's efficacy only partially, just like the contemporary crowd. Some were Confucians who loathed superstition, and others might not have trusted certain performers. Today, some are devoted Christians, and others embrace atheism. Still, many people in the audience participate eagerly by offering donations and asking for personal blessings and divinations. For them, the main message is the centuries-old religious concept about the connection between humans and other entities.

APPEARANCES MATTER: DRESSING FOR THE SHOW

The appearance of the ritual stage, the mansin's skill in dance and song, and the quality of the musicians are crucial for the spiritual message to earn respect from the audience, scholars, and media representatives. All must look simultaneously well prepared and authentic. In the World Cup Stadium yard, the workers run back and forth with last-minute altar adjustments. Mansin Sŏ, her senior apprentices, and the elderly drummer enter one of the sheds that has been arranged as a dressing room (*taegisil*). They change into their ritual uniform—a white hanbok with a crimson sash. A uniform for the performing team has become a common sight at staged kut but not in private rituals. The outfit is supplied by the presiding mansin and constitutes a significant part of the mansin assistants' compensation. Each hanbok of such quality costs at least two hundred thousand South Korean won (about $200), and the assistants seem pleased to receive it. The uniform is also another marker of the professionalization of kut teams, which might result from the increased commodification of Korea in general. The hanbok uniform symbolically differentiates the mansin from other workers, helpers, and crew members. In village kut, everybody knew each other, and mansin did not need such external markers to tell the audience who they were. In urban, staged kut, mansin follow the Korean norm of wearable group markers to legitimize their work and increase public acceptance (M. Clifford 1994, 10–11). The tendency to standardize outfits is also visible in the costumes worn to represent the various possessing spirits during kut. Because most such outfits are bought in stores, they are similar from one mansin to another and allow the audience to recognize which spirit is "attending" the feast by its conventional outfit. Commodification has homogenized the visual vocabulary of musok to some extent. It has certainly allowed mansin to purchase ritual artifacts with much more ease at large specialty shops.

The men bring handfuls of such costumes to the shed, and the female apprentices hang them on metal racks. Mansin Sŏ is being helped into the full attire of a *sansin* (mountain god) over her hanbok. This elaborate costume, which has become one of the trademarks of musok, includes a red skirt and jacket with long, white sleeves; a wide, embroidered sash; a tall, red cylinder hat decorated with lines of paper flowers; and a painted yellow fan (fig. 1.2). The fan depicts gods and spirits and features long cloth streamers with brass bells tied to their ends. This outfit is very common in the Hwanghae-do style of kut, named after the region in North Korea from which it originates. Similar costumes appear in photographs taken by Japanese ethnologists in the early twentieth century. However, contemporary versions are prepared by professional costume designers with sewing machines and synthetic threads. In fact, some owners of musok goods stores have become advisers to mansin about which outfit to buy and how to wear it (Sarfati 2010; Thacker 2004).

Mansin Sŏ's collection of musok costumes (*sinbok*) is impressive. She has dozens of expensive silk and polyester garments hung proudly in special closets

Fig. 1.2 Mansin Sŏ performing as *sansin* (mountain god), 2007, World Cup Stadium, Seoul. Credit: Author.

with large glass doors, on permanent display inside her home shrine in Yŏnju near Seoul. When I first visited her shrine in 2005, tightly packed garments occupied a ten-foot-long closet. By 2007, the closet had doubled in length, and later, storage rooms were used for the surplus sinbok that she had accumulated. Most of these costumes were special-ordered to fit her taste and the spirits' inner image while adhering to accepted norms for their appearance. In long, private rituals, Mansin Sŏ often uses forty or fifty costumes in one day. In a typical kut, mansin can embody several dozen spirits, each represented by a different costume. In small-scale kut by new practitioners, the same outfit might be used to represent different supernatural entities. This was the case in many village kut when Korea was a poorer country. For Mansin Sŏ, any kut is a good opportunity to use and display samples from her exquisite costume collection. However, the World Cup Stadium ritual is short, only a few hours long, and she had to choose only ten costumes from her collection. She chose the very best ones she owns, because they must look dashing in the photos and videos. In contrast, in private rituals, I have seen her wear some older items that had sentimental or spiritual value despite their worn looks.

The attendants finalize Mansin Sŏ's makeup and rush to the festival's main stage. Meticulous elaboration of outfits and grooming has been a crucial part of Sŏ's technology of the self, à la Goffman (1959), which she has established and practiced throughout her career. The men have already set a small altar with brassware, paper decorations, and some fruit and rice cakes. An hourglass drum, gong, and cymbals are also positioned to the right. The preparations are over. Although the religious ritual actually began at the sound rehearsal, now is the moment that everyone has been waiting for. The audience has settled into the stadium's paved yard, and the official event is about to begin. Staged kut are about audience and publicity, as well as gods and spirits.

STAGED CONNECTIONS BETWEEN AUDIENCE AND MANSIN: KUT AS THE OPENING PERFORMANCE OF THE FESTIVAL

The distance between audience and performers is one of the most significant differences between village and staged kut. Under the lights, the performers can barely see their observers. It makes this event more of a spectacle than a communicative performance. This is fine with the festival planners because most items in the program are not supposed to include direct interaction between performer and audience. The mansin, however, finds ways to communicate with audience members and stir them to action within the ritual. The audience is seated in front of the main festival stage on folding chairs. Many hold their umbrellas ready for the inconsistent rain. The chairs are separated from the stage by a black rope, which allows the twenty photographers and media people to choose their positions. I spot an acquaintance, a photographer who is an ardent fan of Mansin Sŏ. I meet him often in Mansin Sŏ's public kut performances, and see his photographs featured in promotional brochures that are handed out at these performances. Thanks to our acquaintance, he arranges for me to join the photographers in the best position, closest to the stage, although I do not possess the name tag required to enter the restricted zone. Everybody is ready and alert for the beginning of the show. They might not all be keen on the event's religious meanings, but they want to see some dancing and singing.

The front rows are full with an organized group of middle-school students in their formal black-and-white uniforms. They are noisy, bored, and impatient. They joke and play with each other. When the commissioner of the Korea Traditional Performing Arts Festival, the famous *samulnori* drummer Kim Tŏk-su (Kim Duk-soo), goes onstage to announce the beginning of the event, he needs to hush them.[2] It is 6:00 p.m. and getting dark. Kim Tŏk-su wears a Korean-style silk suit in green and yellow with puffed pants and a jacket with large, black buttons over a white silk shirt. In his short introduction, he thanks the audience for coming and adds his appreciation of their patience with the difficult weather. He announces that the formal opening of the festival will be at 7:00 p.m. In the meantime, Mansin Sŏ Kyŏng-uk will open the event with blessings from the gods and from the famous deceased General Ch'oe Yŏng, who is her supernatural guardian. The audience applauds, and some of the children even shout in the manner now common in pop-music concerts. One might find this behavior unsuitable for a religious ritual. However, the mansin seems happy to see that the younger audience is showing interest, according to their age-group norms.

Kut is the main performance in this part of the festival. However, many younger audience members are not well acquainted with the revered spirits, structure, and meaning of kut rituals. Therefore, the introductory note by the famous drummer bridges the distance between the kut tradition and the audience through a more often viewed popular genre, the samulnori. The enthusiasm and respect shown by Kim Tŏk-su serves to legitimize the kut. This enables the spectators to better appreciate the religious performance that they are about to observe. The choice of the drummer—as the festival's host and announcer—boosted publicity for the event, and the audience's passionate response to his appearance shows that the festival planners made the right choice.

The drumming begins. Mansin Sŏ steps to the front of the stage. Behind her stand four of the white-clad apprentices and the ten-year-old male apprentice dressed in a blue coat and black hat. Kim Tŏk-su takes off his shoes and, guided by one of the apprentices, bends to pour water into small brass cups on the altar. He lights incense sticks, bows, and prostrates himself twice in front of the altar; then, he bows once to Mansin Sŏ and goes to the back of the stage. He is the patron of this ritual, as the commissioner of the festival. Therefore, he must pay respects to the gods and spirits who are about to bless the event and the whole nation.

The mansin begins to sing ancient *muga* (kut chants).[3] She promises that Ch'oe Yŏng *Changgun* (General) will bless the audience and the nation with strength and health. She spins over and over again. The edges of her coat float in the air, forming a silhouette similar to an open rose. The music gets faster and faster as the mansin turns without stopping. She is in full control, a half smile on her lips. The musicians look attentively at the dancing woman, waiting for her hints about when to stop the music and when to change the rhythm. When they come to a halt, Mansin Sŏ joins her palms and rubs them with her long, white sleeves. Then she lifts her arms so that the left sleeve covers her face and turns around slowly. Suddenly, she drops down to her knees. She lifts her hands toward the sides of her head and tosses the sleeves over her back. She prostrates herself, laying her forehead and the palms of her hands on the ground. The dramatic dance captures the audience's attention. The schoolchildren stop their chatter. Even without knowing the actual meaning of these movements, the observers realize that something serious is happening. The performing team has made its sincerity visible.

In the background, the musicians play slowly. An apprentice hands the mansin a beautifully ornamented brass brazier with smoking incense sticks. She turns it around in front of the altar and puts it down. Then she stands. As the music grows faster, she starts spinning, her red robes creating a gracefully moving circle around her. Then she begins jumping up and down and moving her hands vertically. The drummer shouts encouragement. With a sharp look, Mansin Sŏ signals for her attentive assistant to hand her colorful silk flags and two wooden sticks with white paper streamers. She opens each flag and shakes it, and then, holding them close to her chest, she begins spinning again. She stops to signal her assistants what she will need next, and they run backstage as she unfolds the flags, holds them together, and jumps on one leg. The drummer shouts more encouragement. All smiles, Mansin Sŏ rolls the flags together, and her apprentices return, along with Kim Tŏk-su.

The audience cheers and claps at Kim's appearance. The drummer bows and picks a flag stick from the bunch that the mansin holds in front of him. In musok, possession trance is induced by drumming and swirling, and the red-clad mansin is apparently possessed by the mountain god. In the performance of experienced practitioners, there are rarely feats of dramatic possession with rolled eyes or shaking body. Kim bows his head, with the palms of his hands held together in front of his chest, as Mansin Sŏ unfolds the flag. He chose the white one—a good omen. She spins around and around with the white flag, showing it to the audience. Then she adds it to the other flags and passes the whole bunch several times behind her back. Again, she invites Kim to choose a flag. They play tug-of-war with the sticks—he tries to pick one, and she pulls it away from his fingers. Eventually, he chooses a stick, and she shows that he has picked the red flag—another good sign. The mansin smiles happily as she jumps on one leg with the red flag held high.

She rolls the flags back together, turns to the audience, and signals to my acquaintance, the photographer, to approach the stage. He chooses the stick of the white flag. So far, all the flags predict the success of the event. It is believed that when the gods are happy, they let people choose flags that forecast wellness. Green and yellow flags would be the worst omens and might require a whole set of fortune-reversal chants and acts. The mansin transmits these religious meanings to the audience through facial expression and dance movements. When she unfolds the flags, she looks worried. When an auspiciously colored flag appears, she dances and smiles, waving the flags with apparent satisfaction. Most Koreans use various divination services, even as a pastime, and mainly before the new year (Sarfati 2017). Thus, the audience understands that a good omen has just been announced and is happy with the mansin.

The serious meanings of flag divinations are also apparent in private rituals. In a private kut performed for a childless couple by another practitioner on August 7, 2014, the husband kept choosing green or yellow flags. The young mansin became very worried and ordered the helpers to light two torches. She covered the client with a woolen blanket and began to swirl the torches above his head. When he chose another green flag after that treatment, she took a live chicken and rubbed it on his face and body, chanting various shamanic verses of muga. She then threw the chicken to the ground to get rid of the bad luck. The next flag he chose was white. This is why, in 2007, on the World Cup Stadium stage, Mansin Sŏ continued to smile as she spun with the white flag held up. Three good omens in a row signal strong supernatural approval.

The people chosen for the flag picking in a kut are usually the event's sponsors—namely, the people who hire the mansin team. In this staged kut, the drummer serves as sponsor because he represents the festival authorities. However, the choice of an unknown photographer as the second flag picker is less predictable. In this case, the mansin's personal interests come to the fore and obscure formal hierarchies. The photographer is an avid follower, helper, and professional team member whose artistic photographs Mansin Sŏ uses regularly. She does not hire him; he attends voluntarily, out of sheer fascination, and he rarely photographs the kut of other performing teams. Letting him pick a flag after the famous samulnori drummer, onstage in such a public ritual, shows him great honor. It is the mansin's way of thanking him for his efforts, acknowledging his significance to her enterprise, and allowing him a taste of recognition. His warm and excited response proves that Mansin Sŏ has achieved her goal in this deliberate act. To the audience, he might seem to be an arbitrary choice among the general crowd. To the performing team and the photographer himself, it is a promotion in status—a token of appreciation that will last long after the event. The mansin's acknowledgment will certainly increase his loyalty to her and ensure the continuous flow of quality kut photographs.

Nevertheless, the drummer and the photographer are not the ritual's main stakeholders. Kim Tŏk-su is the formal representative of the festival, but he is not the one who decided what ritual to include or which mansin would perform it—indeed, he did not even know Mansin Sŏ personally before this evening[4]—nor did he sponsor the ritual financially. He is a public figure hired to represent the Ministry of Culture for this event. The photographer is also not a typical kut participant. He helps to document the event, and the moments that he captures with his lens are used later in Mansin Sŏ's promotional brochures, business cards, website, or in the mass media. Consequently, in this urban staged kut, the two figures honored in the festival's opening are professional mediators between the mansin and the public. These mediators are instrumental in the dissemination and publication of musok and its beautiful arts. In premodern settings, mansin relied on promotion by old village ladies looking for a cure to supernaturally imposed diseases and misfortunes. Today, men who belong to other social spheres serve as producers of the mansin's fame. Without them, her song and dance would reach fewer viewers. Audience members who are used to short, modern, staged performances might think that this is the climax of the performance. However, the flag divination sequence signals that the ritual has just begun.

As the music fades, Sŏ gasps for air after the strenuous dance. She tells the audience that the spirits are pleased with the feast and will bless them with health and wealth. The cymbals resume their beat, and the pipe and drums join in. Sŏ unfastens her red hat and hands it to the assistant, who proposes a green silk coat for the mansin to wear over her red outfit. A shiny, black hat tied under her chin completes the costume of a respectable man of the Chosŏn era (1392–1910). The mansin is about to be possessed by an ancestor. She spins, holding up the two white paper sticks, as her green and red coats swirl together in the air. She walks back and forth, swaying a bit to the sides as she goes. Behind her, her assistants prepare additional costumes from her exquisite collection. She changes into these costumes to invite other spirits. She speaks while possessed with each divinity so the audience can follow the meanings of the dances.

The drizzle strengthens, and the spectators open their umbrellas. Onstage, all continues with little or no attention to the weather. It starts to rain hard, and Mansin Sŏ changes her outfit again—this time to a blue vest and a black hat with a red tassel and a peacock's feather. This costume recreates an official's uniform of the Chosŏn period, informed by traditional norms of kut, academic research in costume history, and pop-culture imagery from historical television dramas. Sŏ jumps up and down and swirls while holding a pair of brass knives. A dramatic peak in the music drives her to arch backward and stab her chest with the knives. She turns around and faces the back of the stage, then she arches her back and points the tips of the knives to her chest. She repeats the same act facing the remaining two directions. She goes on with her dancing while shaking the knives in her hands. Following her hand signal, the musicians stop playing. She stands still and says with a deep, manly voice, "I will bless you with good health and prosperity. All the people in this country will enjoy peaceful days." A few more swirls and she stops again and thanks the audience for their attention, saying in her own feminine voice, "A kut is really fun, isn't it?"

That final statement conveys the general atmosphere of this part of the staged kut. It is a popular event with many young observers and deserves a light ending. Humor is also prevalent in the official opening performance of the festival that follows on the main stage. Many dancers and musicians showcase different performance styles, including some perceived as nontraditional. "B-boys," who developed a unique version of the American breakdance style, twist their bodies beside traditional fan dancers and performers in Buddhist attire.

As the main stage fills with dancers swaying to a hybrid of traditional Korean tunes and Korean pop songs, the kut moves to the secondary stage near the pond, where the large altar was set throughout the afternoon. A more serious and detailed presentation will be possible there. The altar, the musical instruments, and the rest of the kut paraphernalia are cleared from the main stage and carried to the waterfront, where the team gets ready to continue the ritual after the fireworks show concludes. Mansin Sŏ takes off her red outfit but remains with the white hanbok that she wears underneath. Her assistants seat her in a comfortable chair and ask her to relax while repairing her makeup—some of it was smeared by the rain while she danced on the main stage.

PROFESSIONAL MEDIATION: SCHOLAR AS INTERPRETER OF THE RITUAL'S MEANING

An older audience of people between thirty and sixty years of age, accompanied by young children, attends the pond-side ritual. The many god paintings on the metal frame create a more religious atmosphere. These ritual sequences are planned to be longer and more efficacious in appeasing the spirits. The full altar discussed earlier was prepared for this more solemn ritual, along with the platform holding the chaktu blades on which the mansin will dance. In this more serene atmosphere, another mediating professional joins the performance team. Professor Yang Chong-sŭng, who organized this part of the festival, will help explain the ritual's meaning to the audience. He will incorporate this ritual into the festival's agenda of heritage construction and transmission, and the mansin will keep her role as a religious performer. No foreigners attend this event, which was promoted in Korea as an event of national identity formation rather than a tourist show. The middle-school students who formed a large portion of the audience at the mainstage kut are missing. Many of them stayed to watch the hybrid music and dance performance there.

It is 8:30 p.m. The large offering altar, discussed at the beginning of the chapter, has been set at the center of the low stage area. The musicians sit to the right. Over her hanbok, Mansin Sŏ is dressed in the basic musok outfit: a long blue vest with delicate embroidery on the chest. She is holding a tray with food offerings for wandering spirits. Rice cakes, fruit, and rice wine should pacify random spirits that might be attracted to the lively music. Although many spirits and gods will be invited personally to join the party throughout the ritual, other spirits might be around that are hungry and unattended. Therefore, before the main rites begin, several small offering altars are set around the performance stage. The mansin lifts a side altar high in the air, swaying in all directions. She announces in a respectful tone, "Any hungry spirit is welcome to eat and enjoy the meal." Then she places the tray at the far corner of the performance area.

It is important during kut not to provoke any supernatural power in a way that might afflict the patrons of the event. The power of supernatural entities is never underestimated in musok, and measures are always taken to prevent any mishap. The material aspects of pleasing the spirits are retained, even in shortened, public rituals such as this one. Interestingly, most mansin agree that spirits and gods understand the need to skip sacred texts and dances in order to fit the tight time frame of a festival setting and still bless the audience assembled for the brief ritual. However, those powerful entities would not accept lesser offerings, especially at such grand occasions. Material expressions trump song, dance, and music in their full manifestation during staged kut. Form and décor are imperative parts of musok, and objects play a central role in its cosmology. This rich materiality is on display at all times before the ritual's audience.

In front of the altar, holding two wands covered with white paper streamers, Mansin Sŏ dances and jumps while the senior female drummer calls all spirits to enjoy the party. The streamers will help channel spirits into the mansin's body. As the mansin prostrates herself several times in all four directions, Dr. Yang carries a microphone stand to the straw mat. His black suit jacket distinguishes him from the other performers and assistants, who are dressed in plain, casual clothes or traditional outfits. As noted, he is a senior curator at the National Folk Museum, a scholar of musok, and the one who chose and coordinated the kut performances for the festival. These roles entitle him to introduce the ritual. He waits for the mansin to finish her veneration gestures with a bow to the audience and then takes over:

> I really thank [the performers] very much. Let's thank them for their lovely dance. [The audience claps.] Now, I am a committee member of the Korean Traditional Performing Arts Festival, and my name is Yang Chong-sŭng. [He bows, and the audience claps.] Thank you so much. Today, right now we have a bit of rain, but we will proceed with our plans. We are presenting the traditional ritual, the original form of the belief of the Korean people. We have the main stage, where Kim Tŏk-su already gave his opening note, and here we have the kut shrine. Now that you have waited so long, the ritual will last a few hours. I would like to introduce the plan for this kut shrine. Today you came here to see the ritual, didn't you? You can also tell your family and friends that tomorrow we will have a Seoul-style ritual.... Soon, Mansin Sŏ Kyŏng-uk will return to the stage wearing the mountain god's outfit. He is her guardian spirit. She will also show you many other spirits, and the last one will be General Ch'oe Yŏng, and then she will also climb the chaktu blades.... I know that it is raining now, but I ask you to stay the full hours, and in the end you will receive many festive rice cakes. This is for today. Tomorrow umaji-kut will be presented here.

Dr. Yang introduces himself as an unquestionable authority. He is a scholar and a committee member of the festival. He legitimizes the whole event. He awaits the audience applause that confirms his position. The mansin team welcomes his introduction, although it is an interruption of the ritual's flow. It is thanks to him that they have been invited to perform tonight, and his official speech adds a serious aura to their work. His brief explanation of what should be expected in the coming hours mediates the ritual's meaning for an audience that might be only partially aware of this traditional kut style. Dr. Yang does not dwell on the reasons for holding kut, which he assumes the participants know well. Rather, he uses the occasion to promote tomorrow's kut, as some of the audience might be unaware of it. Mentioning the other rituals planned for the festival aligns today's kut with the listed festival performances. Nevertheless, he singles it out as a unique religious occasion. This act also affirms the importance of kut in Korea's traditional folk arts and demonstrates its diversity. When Dr. Yang finishes his short speech, the mansin can resume her ritual.

The music begins again, and Mansin Sŏ is back onstage, fully clad as sansin (mountain god) in the same red outfit that she wore on the main stage. She is holding a pair of brass cymbals and a fan with a red rim and many depictions of gods. She begins singing praises to the mountain god as the music plays softly and rhythmically. She asks the mountain god and General Ch'oe Yŏng to bless the country and its people. The ten-year-old apprentice sits with the three musicians and plays the cymbals. They are considered the simplest instrument to play, although their sound is strong and significant. He seems to be doing well, and the drummer and gong player keep glancing at him with encouragement.

Most mansin apprentices are older than eighteen years, and the boy's presence in this public kut is striking. An elderly woman seated beside me tells me that he has probably been very sick if his parents agreed that he could become a mansin's apprentice. Mansin Sŏ's other spirit children told me that she bargained with the spirits to allow the boy not to become a full mansin until he is eighteen. The spirits agreed to let him finish school and, in return, he performs with the musicians whenever there is a ritual in the afternoon and not too late into the night.[5] For the audience, his presence does not seem questionable or strange. The young apprentice manages to keep up with the changes in the music's beat as it slides between different muga parts.

After a few stanzas, the mansin signals to the musicians that they should play repeatedly and quietly, to let her voice be heard. She says, "Venerable mountain god, please bless the nation again." At the end of her phrase, the music resumes at full volume, and she begins to spin around and around, holding the fan open. In her other hand, she replaces the cymbals with two wands with white streamers and colored divination flags. She puts down all but the wands and shakes them up and down while dancing, facing the altar and then the audience. The wands are a symbolic *axis mundi*, through which spirits can descend into the mansin's body. She walks back and forth as the music grows faster, then circles repeatedly in one spot. An apprentice gives her two bunches of hemp-cloth streamers, which she shakes wildly. Now everyone knows that she is possessed.

The assistant hands the mansin long strips of hemp and white silk, which she tears dramatically into shorter pieces. The audience understands that the spirits are causing these frantic shaking and tearing motions. She scoops up the pieces of hemp and silk into her hands and circles around until she falls prostrate in front of the main drum. She gets up and circles again, then prostrates herself in front of the altar. She does this several times while facing the audience, which applauds. She pours drops of rice wine from a brass bowl in all directions of the straw mat, as offerings to the supernatural entities present there. These offerings, proudly exhibited before the human and supernatural audiences, are simple commodities that have not undergone special shaping into musok artifacts. An abundance of cloth and wine is perceived as a sign of generosity toward the spirits. Finally, Mansin Sŏ stops her constant motion to deliver the words of the gods. Possessed by sansin, she announces, "I [the mountain god] am pleased with the kut. I will help the people and bless them."

The next spirit to possess the mansin is *sinjang*, a spirit general. Just as she did on the main stage, she dances with two brass knives, pointing them at her white silk coat and stopping to arch backward in all four directions and stab her chest. Jumping up and down, shaking the knives around her body, she smiles as she embodies the spirit of the warrior. When the music stops, she says, "Dear noble people (*yangban*), know that there are many warriors, not just Ch'oe Yŏng [pointing at his painting behind the altar], who is so famous. I am not him, but as an important warrior myself will bless you with good fortune."

The ritual has been shortened significantly in these parts, and only a few selected spirits are invited to possess the mansin. Still, in a staged festival performance, it is challenging to maintain the audience's interest. The mansin moves to the part where she walks among the audience and offers personal blessings. Sŏ invites all participants to venerate the spirits of their ancestors. It is a signal for the participants to begin offering money to please their ancestral spirits. The practitioners and apprentices walk among the observers and collect donations.

The mansin walks within the audience and points her spread fan toward them. Many people place ten thousand–won bills (about $10) on the fan. Some approach her and some just wave the bills and wait for her to come. She blesses each donor. She takes the bills, hands some to each musician, and then says, "I have only one bill left. How can I place that on the altar?" More people open their wallets, and she walks back and forth among them. When a person hands several bills, she says with a humorous tone, "Look at this generous gentleman," and the audience laughs. Sometimes she says, "Thank you" in English to Korean contributors of money. As she walks around collecting more and more bills, she says, "You really make me walk so much that my feet hurt. But the children [who often run to hand her the bills] are so cute that it is all right with me." She hands the bills to her assistant and continues talking fast. "I am walking back and forth, and my feet really hurt, but be blessed. You will not be sick and you will possess much money." Not all the audience members donate, but those who do smile and look happy. It is rare now to attend a private kut of others, and even some musok believers have few opportunities to participate unless they sponsor a kut themselves.

Kut are expensive affairs. Several million Korean won changed hands before the ritual. Paid by the festival authorities, this money was used for the preparations, the assistants' wages, and the mansin's compensation. In addition, at every ritual, audience members who are not the main sponsors are also expected to contribute money to appease the spirits. At this ritual, where the audience is composed of people who are not personally connected with each other, the pressure to donate large sums of money is far less than in a village setting. At a performance, people give as much as they wish; many do not open their wallets at all. The mansin uses humorous gestures to create a favorable atmosphere, which might increase the observers' contributions. Some audience members say that they put money on the mansin's fan as "part of the show" or as "a token of respect to her superb performance," rather than for religious reasons. She is a gracious dancer, and the elaborate costumes and decorations add theatricality to the entertainment function of the ritual.

A blue vest over a red coat and a tasseled hat replace the white robe and tall silk hat. The spirit of another warrior has arrived. He also makes the mansin spin and stab her chest in all four directions. A vest with colorful cut edges is handed to Mansin Sŏ; wearing it, she becomes possessed by a warrior of a higher rank. She grabs a pair of chaktu blades from the altar. These blades are used in agricultural villages to chop fodder. In kut, they symbolize the bravery of warrior spirits that possess the mansin. These spirits engaged in dangerous practices during their lives, and they miss such adrenaline-stimulating acts. During the dance, the possessed mansin presses the blades to her face and hands. She passes the length of the blades on her tongue but does not get hurt. No blood pours, and the only visible effect is a temporary mark against her flesh. This sturdiness is attributed to the supernatural protection of her body during possession. One of the reasons for Mansin Sŏ's many public performances is her spiritual connections with generals' spirits, which make the ritual more exciting and fast-paced.

After this dangerous stunt, another layer is added to the outfit of the entranced performer. This heavy, velvet garment is designed as armor with golden, metal scales attached to arms, shoulders, breast, and back. A wide sash with a circular, golden buckle depicting the face of a lion is fastened to the mansin's hips. A long sword completes the look. She is about to be possessed by another famous general. After some turns and dancing in front of the altar, the general delivers blessings and promises good fortune to the festival viewers and the nation.

Because time is short, the next outfit change is quick, revealing a more peaceful god. It is *ch'ilsŏng*, the spirit of the seven stars of the great dipper. The white hanbok is now topped by a red sash embroidered with many pink lotus flowers and depictions of turtles, deer, and cranes. These symbols are understood in Korea to represent longevity and inner peace. Over the sash, Sŏ wears a long, wooden Buddhist rosary and dons a triangular white hat. In her hands, she holds a small brass gong, a pair of brass cymbals, and a white fan with paintings of gods. This extremely elaborate costume resembles a festive dancing outfit of Buddhist monks and nuns, as ch'ilsŏng is perceived as a merciful, vegetarian, Buddhist character. A large clay jar has been placed in the middle of the performance area, awaiting its role in the ritual. Even peaceful spirits like being entertained with moderate stunts.

To the left, Dr. Yang holds a microphone and begins to explain how kut rituals function in Korean folklore. He lists the qualities of ch'ilsŏng spirits and some related beliefs. The musicians appear impatient, but the mansin is all smiles, waiting to begin her part. Again, Dr. Yang's presence is accepted for its promotional qualities, although now it seems to bother the performers and divert their attention from the ritual. Dr. Yang explains that rituals of this kind usually last several days. However, because of the festival's structure, today's ritual will end before midnight. He goes on to emphasize the regional diversity of the kut that he chose to feature in the festival and adds that all rituals will be presented in shortened versions. Again, he uses the stage to promote future events. Dr. Yang's personal interest in having large audiences throughout the festival overcomes the uneasiness of interrupting the flow of a sacred moment. Mansin Sŏ, dressed in an accessory-laden costume, waits patiently for Dr. Yang to withdraw. She is ready to begin dancing on the straw mats.

As ch'ilsŏng, Mansin Sŏ dances with a spread fan and shakes the cymbals to symbolize the descent of the god into her body. At this point, she is both the mansin, who performs the ritual in full control, and the god, who is embodied in her and enjoys dancing. The cymbals are connected to each other with a long strip of white silk; as the musicians play along, she lets the cymbals fall to the ground, holding the white strip in her hands. She repeats this movement in all four directions to purify the kut arena symbolically. Then she tosses the cymbals to the back of the stage, where her assistants immediately collect them. She begins spinning, holding the fan in her left hand and a long, white, silk streamer in her right hand. An assistant hands her an adorned brass brazier. She turns around slowly until she completes a full circle and is again facing the altar, with the brazier held high. The brazier contains rice and incense sticks and is shown as a communal offering to the other spirits that have come to enjoy the ritual. She returns the item to the waiting assistant, who receives it with a slight bow. Koreans know that such braziers are used to light incense for the souls of departed people. The constant use of this artifact reminds everyone that the dances and songs are addressed to the dead.

Now the mansin and her apprentice both sit on their bent knees in front of the altar. The heavily clad mansin needs to adjust her many robes before she can come to a full cross-legged position. Then she receives a metal spoon and knife, which she clangs to the beat of the music. She moves to sit in front of the drummer, lifting her long sleeves rhythmically and swaying from side to side. The music is slow and repetitive, and the drummer chants. The mansin looks entranced.

As the music grows faster, Mansin Sŏ stands and begins spinning. She walks to the large clay pot and climbs onto it, her feet resting on the thin edge on either side. Facing the altar and banging a pair of cymbals, she maintains her balance as she sways and dances with her hands and upper body. She slowly jumps up and down on the rim of the pot, turning to the right until she faces the audience again. The drummer plays fast and shouts encouragement. The mansin's face holds a new expression—her slight smile throughout most of the show has changed into a broad grin with glazed, half-shut eyes. It is an expression of sheer joy, to which she also attests in our conversation after the event. She opens her arms wide while holding the cymbals. As she faces the audience, everyone cheers loudly. Still on the clay pot, she shouts, and the musicians stop playing. Ch'ilsŏng is about to speak. The crowd grows silent, and the pipe player adds a few notes here and there to emphasize the spoken words: "I [ch'ilsŏng] am happy with these paper flowers and tasty fruit [pointing at the offerings on the altar]. You will be blessed with happiness and good health." The words spoken by the mansin emphasize the god's presence in the place through his mention of the material aspects of the altar. This close connection with the audience is mediated through the objects consumed both symbolically and literally.

In a sharp move, the mansin jumps off the pot and changes into a blue coat and red vest with edges cut into colorful stripes of embroidered silk. She adds the tasseled black hat and becomes the spirit of Ch'oe Yŏng Changgun, the historic general who is her main venerated entity. Most audience members know that spirits of generals like dangerous games and that mansin can stand on sharp blades, but not everyone has seen this in real life. This moment is exciting for all.

DANGER AS EMOTIONAL MEDIATOR OF RITUAL EFFICACY: THE MAIN VENERATED DEITY ONSTAGE

At this point, many in the audience are already tired. The rain has been coming and going, and the performance has lasted for more than two hours. Still, few people leave. They are waiting for the anticipated act of bravery performed to entertain the spirit of Changgun, the main guardian entity of Mansin Sŏ. Dangerous practices are not merely exciting extravagances—such acts are deemed crucial to the ritual's success. The mansin's ability to perform them unharmed is perceived as proof of her spiritual abilities and the ritual's efficacy. The audience and the mansin's team are eager to see how this important feat will proceed. The intense feeling of danger serves as an emotional mediator of the ritual's significance.

Embodying the spirit of Changgun, Mansin Sŏ holds a pair of knives that shake and cut the air as the possession intensifies. Sŏ dances and whirls, with the colorful edges of her vest flaring in the rain and wind. She asks her assistants for a special hat to mark her upcoming climb onto a pair of chaktu blades. The blades are sharpened before the ritual to please the danger-seeking warrior's spirit. The chaktu must be ritually placed on a six-foot-tall wooden platform decorated with silk streamers that is carried center stage by three male assistants. The music is loud and fast, and the mansin spins faster and faster at the right edge of the stage. She is getting ready to entertain the strong spirit of her supernatural personal guardian (*momju*).

Dr. Yang, holding a microphone in one hand and an umbrella in the other, speaks from the left edge of the stage. He speaks in a loud, clear voice, appropriating the close attention of the audience. He repeats his previous announcement to promote tomorrow's performance: "Dear people of Korea, I hope all of you are enjoying the performance. Tomorrow there will be another kut here and you are all welcome. Now, the mansin will honor the famous General Ch'oe Yŏng by stepping onto sharp blades."

Two long bamboo poles, decorated with red, green, yellow, and blue silk, are fastened to both sides of the platform's top. On the platform, a low wooden table is placed over a clay bowl with rice. On the table, a wooden barrel is set. On top of the barrel, the two notorious blades are held together with long screws and purifying white cloth. Mansin Sŏ's ability to stand unharmed on those sharp metal pieces will demonstrate the sincerity of her ties with the supernatural. It is a moment of intense activity for the assistants. They check the stability of the tall, complicated structure and show signs of stress in their sharp movements and worried faces. It is evident that even the mansin and her apprentices are eager to conclude the act with a positive response from the general's spirit. They all fear the outcome of an unsupportive reception, although Mansin Sŏ claims she has never been cut by the chaktu blades while dancing on them possessed. Other mansin acknowledge having been cut in moments of distraction. In the Korean cosmology, spirits of the dead are characterized as yearning for their lifetime activities. A central role of mansin during rituals is to entertain the spirits by engaging in symbolic activities that will satisfy their desires. Spirits of children are given sweets and toys, whereas spirits of warriors are offered knife stunts and dangerous games. When these supernatural entities are pleased, they adhere to the mansin's requests and help the people who worked to provide them with entertainment.

Sŏ places another coat over her outfit. It is heavy, velvet armor reaching to her knees. With the bulky costume, she climbs the stairs to the platform—she is a bit unstable but fast and vigorous. She holds a pair of brass knives in her clenched teeth. Two men hold the handles of the chaktu blades to keep them steady as she slowly places each bare foot along a sharp blade. She holds the two bamboo poles, and her facial expression conveys deep concentration. There are no smiles now. Her feet are above the assistants' heads, and they look up to see how she is doing. She arches backward, the knives still held in her teeth. The music slows down, but at a sharp glance from the mansin, the musicians resume speed. She turns on the knives, her feet slowly changing positions. First, each foot rests on the two knives. Then, each foot stands on a single blade. She stands with her back turned to the audience and, after completing a full turn, she faces the audience again. Now she takes the knives out of her mouth and, finally, smiles. She waves the knives and looks straight at the audience, which cheers. The danger has almost passed, as the successful stunt was performed in perfect control and marks the ritual as efficacious.[6]

Sŏ lets go of the bamboo poles and spreads her arms wide. With a shake of one knife, she signals to the musicians, and they slow down. Bending down to reach the stretched hand of an assistant below her, she takes a bunch of silk flags. She waves them left and right. The music stops completely, and she begins to chant and deliver the words of Changgun, all while standing barefoot on the blades. Unfortunately, the wireless microphone is not working—with the rain and wind, the mansin's voice is lost. When the sound system is repaired, she can be heard again as she chants, "To the honored general of the blades (*chaktu changgunnim*) and the honored god of the blades (*chaktu sillyŏngnim*)." Her voice is lost to the weather again as she continues her chant. With the concluding words of the spirits, however, she rises to a shout that all can hear: "General Ch'oe Yŏng will bestow on all of you health and good fortune." This blessing is accepted with cheers as the audience feels the danger of a woman standing on blades. Many interpret it as a sign of true possession, which means that the words she says are really the voice of a powerful supernatural entity.

An apprentice stands on a plastic chair and stretches to hand Mansin Sŏ a straw basket full of small, embroidered silk bags. The bags are *pujŏk* (charms and talismans for good fortune) and contain yellow pieces of paper with an inscription in red ink. The mansin scoops them up in her hand and throws them to the audience. Everyone gets up and runs closer to grab the little bags and the blessed candies that begin flying in the air. A cluster of umbrellas blocks my view, shakes my camera, and wets me completely. I worry that the crowd may get too close to the platform and bump the mansin off the chaktu blades. A middle-aged woman asks me whether I caught any pujŏk, and when I say no, she grabs a green bag and some sweets and hands them to me. For many people, it is especially important to take home this talisman from the possessed mansin standing on the sharp blades. By endangering herself, the mansin mediates between the audience and the powerful spirit, rendering his blessings at this moment especially efficacious.

As the umbrellas begin dispersing, I see Mansin Sŏ slowly getting off the blades and down the wooden stairs assisted by one of her *sinttal* (spirit-daughter or apprentice). The relief that the mansin, her apprentices, and other staff express reflects the difficult and dangerous character of the moment. Several male assistants begin dismantling the platform and stairs. Female assistants draw the crowd to the left end of the stage, handing out packages of spongy rice cakes (*ttŏk*) from large cardboard boxes. The music resumes a quick tempo, and Mansin Sŏ dances on the straw mat with several more turns and chants to send the spirits away.

She leaves the stage abruptly and walks to the dressing room. The crowd quickly disappears, and the assistants begin to pack the offerings and decorations. It is only 10:15 p.m.—two hours before the presumed ending of the performance around midnight. The weather and the failure of the sound equipment were too much to bear. Both performers and audience struggled but eventually conceded defeat. The natural elements affected the ritual process in ways that could have happened decades ago. In earlier times, rainproof plastic sheets could not cover paper offerings and paintings, and artificial lighting depended on candles and torches that could die out with wind and rain. This time, the failure of electronic equipment led to the event's abridgment. The material and performative aspects of the event have changed over time, but the need to please the spirits has persisted.

MEDIATION AS THE KEY TO THE SUCCESS OF CONTEMPORARY STAGED KUT

Mediation is a key concept in musok. Mediation between humans and supernatural entities is the core of every kut. The main role of the mansin is to enable communication between different realms of existence, which is believed to solve difficulties and misfortunes in people's lives. This traditional concept of mediation is performed through the embodiment of spirits and the presence of material offerings. Spiritual mediation has always been assisted in private and public kut by music, artistic artifacts, and foods. The objects serve as vehicles of meaning, expressions of devotion, and manifestations of the mansin's knowledge of traditional arts and crafts. The offerings and ritual implements stand among the mansin, the audience, and the supernatural. But has mediation, as a process, remained the same as in early modern musok performances? How can analysis of the changes that such mediation has undergone enrich our understanding of the appeal that kut still holds for contemporary Koreans?

The concept of mediation serves here as an overarching framework for examining differences between village settings and top-notch stages for kut rituals. Mediation has been increasingly characterized by new forms of professional handling and the use of contemporary technology. Professionalization and the replacement of human interaction with technology characterize urban South Korea in general, and much face-to-face communication is increasingly replaced by technological platforms such as cellular phones and online social networks. In kut, voice amplification, artificial lights, transportation, and media-enhanced publicity have become inseparable from public performances of this vernacular religion. Furthermore, the professionalization of musok is apparent when common people, who no longer perform daily house rites for supernatural entities, turn to mansin to console the spirits. The World Cup Stadium kut represents a new genre of ritual that has become increasingly common. However, not all two hundred thousand practicing mansin in Korea achieve such honors as staged kut. Moreover, even famous practitioners spend most of their time working with private patrons.

An important role of women in premodern Korea was to take care of spirits and gods on a daily basis (Kendall 1985). They used to pour wine and water around the house for wandering ghosts, offer rice to the earth deity before meals, and pray for the help of various powers (C. Im 1996). In stressful times, many Koreans still feel the need to communicate with the supernatural, but they lack the knowledge to do so on their own. Their source of spiritual guidance has increasingly become professional mansin rather than older, female, family members. Clients expect the mansin to be well versed in the traditional forms of ritual; to use the expected, standard implements; and to look professional. Moreover, mansin make sure to invite all their clients and acquaintances to any public, staged performances. After these events, they upload images and videos to their websites and social media profiles.

Most clients speak proudly of their favorite mansin's stage performances and media appearances. They perceive public visibility as a legitimizing aspect of the religious work and as proof of authenticity. As a young new client of a famous mansin said, "No famous scholar would have written a book about her had she been a fake mansin. She must be very good to achieve such fame. The television producers like her, too. She is a real master of the traditional arts." Clearly, choosing which mansin to hire may depend on her performance competence, as measured and assessed by professional scholars of the field. The standards of artistry expected from stage performers exceed those that a rural, small-scale practitioner needed to exhibit.

As discussed, scholars are often invited or hired to interpret at staged performances. In this role, scholars mediate between the mansin team and observers who might not be well informed about musok. Some young participants in the World Cup Stadium kut said that this event was their first acquaintance with this dazzling display. In village kut and in private rituals—where a person who wants to know more about musok or a specific rite can ask another participant or one of the assistants to explain—mediation between audience and mansin is informal. In staged kut, most participants do not know each other, which makes communication between them more problematic. Assistants are onstage and thus unavailable to take questions. Consequently, the scholar-announcer's role is indispensable.

Being endorsed by a scholar lends a mansin an important promotional tool. A mansin who is nominated as a "Holder of Intangible Assets" or who appears in television shows and staged kut typically reports increased appreciation by the public. Mansin see an evident surge in their clientele after their nomination or media appearance. The government's program for preserving traditional arts has become instrumental in mediating between the mansin and the public beyond artistic displays. Its procedure has become complex, personal, professional, and political (Choi 1987; K. Howard 1998; Yang 1994). There have even been rumors of mansin who tried to bribe scholars for personal promotion. Apart from their academic articles and books, many Korean folklore scholars write introductions to mansin websites and promotional materials.

The colorful printed booklets distributed during staged kut meet the audience's need for immediate explanations (fig. 1.3). In a typical brochure, the lead mansin tells her life story and the main attributes of her ritual style. This is followed by a list of her honors and staged performances. In the Korea Traditional Performing Arts Festival brochure, there was also information about the kut structure, its history, and its uniqueness and importance, as described by scholars and festival management. This aspect of professionalization in kut performance follows conventions of Western concerts and theater shows. It can also be viewed in other contemporary traditional performances, such as

Fig. 1.3 Mansin Sŏ's brochure, 2007. Credit: Author.

mask dances (*t'alch'um*). It marks the performance as artistic entertainment for nonparticipant viewers.

The separation between knowledgeable performers and audience is also manifest in the kut's spatial arrangement. Urban rituals usually occur in large spaces where the mansin performs on elevated stages, far from the audience seated in European fashion on chairs. The physical distance between the audience and the mansin team requires electronic voice and light amplification. Technology and the professionals who can operate it have replaced the natural mediation of sound between mansin and audience, which used to require only a strong voice. Except for one or two moments in which the mansin and the audience interact to exchange money and amulets, there is complete detachment. The alienation between the random urban audience and the mansin team is also expressed by the content, which has changed from personal and improvised to general and prescribed. There are no inside jokes and anecdotes, and no dark secrets are revealed and discussed.

Moreover, in the villages, much of the ritual's paraphernalia was prepared with the help of many local people. Consequently, the viewers had sentiment toward the artifacts on the altars. They were invested in cooking, cutting, sewing, and arranging them. This practice has mostly disappeared, even in private kut. Instead, consumerism has become the common way to obtain the needed props for kut rituals. Dealers and merchants of folk art have become the main agents mediating between producers of religious artifacts and the mansin, who in turn make this rich material culture accessible to kut audiences. In large-scale kut, the involvement of villagers and mansin in staging and prop management has given way to teams of workers who are hired by famous mansin on a regular basis. When the rite is over, the audience leaves, and dismantling of the elaborate stage is left, again, to professionals.

The ritual continues to live beyond the memory of its participants—filmed and photographed documentation lasts for many years. Photographers, bloggers, and journalists work to mediate between the mansin and the general public, beyond the few hundred who attend each staged kut. Such printed, filmed, and digital representations of musok performances are also studied by less experienced mansin and imitated in an attempt to improve their chances of success. Mansin make sure to invite relevant media figures and celebrities to their public rituals. This increases their attractiveness to broadcasting venues, and many practitioners have begun to upload footage from their rituals to social media and YouTube.

The production of a public, staged kut has become a joint endeavor of professionals from various fields. Some are experts in religion and traditional arts. Others are professionals in the technologies of performance enhancement and documentation. The importance of the event itself is transferred to mass media. Exposure to musok practices has become a media experience for many Koreans. They see it on television but not in a tangible, face-to-face situation. In this chapter, I offered a thick description of a staged ritual that demonstrates the extent to which such rituals have become laden with various levels of mediation and, recently, with electronic technology.[7] Latour's ANT theory, in which objects are perceived as having agency affecting cultural processes, is helpful in explaining these mediation processes. The objects shown on the altar affected the audience's response to the ritual and increased their enjoyment. These offerings and depictions of spirits and gods also marked the event as religious and framed it according to the semiotic social norms. Moreover, scholarly evaluation of the ritual's authenticity, which led to its inclusion in the festival, was also affected by its materiality. The technological devices dictated much of the ritual's pace, as well as its abrupt end.

This grounded account demonstrates that a staged ritual is an occasion outside daily life. It summons various related and unrelated people and objects to cooperate for a designated time. It is "an association between entities which are in no way recognizable as being social in the ordinary manner, *except* during the brief moment when they are reshuffled together" (Latour 2005, 65). The audience for this ritual was composed mostly of strangers. The technological devices were rented by the festival, whereas the ritual artifacts were prepared by the mansin team. Nevertheless, all participated and related to each other to produce the meaning of the performance.[8] In many other staged kut rituals held inside museums or in city festivals as "cultural performances," visitors receive real blessings and amulets from the performing team. In more than a dozen such museum performances that I observed, the mansin team treated these staged rituals with full reverence and religious attentiveness. Such a religious attitude at museum events has been observed elsewhere—in a recreated voodoo shrine in a California museum, at a Tibetan mandala ceremony in a Virginia museum, and at a Hindu blessing ceremony in a Glasgow museum (Arthur 2000, 18–9; Cosentino 2000, 102).[9]

Staged kut are cultural performances with the complexity of maintaining a traditional belief system in an ultramodern urban society (Bauman and Ritch 1994; Stoeltje and Bauman 1988). The description unfolded by exploring the characteristics of musok and the major roles played by objects and technology. It also addressed issues of scholars' interventions and the importance of media coverage. The proliferation of such staged musok events demonstrates how, in the government preservation system, the performative aspects of this vernacular religion have been framed as folk art. The ritual as cultural performance has been augmented and become the center of preservation efforts, whereas its religious aspects have been disregarded. Official endorsement by academically trained scholars has added to the emphasis on the artistic value of musok while allowing the mansin to use such sponsored occasions for their own religious goals.

In chapter 2, I analyze another contemporary form of mediating musok knowledge to audiences: films. Films are both an entertaining medium and an accepted form of professional mediation between the general public and cultural values and behaviors. Whereas the discussion of staged rituals focused on the present condition of musok, the next chapter takes a historical perspective. Films about musok span from at least the 1960s to the present. I use that medium to explore how the image of musok in Korea has changed over the past fifty years.

NOTES

1. In 2012, locations were listed on the official festival website, which is no longer available.

2. *Samulnori*, the song of the four instruments, is a modern transformation of traditional Korean *p'ungmul kut* music. Unlike p'ungmul kut, the new form includes only an hourglass drum, a small rotation drum, a round drum, and a brass handheld gong. A symbol of Korean traditional arts, samulnori is a well-respected art form (Hesselink 2004).

3. Full chants of Hwanghae-do–style kut were transcribed by Ch'oe Kil-sŏng (K. Ch'oe 1991) and Hong T'ae-han (T. Hong 2006). Translations of muga chants into English were prepared by Alan Heyman following transcriptions by Yim (2005). Descriptions of Hwanghae-do–style kut can be read (in Korean) in Yang's article (2003). For more about muga's content and form, see B. Yi (1986), and T. Kim (1966).

4. Their meeting at the festival proved an excellent networking opportunity for Mansin Sŏ. Several joint performances resulted, among them a concert in October of that year at the National Theater of Korea.

5. The apprentice was initiated to become a fully accredited mansin in September 2017. His performance photographs and videos were uploaded to Mansin Sŏ's Facebook page with an excited text telling readers that he had been an apprentice since the age of eight. Now, at twenty, he was a freshman in college.

6. A video filmed and edited by me and Shai Sarfati that depicts moments from this and other rituals, in addition to interviews with Mansin Sŏ and Mansin Kim Nam-sun about possession by the spirit of Changgun, can be watched on YouTube (Sarfati and Sarfati 2007).

7. For more on thick description, see Geertz (1973, 3–30).

8. The presence of an audience in kut rituals cannot be overestimated. In 2020, during the COVID-19 pandemic, I observed several filmed rituals that were held in museums without audiences. The lack of nonperforming participants clearly affected the rituals. There was much less humor, and only a

few exchanges of encouraging shouts among the performers. With no people to divine for or give away the offering foods to, the event was quite formal. In one such event, the mansin was perplexed about how to handle the flag divination, and eventually asked one of the producers to approach the performance area for this. The producer seemed quite reluctant to be filmed as a participant and the whole situation seemed awkward, to say the least.

9. I am grateful to Pravina Shukla, who pointed out this interesting feature of religious exhibits in a seminar discussion in March 2005.

TWO

The Changing Image of Musok in Films

MASS MEDIA HAVE BEEN CENTRAL in the culture of South Korea since its founding in 1948, when the government began using film, among other media, to promote its cultural policies. In the 1950s, the South Korean authorities, headed by Yi Sŭng-man (Syngman Rhee), decided to encourage film production to improve people's morale. They exempted films from taxation after the armistice that ended the Korean War in 1953, and the number of films produced each year rose from 18 in 1954 to 111 in 1959 (Koreanfilm.org 2011a).[1] Very few mansin appeared in films during this time. As South Korea was modernizing, perhaps filmmakers preferred not to portray this kind of old-fashioned, controversial tradition. Most anthropologists in Korea likewise ignored musok as a topic of thorough ethnographic research in this period and focused on other social and structural issues (K. Kim 2004, 65). Folklorists mostly sufficed with documenting the ancient heritage of musok as historical evidence of regional and national uniqueness rather than as a living tradition (Janelli 1986). This trend changed significantly in the 1960s, when mansin began to have meaningful roles in several feature films.

Musok is an especially rich arena to explore in film. It offers stunning audiovisual experiences, and it can represent the tensions between traditional, rural Korea and contemporary, late-modern, urban South Korea and between cultural hierarchies and social mobility.[2] Compared with the staged ritual described in the previous chapter, films have broader and more diverse audiences.[3] Their depiction of behaviors and objects reflects the values, emotions, and worldviews of their protagonists and the broader society. Moreover, most films discussed in this chapter received minimal governmental support and had successful commercial distribution with many thousands of viewers.

Feature films offer a unique opportunity to explore the image of musok in genres that do not always depict reality. Documentary films about musok also gained popularity and were screened in commercial theatres in the 2000s, which demonstrates the Korean public's interest in the subject.

This chapter surveys the changes in depictions of musok in films from the 1970s, when it was shown as a dark and scary practice, through the 1980s and 1990s, when it was framed as a vanishing tradition in need of preservation, and up to today, with mansin shown as creative, evolving practitioners with sincere intentions to help others. Female supremacy in musok is reasserted when films show female mansin as powerful and dominant. The underlying statement of films with strong female spirit mediators is that women can become eminent thanks to their supernatural gifts. However, each period reflects differently on this kind of power and its outcomes.

DID THE EMERGENCE OF FILM TECHNOLOGY CREATE A SHIFT IN MUSOK'S IMAGE?

The paradigm of technological determinism views innovative materiality as the main catalyst in contemporary cultural life. In 1964, Marshall McLuhan famously stated, "The medium is the message," describing how changes in technology affect culture and perceptions. In his view, "the personal and social consequences of any medium—that is, of any extension of ourselves—result from the new scale that is introduced into our affairs by each extension of ourselves, or by any new technology" (McLuhan 1964, 1). In other words, changes in technology affect the messages that new venues convey, not because of societal or cultural processes but because of qualities inherent in the technology. "The 'message' of any medium or technology," he continues, "is the change of scale or pace or pattern that it introduces into human affairs" (1). According to McLuhan, technology is the main factor in the content that it conveys. Several musok practitioners acknowledged the truth of this view, referring to their use of technology while travelling for pilgrimage, and as a basic requirement for preparing sumptuous rituals. Nevertheless, it might not explain how the same medium can produce different and contradicting messages, as will be shown in this chapter.

Technologies that are different in scale and pace—for example, film and television—can produce similar messages. Moreover, the dialectics between choice of medium and message are not tackled by McLuhan (1964) at all. Conversely, in musok, one can clearly see how mansin cater to the needs of the medium—for example, by shortening reperformed rituals to fit the length of a documentary program, scheduling events according to media producers' demands, and consciously staging nice photographic angles. Diversity in audiences' responses to the message is another crucial factor that McLuhan does not thoroughly consider. These different agents in media representation processes need further addressing, as this and the following chapters offer. By separately exploring each medium that represents musok, some technology-related consequences become clear and will be discussed.

McLuhan's (1964) thesis has been verified in some aspects of human cognition, such as the effect of the medium on the level of imagination (Greenfield et al. 1986). However, I and others argue that technological innovation depends on fertile cultural soil to generate new messages—and that the culture also determines the extent and manner of reception of new technologies (Jensen 2002; Meyrowitz 1998). Any significant change in the musok-related message arises from the use and reception of the medium discussed, which is largely determined by broader cultural tendencies rather than by the medium's inherent qualities. Lemish (2006, 1) explains why "the message is the message" in children's television programs, whereas the medium is mostly a means to convey it. She agrees with the strong statement "Marshall McLuhan appears to have been wrong. The medium is not the message" (D. Anderson et al. 2001, 134, quoted in Lemish 2006, 1). In relation to film, technology alone did not create the message about musok.

The same medium has been used to promote various contradictory messages about musok. The dramatic change in musok's image in films demonstrates that the medium does not necessarily affect or produce the message of its content. In the 1960s, when McLuhan discussed films, he stated, "The message of the movie medium is that of transition from lineal connections to configurations.... We return to the inclusive form of the icon" (1964, 3). This assertion might have been true for its time, and it resonates for some Korean movies from the 1970s, when artistic and experimental films showed musok as a kind of curiosity. Today, we find movies that do not use the medium to produce such complicated depictions of illusion and strangeness; rather, many mansin are depicted in realistic, linear stories. The grandiose productions from the 1960s that McLuhan views as "a world of triumphant illusions and dreams that money could buy" (1964, 3) turned out to be only one form of this medium. Other messages became increasingly possible in movies, and cinema became a conglomerate of diverse and contradictory genres and messages. McLuhan states that "the effect of the medium is made strong and intense just because it is given another medium as 'content'" (1964, 8). In contrast, I look at Korean films about musok through a cultural–historical lens rather than a technology-focused perspective.

In Korea in general, and in the Korean film industry in particular, I see clear connections between historical and cultural processes and how musok is depicted in film. Films about musok define and articulate meanings, values, and social roles of cultural displays through differential applications of humor, fear, and sympathy related to the period and sociohistorical realities. Most changes in relation to musok do not stem from technological innovation but rather from historical, social, and cultural developments. Therefore, I cannot agree that "the medium is the message" when it comes to musok in film. I argue that the ways in which musok has been mediated for Korean and international audiences through film has evolved alongside historical, social, and artistic norms and expectations. Films from the 1970s would likely be impossible to produce, or at least be perceived as irrelevant, in the contemporary cultural environment. Similarly, it would be difficult to imagine that contemporary films about musok would be appreciated by 1970s viewers.

I will unpack this argument by analyzing four aspects of each film presented here: plot (how mudang fit in the film's narrative), depiction (visual and textual representation of mudang and musok), social acceptance (how the film shows the social relationships of mudang), and presumed futures (how musok is expected to develop). (I use the term *mudang* because the films depict both possessed and hereditary practitioners; in some cases that will be discussed, the boundaries between these regional ritual styles are far from clear.) At the end of the chapter, I analyze documentary films to understand whether they demonstrate similar changes in how musok is interpreted.

The analysis reveals clear chronological development in musok's depiction through three periods: 1960s to mid-1980s, mid-1980s through the 1990s, and 2000 to 2018. This division is significant in terms of historical changes in Korea and its film industry and the changing presentation of musok in films. The first period reflects the dictatorial regime of Pak Chŏng-hŭi (Park Chung-hee) from 1961 to 1979 and his successors in 1979–1987, with harsh censorship and government control of the film industry. The second period is related to democratization and a renewed appreciation of indigenous folklore through the *minjung* (people's) movement beginning in the 1980s. Some have called the film industry from the mid-1990s the "New Korean Cinema," as a result of new business ventures in the industry and different artistic aspirations after democratization (Shin and Stringer 2005). The Korean film industry enjoyed increased popularity at that time. Controversial laws limiting the number of foreign films allowed into Korea each year helped the local film industry gain influence

(C. Kim 2000). However, the 1990s yielded few films centering on mansin. The minjung ideals, promoted since the 1980s, related to Korean culture as worth maintaining. Such indigenous cultural traits were viewed as instrumental for nationalism and democracy in their modern, western style (N. Lee 2007). In contrast, musok did not fit as a religion but rather as an emotionally stimulating performance and art form. The minjung movement led to mediatized depictions of less controversial traditions, such as *p'ansori* epic singing (e.g., in the film *Sop'yŏnje* directed by Im Kwŏn-t'aek, 1993) and funeral and ancestor rites (e.g., in *Ch'ukje*, also by Im Kwŏn-t'aek, 1996). For this reason, I group the 1990s with the 1980s, as these decades show little change in the representation of mansin. The new perspective on musok as an integral part of an urban, late-modern society begins in the 2000s.

PLOT: HOW DO MUDANG PROTAGONISTS FIT INTO FILMS?

The cases discussed here include sample representations of the rich ideological and material culture that are mediated through cinematic representations of musok. *Mediation* here refers both to the technological means that connect mansin and audiences and to the use of the media as a means to depict and represent culture. The two-dimensional image on the screen is elevated by the ability to cross long distances and cultural barriers that might otherwise prevent the spread of knowledge about musok practices among younger Koreans and Western audiences. As discussed in the introduction, most Western scholars of religion and culture agree that dichotomizing sets of ideas—for example, rationality/spirituality or tradition/modernity—does little to convey the reality of late-modern societies (Satlow 2006; Glassie 1995). Nevertheless, popular imagery in Korea is still drawn to such distinctions, and films on musok are no exception (Douglas 1966). The films discussed in this chapter juxtapose modernity and traditional culture, manifested in the vernacular religion of musok. Each film takes a different stance that concurs with the film's production period and context.

Musok as an Obstacle to Modernity and Progress

In the 1960s and 1970s, films depicted musok as a remnant of an older social and cultural order that might halt modernization and the introduction of new technologies. South Korea underwent colonialism and a painful civil war that ended in 1953. The 1960s were a time for nation building, restructuring the underdeveloped agrarian system, and strengthening the economy. Musok did not fit into this agenda. The government asserted that mudang took money that was needed elsewhere, in technological projects, and that musok (also called *misin* [superstition] at the time) distracted people from working hard to change their own fates. In 1970, the government launched the New Community (*saemaŭl*) movement to reinvigorate rural Korea. In particular, the government worked to eradicate what it deemed harmful superstitions and their practitioners (Kendall 1988). Moreover, Pak Chŏng-hŭi's regime exerted tight control and censorship over film content, culminating in the Motion Picture Law that restricted much of the film industry. By the end of the 1960s, given the limited topics and content allowed in films, the public's interest in visiting movie theaters had diminished significantly. To reinvigorate the film industry, the government created the Korean Motion Picture Promotion Corporation (*yŏnghwa chinhŭng wiwŏnhwa*) in 1973. Many films produced with the help of this office were essentially propaganda, but financial support was also provided to quality films (D. James 2001, 16).

Within this government-supervised atmosphere, mudang enriched film plots as scary, unwanted, and harmful personas. In the film *Ssal* (*Rice*, 1963, directed by Sin Sang-ok), which attracted more than fifty thousand viewers in Seoul, the main protagonist wishes to build new irrigation systems to save the starving villagers (Yecies and Shim 2015, 27–30). A mansin confronts him and tries to frighten the villagers to prevent them from participating in his project, saying that the mountain spirits might get angry. This view matched government policy, and its director—an avid supporter of this view—became a leading figure in the government-supported cinema of the 1960s (Yecies and Shim 2015). *Munyŏdo* (*A Shaman's Story*, 1972, directed by Ch'oi Ha-wŏn) depicts a mansin in a remote fishing village, whose powers decline when Christianity challenges her worldview. The mansin's son wants to be an evangelical Christian. Rather than understanding this as his personal choice, she thinks he is possessed and needs exorcism. She kills him in the process of trying to eradicate the "Christian spirit." Later in film, she dies while trying to exorcize another villager by the river. A grim end for musok is suggested metaphorically by the mansin's drowning.

The colorful footage of the home shrine and rituals in this film offer a somewhat nostalgic peek into a tradition that was perceived as vanishing in the 1970s. The material aspects of kut are depicted in their full glory of colorful costumes, beautiful paintings, and rich offerings. The artistic aspects seem to pose no problem with modern esthetics. However, the religious bases of the creed are depicted as dangerous and not fit for the modern world. The original story was written by Kim Tong-ni in 1936, when Christianity was new in many remote areas and colonial modernization was in full swing (T. Kim 1936/2004).

He used a modernist literary style to describe these new social tensions (Poole 2014). The view of musok as dangerously outdated, proposed in the 1936 novel, pervaded the social and political atmosphere surrounding the 1972 film. Some people even remember how the film *Munyŏdo* caused a sensation when it was released because it featured the dancing feet and singing voice of a real mansin. This use was viewed as a wrongful legitimization of the practice.

Among the films of that period that represent musok in much detail, the most celebrated is probably *Iŏdo* (*Iŏ Island*, 1977, directed by Kim Ki-yŏng), which was based on a 1974 novel by Yi Chŏng-jun.[4] I discuss it in more detail because it had significant viewership and was named as one of the best Korean films ever made (Koreanfilm.org 2011b). It was shown in 1998 at the Berlin Film Festival in a posthumous retrospective of director Kim's work. *Iŏdo*'s genre is not easy to define. It plays along several different styles and plotlines, including horror, psychological thriller, and drama. Again, a mudang acts as a representative of ancient Korean religious practices that are inappropriate in modern times. *Iŏdo* describes the mythical island of P'arangdo (also called Iŏdo), which, thanks to its detachment from modern urban trends, has maintained the indigenous traditions of Korea.[5] Close to this pristine environment, a tourism company strives to build a luxury hotel. The ground is set for a confrontation between indigenous tradition and global capitalism. When a man disappears, the tourism company's manager is accused of murder. The locals are sure that the legendary sea demon took him into the depths as punishment for intervening in nature. The role of musok in escalating the suffering and drama is revealed when the mudang tells the widow that together they will reclaim the body of her dead spouse. The mudang performs an exorcism ritual that culminates in an extraordinary moment when the dead body floats ashore.

This scene, toward the end of the film, is an affirmation of the mudang's surly character. A local barmaid claims to own the body of the dead man, who seems to have been her lover. She and the widow struggle, and the villagers are called to decide who can have the body. The mudang asserts that the body is hers because she brought it back from the sea. Then she takes the corpse to her shrine. In this grotesque scene, the mudang does not help calm the two women fighting over the corpse. Rather, she is shown dancing and singing with evil-looking stares. Later, the mudang encourages the barmaid to conceive a baby with the corpse moments after she has sexual intercourse with the tour company manager. It turns out that the man's disappearance is related to the company manager's disbelief in the spirits, which led to his plan to develop the haunted island.

The film depicts a place where women are scarce, and, accordingly, they seem to be quite powerful. Several women in this film are evidently in control of their own bodies and do not let any man near them unless they wish it. The Iŏdo mudang even controls the body of the disappeared man and induces bizarre sexual intercourse between his corpse and his lover. Moreover, this mudang is involved in the beautiful bartender's seduction of the tour company manager visiting the island. As the film shows, this kind of female dominance is an uncommon condition resulting from the outlandish place, inhabited mainly by men.

Mudang in Iŏdo, Munyŏdo, and Ssal are symbols of antimodernization. Little about their personalities, lives, and thoughts surfaces in the films, and musok practices do not appear to be helpful in any way. In these films, female mansin are shown as strong and influential in their relationships with men. Their sexual desire and attractiveness are portrayed as dangerous and even destructive.

Musok as an Important Tradition on the Verge of Extinction

A shift in the social role of cinema occurred in Korea in the late 1970s and throughout the 1980s. The democratization movement, which included many intellectuals and artists, began to make films for less state-sanctioned productions. Many directors gained more independent status than their tightly state-supervised predecessors. The beauty of folklore and heritage was central to the movement in general and became incorporated in the period's films. From the mid-1980s, the industry enjoyed more liberty. The combination of prodemocratization protests, the anticipated 1988 Olympic games, and the resulting global pressures brought about change that many had been working for. Indigenous features of Korean culture and religion increasingly became the topics of films that were acknowledged in international film festivals. Presenting beautiful Korean tradition to the world became a national quest. No longer a government propaganda tool, films came to be perceived as a way to express the sentiments of the people. A group called *madanggŭk* (literally, the space of folklore performances) asserted that films should be related to their audiences' lived experiences and their folkways. The increased interest in the culture of "the people" was expressed in the minjung movement as a discourse against hegemony and part of the struggle for democratization and personal success (Abelmann 1993, 1996). Everyone, including filmmakers, must "revive traditional performing arts against the flood of foreign cultural materials" (Min, Joo, and Kwak 2003, 87). Film director Chang Sŏn-u (Jang Sunwoo) wanted to revive the humor, communicability, and interplay between fantasy and reality of Korea's folk drama, as was common in the minjung ideology. This view was expressed in the film *Gum* (written in 1986), about the ghosts of anticolonial Korean soldiers who visit the world of humans one hundred years after their deaths. The plot demonstrates the complicated encounters of the ghosts with the humans, who can see them only when they are chewing gum (Min, Joo, and Kwak 2003, 92–95). This film and others from the last stages of censured media relate to the musok worldview and cosmology, where ghosts can interact with people, but do not clearly show mansin and their practices.

Film directors began incorporating mudang characters into film plots not as symbols of harmful, occult superstition but as carriers of important national heritage and desirable members of society. In the film *Pimak* (*The Hut*, 1981, directed by Yi Tu-yong [Lee Doo-yong]), a man becomes afflicted with what seems to be *sinbyŏng* (spirit possession sickness, the first stage in the process of becoming a mansin). His grandmother invites a mudang to perform a healing ritual. After this ritual fails, a more powerful spiritual mediator is called to perform a rite. The healer finds a bottle revealing an old family secret, and an opportunity arises for belated justice. Musok is shown as efficacious and needed. Similarly, in *Pul-ŭi ttal* (*Daughter of the Flames* 1983, directed by Im Kwŏn-t'aek), the protagonist has a sick daughter who seems to be possessed. His wife and mother-in-law attempt Christian healing, but he is reluctant to join these efforts and becomes haunted by nightmares. He dreams of his mother making love to men and is not sure who his father is. Whether she is a seducer or a victim of abuse is unclear in these visions, but her sexuality is an undisputable driving force in her life. He then searches for her and discovers that she was a mudang who committed suicide after being persuaded to quit her musok performances in the 1960s. The persecution of mudang in that period is represented as cruel and unnecessary, and the powerful desires of spirits are depicted as unquestionable and requiring attention.

In *Pul-ŭi ttal* and *Pimak*, the protagonists are men who suffer from supernatural afflictions because of the women around them. Musok is shown as a powerful spiritual resource, and the message is that it would have been better if the persecuted mansin were accepted and respected by Korean society. Legitimizing musok could have prevented much suffering experienced by the female mansin and her male kin. In *Pimak*, the sinbyŏng patient suffers because of the wrongdoing of family elders. In the *Pul-ŭi ttal*, having a mudang as a mother—and, specifically, having her persecuted—ruins the protagonist's childhood and family, and his daughter suffers supernatural affliction. In both films, angry ghosts are the reason for possession, and musok seems to have been driven out of society to the verge of extinction.

The idea that musok can expose and reconcile past wrongdoings that resulted in death is also expressed in a 1989 play that was later adapted into the popular and critically acclaimed film *Ogu: A Hilarious Morning* (2003, directed by Yi Yun-t'aek). This play seems to have been inspired by the story of *Gum*. Here, too, the plot is based on the mission of three ghosts in the human world. Their adventures intertwine with the story of Grandmother Hwang, to whom one of the ghosts used to be married. This widow wishes to conduct an *Ogu kut* ritual before she dies. This ritual is usually performed after death to smooth the transition of the deceased's spirit to the underworld. However, Grandmother Hwang wants to sponsor this ritual while she is still alive. She worries that her greedy offspring might not use her savings for such an expensive event after she dies. She persuades the old mudang who lives in the village—and who has not performed kut for many years, under the village elders' orders—to perform the ritual.

The play and film portray the ritual's preparation and the various layers of interaction between the living and the dead. The younger generation of the old mudang's family, initially unwilling to take an active role in the ritual, eventually becomes engaged in it. However, there is no hint that they will continue to perform it beyond this particular event. The audience learns that years earlier, the mudang's daughter was raped and her boyfriend committed suicide as a result. Now he comes back as a spirit to expose the rapists and achieve some reconciliation. It is interesting to compare the funeral in the film *Ogu* with the one depicted in *Ch'ukje* (*Festival*, 1996, directed by Im Kwŏn-t'aek). In the two funerals, events that happened in the older generation's youth lead to drama that incorporates similar tensions between generations and between urban and rural Korea. However, *Ch'ukje* (which does not center on musok) ends with a more pessimistic tone than *Ogu*. *Ogu* portrays the coexistence of humans and spirits and the possibility of direct interactions between them through the mediation of a mudang. The film mourns the decline of musok tradition as it used to be practiced in rural Korea. However, it also suggests that the belief system underlying musok activity is firmly anchored in contemporary Korea.

Musok as a Prosperous Tradition in Urban Korea

Since the mid-2000s, musok has been depicted in a new way. Contemporary films reveal musok as a living, beautiful, and indigenous cultural trait. Far from being portrayed as mean or cunning, mansin are shown as dedicated to helping suffering people. Stories focus on mansin who live and practice in the city. As South Korea has become a globally appreciated economic dynamo (Garran 1998; Vogel 1991), it has been unnecessary to abandon indigenous traditions in the name of modernization. As discussed in chapter 1, musok has survived the rapid industrialization of the past several decades and has not hampered Korea's ability to prosper. In the 2000s, there have been fewer attempts to disparage mansin through cinematic depictions, as was done in the 1970s. Furthermore, because everyone knows that mansin work in the large cities, there is no point in showing them as a part of rural culture or a vanishing tradition.

Recent films have often depicted mansin as celebrities. The culture of media celebrity has increased acceptance of behaviors that deviate from normative gender and status roles. As will be discussed, these social changes include representation of mansin as people who live within Korean society and are approached by various clients. In contrast, earlier depictions showed mansin as outcasts called upon only when people were in dire crises. Interestingly, two successful films use comedy, demonstrating that musok is not just a serious spiritual business. Mansin can be integrated into the narratives of commercially oriented film productions.

Ch'ŏngdam Posal (*Fortune Saloon*, 2009, directed by Kim Chin-yŏng) is a romantic comedy, like the other slapstick films by director Kim.[6] The lead actors, beautiful Pak Ye-jin and funny Im Chang-jung, are known for their comedic acting. In its opening weekend in November 2009, the film sold more than three hundred thousand tickets. The Korean title, *Ch'ŏngdam Posal*, means "the diviner from Ch'ŏngdam." Ch'ŏngdam is a fashionable area in Seoul's Kangnam ward, with many galleries and designer shops, while *posal* is another name for mansin but within the Buddhist tradition. The title points to the posh divination parlor where much of the story takes place. The protagonist, Tae-rang, is a successful mansin and the manager. Her specialty is using divination and love advice to help couples. Many celebrities play themselves as her clients in the film.[7] The clients appear quite comfortable sharing the intimate details of their lives with the mansin. For example, a returning customer reveals, "I never wear underwear on blind dates, but for some reason I wanted to wear them on that day. During the date, I went straight to the bathroom to take them off. For some reason, I forgot to zip my pants. Do you think that she saw it? She thinks that I am a freak, right?" The mansin asks about the size of his penis, and when he reassures her that he has nothing to be ashamed of, she promises, "She will call you, just wait." Her half-serious comment is appreciated by the client as fortune telling, and he leaves hoping to meet that date soon.

Tae-rang's life gets complicated when she learns that her fate is to marry a man whom she finds ridiculous. Her mother, who is also a diviner, predicted that Tae-rang would marry before she turned twenty-eight, to a man born on a particular date. Every man she dates meets with some kind of accident, as if fate were unwilling to let her marry him. Im Chang-jung's character is a clumsy horse trainer's assistant whose job includes collecting horse urine. He is hit by Tae-rang's car, and she ends up asking him out despite her strong dislike. Then she learns that his birth date matches the prophecy. The strange relationship creates constant misunderstandings in the early part of the film. Later, some scenes can be categorized as romantic clichés, when the awkward beginning of this relationship gives way to feelings of love and appreciation. The film depicts musok not an irrelevant tradition but rather as a necessary profession that affects the protagonist's life. Consulting a mansin is represented as a mainstream activity, and the mansin views herself as much higher in the social hierarchy than the horse trainer's assistant. This presentation is in stark contrast with the traditional status of mansin.

Paksu Kŏndal (*Man on the Edge*, 2013, directed by Cho Chin-gyu) is an action or gangster comedy.[8] It is sometimes titled *Gangster Shaman*, which is closer to the translation of *paksu kŏndal* (shaman bum). This film adds a twist to the well-trod path of this genre. It combines local traditions of spirit mediation with gender themes and exaggerated crime and violence sequences. The combination sold well, and almost four million admissions were recorded during its theatrical run (Hancinema 2013). It ranked forty-sixth in Korea's all-times box hits (IMDb 2013). In addition, its popularity led to the film's inclusion in the Korean Air feature film section, which includes mostly films that are deemed worthy of international promotion and are noncontroversial. The film's protagonist, Kwang-ho, is a gang member and the right-hand man of a mafia boss. He begins experiencing symptoms of sinbyŏng after a knife stabs his palm during a street fight. Mysterious events also occur, such as a long chase by a flying newspaper. Kwang-ho decides to visit a mansin fortune-teller whose advertisement he saw in that newspaper. He wants to learn why he is experiencing such strange events. She explains that he is possessed and destined to be a paksu.

From that point on, he begins to lead a double life, for fear of being mocked and disrespected by his gang members. In his work as a fortune-teller, the gangster hides his face behind a fan or a cloth screen. In a full-scale kut, he dances unhidden except for a thick layer of makeup. After meeting ghosts and spirits, the gangster becomes more sensitive to issues of life and death and develops compassion for human suffering. This experience leads to conflict between his vocations. He fears his spiritual mother no less than his mafia boss and leaves important mafia meetings in response to her phone calls. This theme is counterhegemonic because in most of Korean society, men are expected to be subordinate to other men—not to female figures, and certainly not to mansin. Both these comedies portray mansin and paksu as struggling mainly with romance, work, or friendship, not with sexual desire. As mansin have become more human and less scary, their sexuality has stopped being depicted as dangerous or non-normative.

DEPICTION: HOW ARE MUSOK PRACTITIONERS REPRESENTED VISUALLY?

The cinematic depiction of mansin always includes colorful costumes and artifacts, music, and dance. However, different approaches channel the audience's emotions toward either respecting and sympathizing with the mudang characters or fearing and loathing them.

Musok as Dark and Scary

The opening scene of *Munyŏdo* (1972) shows a kut ritual held near the seaside. The mansin looks exhausted and can barely walk. She is quite young but is not a cheerful dancer, in contrast to mansin in more recent films. Next, the home shrine is shown. It is a shabby hut that seems to be dark even during the day. Some religious acts are depicted as held at night, in the dark, with the people barely visible. The most extreme scene, in which the mother tries to exorcize her son, shows close-ups of her angry, scary face. Shadowy paintings of gods on the wall contribute to the forbidding atmosphere. After the mother tears and burns pages from her son's bible, they fight and push each other. This intense scene, accompanied by dramatic music, ends with a depiction of the destroyed shrine and the mother mourning her son. In this film, as in *Iŏdo*, the mansin never looks happy.

Iŏdo (1977) depicts rural Korea—and musok, as a part of it—as the extreme opposite of modernity. Accordingly, it presents no beautiful, slow dance and music in the island's exorcisms. Instead, dramatic and menacing talk and spells by the mudang are the main features of these religious events. Grotesque images of a dead body, bewildered women, and fighting villagers emphasize this stance. Debates around this belief system drive the plot. In this respect, musok is no less central than in the other films discussed below. However, in *Iŏdo*, the mudang adds further complexity to an already convoluted net of past and present interactions. Although some graphic depictions are of an erotic nature, the main emotions prompted by the film are bewilderment and suspicion toward the mudang. A consistent feature throughout *Iŏdo* is the artistic use of color. The island's natural settings are shown in monochromatic gray and brown in contrast to bright red for the mudang's outfits and house. This color scheme emphasizes the gulf between the mudang and ordinary villagers. The mudang is not depicted as an integral part of her community. The brown and gray symbolize the peaceful rural scene, whereas the bright red disrupts the harmony and is alarming.

Im Kwŏn-t'aek's film *Sin'gung* (*The Divine Bow*, 1979), which depicts shamanic rituals, was filmed in a location so remote that a technical problem causing blurriness in the right side of the frame was discovered only after shooting ended; this caused the film to be shown very little (Koreanfilm.org 2011b). Some people commented at the time that the blurry image fit the general view of musok as vanishing and that it was an appropriate way to present musok.

Musok as Beautiful and Efficacious

Toward the end of the 1980s, the depiction of musok in films became more admiring and artistically appreciative. Rituals were shown as beautiful performances that include long, popular dances and songs. In *Pul-ŭi ttal* (*Daughter of the Flames*, 1983), the beautiful and colorful depiction of musok stands in stark contrast to the dull depiction of Christianity. Traditional ceremonies and costumes are brightly colored, and people express happiness as they dance and sing. The mudang mother that appears in flashback scenes is very pretty. In contrast, the Christians wear plain, somber clothes and do not express happiness or enjoyment when they protest or sing religious texts.

Twenty years later, in *Ogu* (2003), kut seems to be an even livelier and more enjoyable social occasion. The main kut is an arena where disputes and social discord are settled through beautiful song and dance. The entertainment aspect of this film is also prevalent in the way that the staged and scripted kut is shown. The initial part of the kut, when the mudang perform a purification rite on the riverbank, is filmed as a joyous spiritual experience for the participants and observers. Ritual song and dance are depicted artistically, with professional performers and occasional breaks for humorous depictions of old men dancing or children at play. Even the climactic clash between the raped girl and the rapist's father ends mildly. Grandmother Hwang hugs the young woman and offers her little boy a chance to become part of a respected family. Conflicts and sorrows are resolved in *Ogu* through traditional musok rituals and old-style community gatherings.

In *Ch'ŏngdam Posal* (*Fortune Saloon*, 2009), the divination hall is a fashionable, clean, and organized establishment, and the mansin is smart and stylish. The shrine where she divines for her clients is well lit and full of colorful and decorative musok artifacts. It does not seem like a scary place. Moreover, it is a place where many clients come to seek comfort and help.

Musok as Thrilling and Funny

The acceptance of musok as lighthearted and even funny can be seen in the first sequence of *Ogu* (2003). It begins with a beautiful, scenic view of a cloudy sky above a small lake, within a dense forest. From the lake rise three faces, followed by the naked bodies of the three ghost characters. One of them says to his friends, "Now, let's enter the human world." They begin walking naked in a small-town street. They encounter shocked responses to their nudity and especially to their unnaturally large genitals. They manage to blend into the human world after they don clothes that they pick up on the street. They are not frightening but funny. Their facial expressions and body movements are awkward but not scary.

In *Paksu Kŏndal* (*Man on the Edge*, 2013), the camera takes an active role in emphasizing the conflict between the main character's two roles. Close-ups show the confused expressions of the *paksu* (male mansin), and wide long shots encompass his contradictory social contexts. These shots demonstrate the grandeur of the ritual's setting, the large audience that comes to observe the performance, and the power demonstrations of many gang members. The different angles of the individual frames are shown interchangeably. This choice emphasizes the conflict between the individual and the different social expectations of him.

It is interesting that the trailers for this film emphasize action and racing scenes over musok. Film trailers are a little-discussed genre (Johnston 2009). However, they raise important visual and thematic considerations because they are planned for effective marketing (Maier 2009). The two *Paksu Kŏndal* trailers begin with car chases, mob gatherings, and fistfights—all with very fast cuts. Next appears the gangster's life-changing event: the moment when a knife cuts his palm and he becomes possessed. In the two trailers, a brief sequence of only about three seconds shows a divination session. In this scene, the gangster sneezes, creating a huge cloud of dust and disrupting the shape of the divination rice during a meeting with clients. In that brief moment, a shrine and a traditionally clad mansin can be seen. The next depiction of musok in the trailer goes back in time and includes two women clad in traditional hanbok sitting in front of the gangster and telling him that he is destined to be a paksu. He protests, and the next scene shows him upset and kicking a wooden fence. A wolf appears to the gangster and talks to him. Then the trailer features a series of musok scenes in fast snapshots edited into one long sequence: him putting on colorful makeup while dressing for kut, dancing and jumping, eating, losing his temper while seated behind a curtain at a divination table. In the trailer, it is evident that he becomes a paksu, but the scenes shown are humorous. The fast background music fits the comedy genre. No serene musok activities were edited into these film trailers. In this way, contemporary cinema depicts the religious aspect of musok matter-of-factly, without delving much into value judgments or cultural critique. Musok's vivacious visuals are harnessed to enhance audience entertainment through comedy and thrill. A nostalgic yearning for a vanishing or debated cultural heritage was more evident in older films like *Ogu* and *Pul-ŭi ttal*.

The film's poster also features the main character with symbols of his contradictory roles. His work as a paksu is represented by his posture, seated at a table with an old divination textbook, a yellow pujŏk charm, and typical brass bells (fig. 2.1). His role as a mafia man is portrayed by his wearing a shiny black suit and a colorful shirt, open to midchest. His hair points up "porcupine style" to show his contemporary fashion consciousness. In the poster, his expression is unhappy. The audience sees the difficulty of a mansin's lifestyle and expects to see an internal struggle in the film. These expectations are met when the audience views the gangster as a novice paksu and laughs hard when misunderstandings occur.

SOCIAL ACCEPTANCE: ARE MUDANG OUTCASTS?

As discussed in the book's introduction, mudang have not been perceived as equal members of Korean society. Their social standing as liminal figures who mediate between the human and the supernatural have given rise to fear, respect, and disdain, all at the same time. This multifaceted cultural response is present in the cinematic representations of musok. In *Ssal* (1963) and *Iŏdo* (1977), mudang are shown as outcasts who cause only trouble. The reason for their survival in Korea's modern society is people's irrational fear and superstition. However, in *Pul-ŭi ttal* (1983), the social perspective becomes more complex. The mudang mother tries to practice musok, but several men prevent this. Later, her son thinks that musok is nonsense and consults a psychologist when he has visions. Nevertheless, he continues to have these visions and dreams. He—and, with him, the film's audience—comes to understand that the persecution of his mother was harmful, even disastrous. Unlike the earlier films, the mudang in *Pul-ŭi ttal* is not the miscreant but the victim. Similarly, In *Ogu* (2003), a flashback scene shows the mudang's youngest daughter being asked by her sweetheart to run away together. He cannot endure his friends' ridicule about "dating a witch." Later, when she is raped, the village elders refuse to support her because of her mother's lowly status. The film emphasizes

Fig. 2.1 *Man on the Edge* poster, 2013. Credit: Showbox.

how ostracized musok is. The old mudang's children prefer to work in other jobs rather than continue their family's despised musok heritage.

In *Ch'ŏngdam Posal* (2009), there are signs that the mansin's image is improving. When the mansin tells a couple that they are not meant to be together, the woman frowns and insults her. In response, the practitioner throws money at the couple, saying indignantly, "The gods are angry. Don't ever come back." The startled woman complains to the secretary about the mansin's behavior, but the secretary answers, "Who dares talk like that these days? Mudang are Intangible Cultural Assets now. The fortune-telling market is worth 3 billion US dollars. Disrespecting fortune telling... How ignorant!" This rebuke indicates the contemporary change in the perception of mansin, which results from official acceptance by the government rather than from fear of the supernatural. This kind of respect runs throughout the film's narrative.

However, not all the characters in *Ch'ŏngdam Posal* think that mansin are respectable. In another scene, the mansin visits the home of a rich man she is dating. He tries to touch her legs, and when she refuses and wants to leave, he remarks, "You are nothing but a mudang." He tries to touch her again, aggressively. As she flees, he slips on marbles that have fallen on the floor, drops into his swimming pool while holding onto a lamp, and is electrocuted. This strange coincidence is a seemingly supernatural intervention by the mansin's guardian spirits. Although the mansin's connection to the spirits is shown as unabated, other diviners are shown as false. For example, when she visits a street fortune-teller because she is anxious about her own love life, he predicts that there will be rain and sells her an old, half-broken umbrella. After she leaves, he is shown looking at the newspaper's broadcast saying, "The weather report brings me good money. It worked again!" Despite this cynical remark, that scene and others demonstrate that the main characters are sincere believers who seek the divination abilities of other mansin and diviners.

The film ends with several short, scripted "interviews" with the fortune saloon's clients in extreme close-ups. Some praise the place, stating that it has changed their lives for the better. Others tell how the predictions were wrong or led to misfortune. The film does not state whether fortune-telling is worth the money and effort. Instead, it ends by addressing this practice as an individual whim that sometimes makes people happy and sometimes not. The film consistently refers to the supernatural as part of reality and to mansin as whole persons. However, it does not state a clear resolution about musok's role in society.

Paksu Kŏndal (2013) depicts the paksu as a social anomaly. Musok is perceived as allowing a subversive hierarchy to exist within Korean society. South Korea is a male-dominated society. Constraining social etiquette has resulted in little social mobility for women (Abelmann 2003; Chong 2006; Deuchler 1992; Kendall and Peterson 1983; J. Song 2014). Musok is viewed as a reversed hierarchy because women are the dominant and most successful practitioners, and they advise both genders. This hierarchy is further emphasized as the protagonist behaves like a shy novice with the female practitioners. He fully acquiesces to his spiritual mother, in contrast to his rough relationships within the gang and with other women. In one scene, two gang members strain to see who the diviner is behind the white curtain. They push the curtain aside, and he shakes his brass bells and shouts. The men become upset, tear down the curtain, and turn the divination table upside down, making cups smash on the floor. An alarmed supervising female mansin enters and tells the paksu that he has to go with the clients and perform the ritual they are demanding. He heeds her request to participate in the ritual. This depiction of the paksu's behavior demonstrates how gender hierarchies work subversively in the musok world, even when the mansin's apprentice is actually a macho gangster.

In another scene, a procession of several mansin and many observers is led by a paksu dressed in a colorful costume. The procession crosses the narrow bridge onto a temporary outdoor shrine on a floating platform at a port. The same paksu suddenly enters a dressing room and talks on the phone. He uses harsh, mafia-style speech with a mafia elder who is apparently the event's sponsor. The elder demands to see him. Hastily, the paksu takes off his costume and dons a formal suit. He removes the heavy makeup from his face and runs out to meet the elder. During the meeting, one of the younger men happens to ask the elder whether he has seen the curtain paksu. He suggests that during the ritual, they will tear the mask from his face. The paksu (in a mafioso's outfit and behavior) looks worried but laughs with the others to hide his fear. "It sounds like fun," he says. Then his phone rings, and a woman's voice asks him, "Where are you? It is time for you to perform." He apologizes and runs back to the dressing room to prepare for his dance sequence. He dons the costume again and applies thick makeup. A few minutes later, he dances on the chaktu blades right in front of the mafia elder, who does not recognize him under the makeup and costume. This climactic scene depicts exciting shamanic activities and mafia hierarchies. In addition, it shows the personal conflict of a male practitioner who puts much effort into concealing his religious occupation from his partners in the crime business. The film upends conservative gender roles, in which Korean men are expected to express power, dominance, and superiority (Lim 2008). Furthermore, mansin are considered low status. Viewers are entertained by seeing the macho gangster take orders from his female mansin mentor. The female mansin are central and dominating in contrast to the weakened outcast mansin in *Munyŏdo* (1972) and *Pul-ŭi ttal* (1983).

PRESUMED FUTURE: WILL MUSOK SURVIVE THE TWENTY-FIRST CENTURY?

As discussed, films of the 1970s were produced as the South Korean government launched the New Community Movement Campaign. This initiative took pains to eradicate shamanic practices in order to create a fully modern, industrialized society. Many musok devotees and practitioners feared that this tradition would disappear completely. Filmmakers who portrayed musok in the 1970s also perceived it as a vanishing culture that existed mainly in remote areas of Korea.

Even *Pul-ŭi ttal* (1983) expresses this view that musok will be replaced by modern ideas. Christians and intellectuals in the film assume that psychology will come to explain many phenomena that were once considered to be the acts of ghosts and spirits. However, as the film continues, the audience senses that musok has survived its persecution and is still needed in the 1980s. For example, the possessed protagonist's daughter cannot be cured by modern medicine or Christian healing.

Ogu (2003) shows a different musok tradition. The role of mudang is inherited rather than induced by a spiritual experience. This tradition-based transfer dooms the practice because the younger generation avoids practicing it. In the beginning of *Ogu*, the old mudang's four children are shown at their jobs—teacher, bar owner, fish vendor, and singer. None has taken an active role in maintaining the tradition of musok. Even the old mudang laments, "I don't do the kut anymore, but I am still a mudang." In this case, Korean traditions that used to be transmitted from parent to child but have become formal art classes or died out. The generation gap goes beyond the mudang family. It is also expressed as a direct conflict between the dying Grandmother Hwang and her son, who tries to convince her to give up her expensive kut plans. The village leaders also demand that a large-scale kut not be performed in the village. The film highlights the fear that hereditary musok is dying out.

In *Ch'ŏngdam Posal* (2009) and *Paksu Kŏndal* (2013), the survival of musok in the twenty-first century is no longer questioned. The two films depict the lives of mansin in urban settings and their popularity among various social strata in contemporary Korea. They are depicted as fully adjusted to new technologies, ideas, and cultural values. Musok has become part of the nationalistic effort to produce and maintain a unique Korean identity. It is also a resource for individuals who seek spiritual support.

Nevertheless, some recent films depict mudang with disbelief and ridicule. The popular horror comedy *Kwisini Sanda* (*Ghost House*, 2004, directed by Kim Sang-jin) shows a young man who moves into a new house where mysterious things happen. He discovers that the house is haunted and, in his search for a peaceful life, invites various exorcists to expel the resident ghosts. All are portrayed as ineffective, and their dances and spells are burlesques. One scene uses a split screen to depict segments of Christian, Buddhist, and shamanic exorcisms, each in a different frame. The rituals are represented in a segmented manner, with exaggerated behaviors. The loud, chaotic mix of the various kinds of music adds to the confusion onscreen. But even in this comedy, there is no doubt that musok is alive and well in contemporary Seoul.

FILMS AS VEHICLES OF CULTURAL PROCESSES

Organizing the films discussed along a historical timeline demonstrates how the social perception of musok has evolved. The suspicion and hostility toward this vernacular religion in the 1960s and 1970s faded in the 1980s, when musok became the object of national identity construction and cultural preservation.[9] In the 2000s, films began to depict the contemporary musok world as a living tradition. Consequently, we see several comic depictions of practicing mansin.

Films are vehicles of cultural processes in several ways. First, when they reach broad audiences, cinematic representations affect many viewers and shape public opinion on musok. Second, the cinematic medium emphasizes the visual and artistic expressiveness of musok and thus reduces stigma. Third, musok is such an intense practice, in both meaning and form, that kut rituals offer a cinematic opportunity to make beautiful, scary, exciting, and innovative films even with modest financial and technological means. This religious practice allows for such a diversity of perceptions given to its own variations and the versatility of the medium.

Films are entertaining as comedies and thrillers. They allow people to engage in nostalgia, and they offer an escape to an imaginary world. In musok-related films, viewers might perceive the belief system and practice as scary, interesting, funny, beautiful, or helpful, depending on the film's production design. All of these possibilities allow musok representations to be entwined with various artistic purposes and production schemes. Moreover, as the Iranian filmmaker Mohsen Makhmalbaf observed, "Cinema is a potent generator of change" (Klein 2013). Film viewers were shown musok as a dying tradition in the late twentieth century and were led to think that few practitioners would be left, in a marginalized existence. In the early twenty-first century, films have increasingly portrayed mansin as humane and sensitive members of society. Films both reflect and affect the stigma of musok in Korean mainstream culture. I did not interview the Korean public extensively to verify the effect of films on the general perception of musok. However, in the course of my ethnographic fieldwork, I came across many indications that the general public was very familiar with films about musok. When new acquaintances heard about my research, they often mentioned films; my Korean friends would call to tell me about new films on musok; and my mansin interlocutors discussed the cinematic representations of musok, most quite harshly. Moreover, as chapter

4 will show, scenes from films are often used to introduce televised interviews with actual mansin.

The contribution of musok to society, as both a religion and a performance art, has increasingly surfaced in films. What has remained constant is the appreciation of film directors for the beauty and aesthetic complexity of musok. These films emphasize the art encapsulated in both the material and the intangible parts of kut performance. The Korean government also particularly emphasizes the art of musok as worth preserving. In this way, films parallel other societal mechanisms in transmitting musok's art to the audience.

Another recent trend is the use of musok in experimental films. The most notorious one is *P'aranmanjang* (*Night Fishing*, 2011, by Pak Ch'an-uk and Pak Ch'an-gyŏng).[10] *P'aranmanjang* is a thirty-three-minute horror mystery that was shot entirely with an iPhone, cost about $130,000, and took only ten days to create. It retells a folktale about a fisherman who catches a seductive woman. In the film, the man catches a fish that transforms into the body of a drowned woman in a white funeral robe. He gets entangled in the fishing lines and faints. He wakes up to discover that he is now wearing the woman's outfit. The movie turns to the man's family, which orders a kut to learn the reasons for his drowning and to help his possessed daughter. The boundaries between reality, imagination, and myth are intentionally blurred, and musok is the only way to clarify the situation. Mansin Sŏ Kyŏng-uk, who is discussed extensively in chapter 1, plays the experienced mansin. She assists a younger practitioner in her attempt to send the drowned man's spirit peacefully to the afterworld. To demonstrate the possession of the practitioner, the young mansin is played by the same actress who plays the drowned woman. This choice suggests that the drowned woman caused the man's death and possessed his daughter.

The filmmakers used a combination of musok practitioners and actors and an innovative technology that creates new opportunities for professional filmmakers. This short feature won the Golden Bear Award for best short film at the Sixty-First Berlin International Film Festival. In view of its success, Pak Ch'an-gyŏng, one of its directors, produced the documentary *Mansin: Ten Thousand Spirits*, which will be discussed below.

The ritual's beauty and the enthusiastic participation of practitioner-actors in the filming have become resources for several film directors. A contrasting recent example is the animated film *Munyŏdo* (*The Shaman Sorceress*, 2018, directed by An Chae-hun [Ahn Jae-hun]), based on the 1936 story by Kim Tong-ni that was adapted in the 1972 film *Munyŏdo*. The animation creates distance from real practitioners, as does the choice to tell a story about Korea's past (M. Lee 2018). As in *Ssal*, the colorful aestheticism of musok stands in sharp contrast to the monochromatic depiction of Christianity. The dramatic death of the mudang and her son reminds viewers that premodern traditions are part of the past. Hope for the future is represented by the art collector who keeps the paintings of the surviving mudang's daughter in his collection.

These examples demonstrate the contribution of musok to films. The reverse, in which mansin use cinematic techniques to promote themselves, is also evident. The ability to film satisfactorily with a smartphone allows mansin to document and broadcast their practices online, as discussed in chapter 5. In light of the growing trend of positive depictions of musok, mansin have begun to show more interest in being part of documentaries about musok. This different genre of films has also shown changes in the norms of depicting musok. It will be discussed here to consider whether a similar cultural change in the image of musok can be traced.

CHANGING TRENDS IN DOCUMENTARY AND ETHNOGRAPHIC FILMS ABOUT MUSOK

When the first DVD edition of a film about Mansin Yi Hae-gyŏng, *Sai-esŏ* (*Between*, 2006, directed by Yi Ch'ang-jae) sold out, she told me, "Why not? Musok is fun to watch."[11] This documentary, like several others produced in the 2000s, was also released to commercial theaters. Thousands of viewers watched these films, including mansin, who viewed it with a critical, professional eye, as a learning experience. Famous mansin try to place their work on broadcast platforms. Such media-savvy, sophisticated mansin become models for some two hundred thousand other mansin who practice musok in South Korea.

Ethnographic or documentary films differ significantly from feature films, not only because of their different approach to reality but also because they adhere to different cinematic norms. Documentaries are expected to be filmed in locations that existed before the filming, with little modification, and to deliver the knowledge and viewpoints of real people. However, the depicted mansin do not always agree that documentary directors understand musok properly and often criticize the filmmakers' choices. In the early 1990s, anthropologist Kim Chongho reported on a meeting between Mansin Kim Kŭm-hwa and television filmmakers who wanted to document her dancing on knives. She felt that the media people knew too little about her and her performance; therefore, she showed them a video of an initiation kut that she had held and two books that she had published.[12] After the filmmakers left, she complained that they wanted to make money from her art and that it would cost her too much to provide for such a kut, which they did not offer to finance, in contrast with the producers of the previous film. She stated that she did not need to "bribe" journalists for good reviews of her work, as she was already well established (C. Kim 2003, 211–5). Her comment suggests that younger or aspiring practitioners pay to be filmed and that perhaps she herself had done so in the past.

Before the twenty-first century, most Korean documentaries about musok aired on television, without a theater release. They showed a scholar discussing musok and a mansin performing a ritual; it was uncommon to interview mansin themselves about their art. Such directors' choices mark a clear division between religious performance, which belongs to the practitioners, and learned commentary, which belongs to academia. Timothy Tangherlini regretted that most documentaries on musok "reflect the rigid structures hypothesized by some Korean folklorists" (1994, 434). Documentaries from the 1980s and 1990s followed the trends of Korean folklore scholarship in general—namely, discussing a certain regional style, presenting the mudang as carriers of ancient tradition, and disregarding them as whole persons. Here, too, how musok was portrayed had more to do with general cultural trends than with a particular genre. Folklore studies in Korea followed structural research trends and focused on heritage preservation.

More recently there has been a shift to greater interest in holistic research on individual performers, their life histories, and their performance choices. Even now, mansin are often depicted only as carriers of tradition, with little attention to any activity outside the religious performance. In the 2000s, Korean directors began to give voice to the practitioners and excluded Korean scholars from their films. In recent films, the mansin take center stage, and the ritual becomes the background to their lives and experiences. These changes in how musok is depicted make ethnographic and documentary productions more interesting to the general public, and several such films were released commercially. This change fits with the recent interest in the lives of mansin, as discussed earlier in relation to feature films. This will be discussed further in chapter 4 as a contemporary trend in television programs.

Treating mansin as the experts on musok and showing them as real people aligns with the current situation in which many clients are younger than age forty. The generation that survived the Korean War and rapid urbanization is now elderly in Seoul. Many were educated in the time of the New Community Movement of the 1970s, which sought to modernize Korea and eliminate superstitions (Kendall 2009, 10, 19). Young clients view musok not as a family tradition or a national heritage but rather as a kind of New Age practice. They approach this vernacular belief system as part of a personal, spiritual search or out of a need for counseling. Musok's endurance in the twenty-first century is related to a nostalgic longing for an authentic personal or national identity, but also to these new cultural choices.

I discuss three films that represent the new trends in the depiction of musok. I have not analyzed documentaries from the twentieth century because I chose productions by Korean directors and producers that were shown in commercial theaters rather than televised or academic documentaries.[13] These three films had outstanding ticket sales. *Yŏngmae: sanja wa chugŭnja ŭi hwahae* (*Mudang: Reconciliation between the Living and the Dead*, 2003, directed by Pak Ki-bok) was one of the top-selling documentaries in Seoul's history, with 13,474 admissions.[14] The aforementioned *Sai-esŏ* (2006) had more than 24,000 admissions.[15] *Mansin* (*Mansin: Ten Thousand Spirits*, 2014, directed by Pak Ch'an-gyŏng) had 35,544 admissions in the first six weeks of screening (Hancinema 2015). This steady rise in admissions, although far from the success of the feature films discussed in this chapter, demonstrates the interest of the Korean public in documentaries on musok and in musok itself. There was also international recognition: *Mansin* was named the Fasken Martineau Best Feature Film, received the Video Award at the Toronto Reel Asian International Film Festival, and was the closing film at the 2014 New York Asian Film Festival (H. Kim 2014).

Like other musok documentaries from the early twenty-first century, these films depict the practitioners' lives, perspectives, and activities, including nonritual pursuits. As discussed in the introduction of this book, the line between the two musok traditions is blurry; *sesŭp-mu* (hereditary shamans of southern and eastern Korea) are not necessarily from the same bloodline because adoption of apprentices is common, whereas many *kangsin-mu* (god-chosen practitioners of northern regions) have relatives who are mansin (Yang 2004a; M. Yi 2004). *Yŏngmae*'s narration restates the common distinction between northern and southern musok practices but also demonstrates that times have changed—possessed practitioners have become prevalent throughout the peninsula. Moreover, the film laments the loss of the hereditary practice by showing the sadness expressed by the older mudang. They did not teach their children the complex traditions of sesŭp-mu because of the social stigma associated with being any kind of shaman during the 1960s through 1980s.

The conventional view held by most scholars is that hereditary shamans must pass the tradition down mother to daughter. However, as in other hereditary traditions, they could have adopted apprentices to allow for continuity in their family's heritage (Mills 2007). In *Yŏngmae*, the loss of artistic practices might perhaps be related to how scholars influenced shamanic traditions in an unintended way by emphasizing the hereditary aspect of sesŭp-mu. The film's structure manifests this change in musok practiced in the eastern and southern regions from sesŭp-mu to kangsi-mu and teaches the viewer that many possessed practitioners are not necessarily well versed in the performance of a full kut ritual.

The film begins with the possessed mansin Yi Hae-gyŏng passing a sharp blade over her tongue and standing on a pair of chaktu knives to venerate Changgun. For most Korean viewers, the choice of this scene to open the film sets musok as the theme; however, Mansin Yi is not interviewed or followed further. Instead, the documentary is focused on the two elderly hereditary mudang sisters, who are interviewed extensively and whose daily lives are depicted in detail. They live in a village and have experienced marginalization and material hardship throughout their lives. The later part of the documentary discusses mansin whose ancestors fled to South Korea after the communists took over the north.

The possessed mansin from the opening of *Yŏngmae* is the main subject of *Sai-esŏ*. The narrative in this later production is the initiation of kangsin-mu practitioners. Mansin Yi is shown diagnosing a young woman, an elderly female cancer patient, and a male child as possessed by gods and spirits. She concludes that the reason for these clients' suffering is their refusal to take on the role of mansin and to serve the supernatural entities that haunt them. She offers the two women an opportunity to become her spiritual daughters and undergo training and initiation rituals. For the boy, she performs a kut in which she convinces the gods to postpone his active role as a practicing mansin until he becomes a young man.

Mansin focuses on the most famous mansin, Kim Kŭm-hwa, who died in February 2019. She is depicted in rituals and interviews, along with staged scenes from her autobiography in which three actresses (Kim Sae-ron, Ryu Hyŏn-kyŏng, and Mun So-ri) play her at different stages of life. These scripted sequences, which are staged according to the conventions of Korean historical drama, can be categorized as docudrama or ethnofiction. Other sequences are documentary or extracted from previous documentaries about this well-known mansin. *Mansin* tracks the development of Kim's life alongside events in Korea's history, such as the Japanese occupation and the Korean War. The difficult history emphasizes her endurance in the face of suffering. During her interview about the war, the director situates the mansin, clad in traditional hanbok, inside a museum. Her words are heard over images of dioramas depicting soldiers and frightened villagers. In one of the dramatic depictions of her hardship, the actress is shown seated on the forest floor while two soldiers try—and fail—to shoot her to death.

The thematic choices of the three documentaries resemble those of feature films of the same period, which all mediate encounters between the audience and personal aspects of a mansin's life. As in the feature films discussed, the ritual and religious tradition serve as backgrounds for individuals' stories, not as the main focus. *Yŏngmae* resembles *Ogu*, which was released a year earlier, in lamenting the dying out of sesŭp-mu hereditary musok. *Sai-esŏ* and *Mansin* are reminiscent of *Paksu Kŏndal*, also of the same time period, in their attention to initiation and personal conflict over becoming a mansin. Both *Yŏngmae* and *Mansin* discuss the difficulties that mudang face in finding spouses, but this is not the main issue, as it is in *Ch'ŏngdam Posal*. The personal life of mansin can be depicted in a livelier manner in a feature film than in documentary interviews. In this case, the genre, rather than the medium, shapes the message that mansin have a tough love life because of their vocation. All three documentaries describe issues related to the social acceptance of musok practitioners. Also reminiscent of the family in *Ogu*, in *Yŏngmae*, the children of the two protagonists are reluctant to spend the many years it takes to learn to recite long chants and prayers and to play indigenous music. An interview with a couple of farmers from the same community demonstrates how mudang have been perceived as lowly members of society and how most people refrain from close social relations with them. One of the main interviewees in the film is Mudang Ch'ae Chŏng-nye, who was in her midseventies. She talks with her husband about his reasons for marrying her, saying that he had no other option. Her husband, who is also from a mudang family, responds with similar suggestions about his wife's nonexistent marriage alternatives. These interviews are interesting and touching, but they cannot trigger the same emotional response from the audience as the depiction of the rape and suicide related to being mudang offspring in the feature film *Ogu*.

In urban contexts, children of mudang can hide their stigmatized backgrounds, and many keep only limited contact with their village families. *Yŏngmae* shows how new career choices for hereditary mudang result in a shortage of spiritual practitioners and a growing trend of people who consult possessed mediums that the film calls *prophesizers*. The old mudang complains how such mediums perform rituals without having been properly trained. The purification rite, which is the most popular in the region, requires that she perform with a team of mudang, and she did not teach it to her daughters. In the past, she could perform with her older sisters, but only one sister has survived, and she is elderly and half paralyzed. Eventually, Mudang Ch'ae takes a young apprentice from another family in an attempt to transmit her knowledge and keep the tradition alive, but there is no interview with that novice. The film ends with an interview with Ch'ae during the ritual marking one hundred days from the death of her sister, symbolizing that she is the last mudang of that family.

With a completely different tone, *Sai-esŏ* follows several young apprentices of the possessed Hwanghedo musok style. While planning the film, director Yi Ch'ang-jae interviewed ninety practitioners and eventually chose Mansin Yi Hae-gyŏng as the protagonist. She has been featured in many television shows and newspapers. *Seoul* magazine (Koehler 2007, 36) called her "Woodstock mudang" because she loves American rock music and advocates making musok more accessible to younger Koreans by updating archaic terminology and texts. Her clientele is the most extensive that I have encountered. She rarely goes a day without several short visits from her clients, and her cellphone rings every few minutes with a client seeking advice, scheduling a meeting, or just saying hello. Thanks to the publicity and success of the documentary film, she estimates that at least eight hundred people attended her triennial public kut in 2006. I witnessed several hundred participants at another such kut, in 2014, held some three hours' drive north of Seoul. In that ritual, which also inaugurated Yi's new countryside home, several famous actors and film directors came to show respect, and folk musicians performed onstage between kut sequences.

Even more popular is Yi's spiritual mother, Kim Kŭm-hwa, the protagonist of *Mansin*. She performed extensively for private clients and organizations and conducted many government-sponsored rituals in Korea and abroad as a representative of traditional Korean culture.[16] Her work and life story have been told in several academic papers (e.g., C. Kim 2003; Cheon 2009; Choi 1987; Hong 2006) and in her own book (K. Kim 1995). Numerous documentary films and television programs showcase her work and ritual. Consequently, creating another documentary about her required a unique perspective, such as the hybrid docudrama genre chosen by director Pak. Her life story is viewed as important enough to be revived in dramatized sequences, and famous actresses portraying her as a girl and a younger woman added to the popularity of the film. Moreover, telling the history of modern Korea through her personal experiences places Mansin Kim at the center of Korean society, as a national emblem rather than an outcast. This message fits with the legitimizing tone of feature films from the same period. Together, the documentary and feature films manifest and reinforce broader cultural changes in musok's public image.

USING THE MEDIUM TO NARRATE REALITY AND SPIRITUALITY IN DOCUMENTARIES

The cinematic devices used in each of these documentaries emphasize the directors' intentions. In depictions of the southern hereditary ritual style, *Yŏngmae* uses black-and-white footage, whereas rituals of possessed mansin are shown in color. This choice highlights the main tradition documented in the film—that of Chindo Island—emphasizing that the mudang performing it is the oldest of the practitioners shown. Black-and-white footage resembles historic documentaries, and in the film, this presentation symbolizes the decline of the southern coast ritual style. The artifacts of the Chindo rituals are made mostly of white paper, which creates sharp contrasts between light and shade in this filmed format. Interviews and ritual preparations by the possessed mansin Pak Min-jung, a beautiful woman in her thirties, likewise offer a sharp contrast to the elderly sisters. The choice of this young practitioner as the example of the northern style emphasizes that although the Chindo ritual is dying out and has few practitioners remaining, the northern style is thriving. The young, sophisticated Pak symbolizes a different generation of god-chosen mansin. She is filmed shopping for a ritual while wearing a light purple business suit and speaking a refined, urban dialect. Interestingly, Pak's mother was also a possessed mansin, but the film does not describe their practice as hereditary because possessed practitioners are believed to be chosen by the spirits.

The film *Sai-esŏ* also celebrates the lively, colorful nature of the Hwanghaedo kut style, but not before trying to put the viewers at ease with the spiritual aspect of musok. The director chose to begin the film without a clear reference to musok. The first shot focuses on a young woman seated on a sandy beach, sobbing. The scene continues for almost five minutes, in which Mansin Yi, kneeling beside the young woman, tries to persuade her to let go of her fear and receive the spirits. The two women look like any other urban Koreans. They are dressed in plain, daily clothes; do not use rural speech, ancient words, or ritual texts; and do not hold any religious objects. The only shamanic artifacts to be seen are colorful flags used by an older woman who stands at a considerable distance. The depiction of the two women easily extracts sympathy and personal identification, even from non-Korean audiences.[17] Later in the film, when a full ritual with costumes, altars, and other items is displayed, the unfamiliar viewer is more likely to feel a semiotic distance from the scene. The symbols might not be recognizable, and the occurrences might seem strange and outlandish. Nevertheless, by that point, viewers already have an initial acquaintance with the protagonists.

Mansin Yi is introduced only after a second scene set in the young woman's typical, contemporary home. When the film turns to her shrine, there is a sharp leap into the material aspects of musok. The scene that introduces the mansin was edited to include abundant musok symbols. In about three minutes, Mansin Yi is shown talking, working, and interacting with clients, whereas various musok goods and items are displayed alongside and between the spoken words. At times, the protagonist's speech provides the background sound while she is out of the frame. Rather, we see lit candles, brassware with incense sticks, handwritten white notes attached to white clay pots, a purple paper flower, the tip of a curved knife, a tall trident, and brass bells, as the voice of Mansin Yi says, "We have to do something about her before she gets married. She is suffering right now. The spirit has followed her into the house .... She is not possessed by some evil spirit; you have to know that." A close-up of Mansin Yi smoking fades into another close-up of an older woman and the young patient, both very attentive to what the mansin is saying. Mansin Yi continues, "So, if we just let the spirits settle down, she will feel better. We must relieve her from the pain now. Do you believe in kut (exorcism)?" The young woman answers, "Half and half, right? I don't completely disbelieve and I don't deny anything." The camera focuses on a statue of sansin and a lit candle. Other god paintings are visible on the back wall.[18]

This three-minute excerpt from the film shows how important the objects of musok are in media presentations of mansin and their practices. Although Mansin Yi says interesting words, and her facial expression might be important to watch, the film becomes more interesting when colorful musok artifacts saturate the screen. These images add a current of unexplained data that the audience absorbs while watching the film. Almost no commentary or subtitles are related to the artifacts, so the audience's reaction to the artifacts' appearance is shaped without verbal interference. Their colorful aestheticism appeals to the senses, and the religious meanings emerge through a diversity of semiotic responses, according to the viewer's knowledge and recognition of the symbols.

The material objects of musok serve as indexical signs when they represent the contrast between the mansin and her new apprentice. The young woman's world is decorated with commercial, Western-style goods, whereas the mansin's world is full of images and objects that are clearly more traditional, Korean, and ritual-related. Electric devices, such as an air conditioner, and mundane, commercial objects in her room mark the contemporaneousness of her existence in the ordinary, human world. The ritual artifacts depicting the spirits mark the fact that she can approach ancestors and the timeless gods of natural elements. The film contains a few rare explanations of the role of these artifacts and the context of their use. The film is not about materiality. It is about a spiritual experience, human emotions, and conflicts among generations, perspectives, and strong personalities. Nevertheless, without the beautiful objects, the film would not be the visual feast that it is. As is common in recent films, fast-paced editing and jump cuts between objects and close-ups of people give this film a contemporary feel. The abundance of aesthetically stimulating musok artifacts enables the director to keep the audience's attention.

Sai-esŏ aims to create emotional impact with little academic narrative, whereas *Mansin* shows interviews with many scholars of folklore. However, *Mansin* is not an intellectually dry film, because it has so many dramatized scenes from Mansin Kim's life story. Such hybridity has become more common in the early twenty-first century. Many scholars of visual ethnography have argued that there is no option such as "objective" or "authentic" ethnographic film; therefore, documentary directors wield more artistic freedom in their work (Cooper 2006). For example, when the elderly mansin talks about visions of gods and spirits, the images on the screen are of deities personified by actors and not paintings or statues. In another scene, a dramatized initiation kut is interwoven with documentary footage of apprentices dancing in a single fast-paced sequence, so viewers may not distinguish the real from the scripted parts. This editing technique enhances not only the film's appeal but also its credibility over feature films. The appearance of the elderly mansin every few minutes and the older documentary footage make the difference. The film also shows the elderly Kim with tears in her eyes as she watches the staging of her initiation kut on the movie set. The image reinforces her support of the manner in which the story was filmed.

Mansin shows the variety of apprentices that Kim has had, from young, sophisticated Koreans to elderly women. Andrea Kalff, a German woman who undertook sin naerim kut several years ago is depicted within them. Her interesting case will be discussed in chapter 4. This variety reinforces the message that the gods might choose anyone to become a mansin, and that mansin are not necessarily from humble social backgrounds, despite the traditional stigma.[19] The film ends with a dreamlike scene in which the actress who portrays the young Kim walks in a recreated version of her childhood village and collects items from the spirits that have haunted her throughout her life. Each actor who has played such a spirit in the film hands her an object, including coins, a brass bowl, a pistol, and a camera. She throws these items into a fire pit, where they melt into a metal liquid that she pours into molds of musok brass bells, a fantastic rendering that hints at traditional musok brass bells' preparation. This surreal ending emphasizes the fictitious aspect of the film and lends a philosophical and mystical aura to the brass bells, which are a central symbol of musok and one of its most commonly used artifacts.

The mudang in these three documentaries are interviewed extensively, shown with relatives and apprentices, and followed on daily routines beyond rituals. This approach gives viewers a holistic view of the people behind the tradition. It is interesting that two of the major documentaries about musok were named after the profession's name and the practitioners' title. However, there is much difference between the two terms. As discussed in the introduction, *mansin* is more specific, while *mudang* refers to both hereditary and possessed practitioners. Furthermore, *mansin* relates specifically to the spiritual aspect of the practice, communicating with supernatural entities. The director of *Mansin* chose the name with full awareness of its cultural implications, as stated by a subtitle on a black screen at the beginning of the film that explains how the film's title is more respectful than the common *mudang*. This might even be subversive criticism of the previous documentary.

All three films gave the documented mudang the freedom to shape their onscreen personae. The mudang are well aware of the power that film and television hold and interested in controlling their portrayal to the public. Mansin like Yi Hae-gyŏng work hard to exhibit the material and spiritual aspects of their work in the best possible manner. Yi even launched a blog while participating in the film. In this beautifully crafted website, which will be discussed in chapter 5, she shared her experiences and thoughts during and after the film's production. Professionalization is one of the outstanding characteristics of hypertechnological South Korea. For mudang, this includes handling the press and other media professionals. This development will be discussed further in chapters 4 and 5. Still, being depicted in a documentary film cannot substitute for sincere devotion and dedication to spirits and clients. The practitioners depicted in the three films have not stopped their spiritual work in favor of media appearances. On the contrary, their clientele increased with the massive visibility they achieved through films, and their spiritual powers are perceived as even more formidable, since in musok, success means being on good terms with the supernatural.

Viewers of a documentary film do not encounter reality as it actually exists. Rather, they watch a carefully edited and planned professional interpretation by directors who have their own artistic, humanistic, and commercial intentions. The final product is prepared to make the audience feel as if the film were a depiction of real life. In fact, it is a processed text, a form that has undergone various mediations, interpretations, and adaptations. The differences among the three films discussed demonstrate the agency of documentary film directors, photographers, and producers in achieving the text's final shape. Each filmmaker promotes a point of view. In *Yŏngmae*, it is the disappearance of hereditary tradition and the rise of a less sophisticated practice. In *Sai-esŏ*, it is the complex and arduous initiation into musok life. In *Mansin*, it is the endurance of musok through turbulent historical moments. These various goals cause the films to look different and to focus on different aspects of this complex cultural phenomenon. However, all three directors share a self-reflective approach, which includes showing the cameras and camera people in the film itself (in *Mansin*), talking about their own feelings (in *Sai-esŏ*), and addressing the production process (in *Yŏngmae*).

Some differences between these and previous documentary films result from changes in technology. An important normative part of a DVD is added features, including longer interviews with film directors and participants, "making of" shots, and explanatory data—features that were less common in videotapes and were not added to older films. These features provide DVD viewers with more information about the production process, the depicted mudang, and the director's intentions in producing the film. It is a discourse external to the film itself; before DVDs, it was available only through printed media and research. Not everyone watches these parts of the DVD, but those who take the time feel increased familiarity with the protagonists. These features represent how changing norms in the film industry have increased the agency of mansin in creating their public image. Such added features are not a result of technological innovation but of film directors' professional choices; they are related to factors that are beyond the musok cultural sphere. Cinematic representations of musok are a part of the film industry in general. In this case, such changes have benefited the practitioners depicted in the films. Yet these changes were but a prelude to the ways in which mansin can actively produce their image on the internet, as will be discussed in chapter 5.

Viewers of films about musok create, enhance, and maintain their knowledge of Korean culture through the entertaining experience of cinema, both documentary and dramatized. However, films can also distort our perception of reality. Viewers might expect all mansin to behave like the professionals depicted in films or be able to solve problems through spiritual work, as shown in cinematic representations. In chapter 3, I reflect on another contemporary form of mediating musok knowledge to audiences: museums. Museums are an accepted form of professional mediation between the public and cultural values related to material objects. Folklore museums are more like documentaries than like feature films, in that they are expected to provide accurate and well-researched images of their subjects. Most viewers expect feature films, and perhaps hybrid documentaries, to be centered in the director's subjective worldview. In contrast, the museum is supposed to be objective. The next chapter explores this expectation, which does not necessarily match the politics of inclusion and exclusion that museums embody.

NOTES

1. A history of Korean cinema exists in, for example, Min, Joo, and Kwak (2003), Kim Kyung-hyun (2004), and Yecies and Shim (2015).

2. The term *postmodern* implies not only a moment in history but also a paradigm of analytic deconstruction and recontextualization. Therefore, I use the term *late-modern* to refer to the late twentieth and early twenty-first centuries (Giddens 1991).

3. Since the 1970s, the average Korean visits a movie theater around six times a year. Korean-produced movies account for a significant share of this audience's film viewing (K. Kim 2004, 270, 282, 286, 310).

4. Kim Ki-yŏng also directed other famous films, such as *The Housemaid* (1960), *Koryŏjang* (1963), *Woman of Fire* (1971), and *Promise of the Flesh* (1975).

5. In reality, this "island" is submerged more than 10 feet underwater, but in the film, it is a hill overlooking the vast ocean. According to Korean legend, it is the place where spirits of drowned seamen live. In the film, the island's residents believe that fishermen are sometimes kidnapped by the sea demon.

6. Kim Chin-yŏng wrote the script and directed *Ch'ŏngdam Posal*, as he also did for *Baby and Me* (2008) and *Love Clinique* (2012). He directed *Police Family* (2013) and produced several other films in the years 2004–2010.

7. There has been a similar shift in attitudes toward the Korean mythical nine-tailed fox (*kumiho*), which appears as seductive and dangerous in folktales but as a cute and amenable young woman in romantic television dramas. This was brought to my attention by an avid fan of the genre, Adi Pozner (pers. comm., December 2014).

8. Director Cho is famous in this genre after having directed the first three parts of the successful sequel, *My Wife Is a Gangster* (2001–2006).

9. For further references on the minjung movement and its cultural stance, see Robinson (1993) and Abelmann (1993).

10. Pak Ch'an-uk is the director of the famous horror film *Old Boy* (2003). For *P'aranmanjang*, he collaborated with his brother Pak Ch'an-gyŏng, a documentary film director and artist who has a keen interest in Korean vernacular religions. The film is available on Vimeo's iPhone Film Festival (C. Pak 2011).

11. The director's attitude, which will be described below, gained *Saiesŏ* a debated categorization as mystery documentary ("Filmmessenger"

2006), observational (or participatory) documentarism (Cazzaro 2006), and documentary-fiction hybrid (Smithsonian Institute 2007).

12. The ethnography did not specify which film she had shown, but several such productions are available from that time. For example, she was filmed for the *Anthology of World Music and Dance* (Kunihiko 1988).

13. This is why I do not discuss the ethnographic film *Initiation of a Korean Shaman* (1991, by filmmaker Diane Lee and anthropologist Laurel Kendall). In this ethnographic video, Laurel Kendall looks closely at a single initiation. Commentators complained that the film was difficult to understand without background knowledge about musok and Korean spirituality (Tangherlini 1994). The intimate filming arena allows viewers to observe complications in the ritual, which deviates from its period's norm of presenting a "perfect" kut. The holistic, ethnographic filming also follows ritual preparation, home decoration, and the behavior of other participants. For many years, this film was the main documentary on musok available with subtitles for non-Korean speakers.

14. See the full list at Koreanfilm.org (2019).

15. Yi Ch'ang-jae, the director of *Sai-esŏ*, is a film professor at Chung-ang University. In 2003, he prepared the film *Edit* that featured in a list of the best documentaries by the Museum of Modern Art in New York. He also directed the documentaries *Suintŭrwi hwimanjide* (*Many Hopes*, 1999) and *Mikuk Chŏncheng ryaksa* (*Summary of American War*, 2002). His latest film *Kirwi-eso* (*On the Road*, 2013) received very positive reviews and attracted the unprecedented number of fifty thousand admissions, which is rare for independent nonfiction films (Korean Film Biz Zone 2013). It showed a Buddhist nuns' training center and explored the various reasons for becoming a nun.

16. A list of Mansin Kim's public performances can be found on her web page at Neomudang (2014).

17. I have shown the films discussed here in many classes and lectures in Korea and elsewhere. My impressions of the viewers' responses are the basis for such interpretations of the films' reception in this chapter.

18. For a detailed list of musok supernatural entities and their imagery, see Sarfati (2010).

19. Other stories from the 1980s demonstrate that this is not always the case. A professor and an actress refused to undergo initiation, despite Kim Kŭm-hwa's assertion that they had sinbyŏng (Guillemoz 1992).

THREE

Agendas, Power, and Ideology in Museum Displays of Korean Shamanism

KOREAN FOLKLORE MUSEUMS HAVE EAGERLY taken a central role in displaying information about musok and Korean spirituality. This popular museum genre exists in most Korean cities and regions and varies from standard exhibits of collected objects to large outdoor folk villages with restored houses.[1] It is another medium in which the material aspects of this performative vernacular religion have moved to officially sanctioned arenas and become supervised by professionals. In this medium, the professionals in charge of representing musok to the public are curators and museum directors. Their displays are often the first encounter young Koreans have with this part of their heritage. Korean grade schools take their students on excursions to folklore museums as a part of their regular curriculum. Min, a thirty-year-old teacher who visited the National Folk Museum in June 2017 with her students, told me in an interview, "The young people of our time know so little about our heritage. We still had grandparents who wore the traditional outfits at home and could tell us of bygone times. Now the children only know what they see on TV. We must take them to places like this [museum] in order to teach them about the real Korean culture."

Min distinguished between television depictions of culture and museum representations, assuming that museums show more accurate data. She believed that by walking among the exhibits, the students would experience their real heritage. She never doubted the objectivity and scholarship of the museum display that she was advocating. Similarly, visitors to the National Museum of Korea who were interviewed expressed that the narratives shown there were historically accurate (Saeji 2014).

When I asked Min specifically about the musok display, however, she was more cautious. "People must know that this part of culture exists, but for children it is too complicated to understand. I am glad that this is not emphasized in the children's section." That religion should be represented in folklore museums is generally accepted. However, among the various people involved in the displays' preparation and consumption, ideas differ markedly as to how it should be presented. Through my ethnographic encounters with curators, I have learned of several cases of internal strife within the exhibition planning team. The basis of the conflict was, in all cases, the level of musok dominance in the exhibition. Some staff members disliked plans to devote a large, central space to musok. Others diverged on which regional styles should be displayed, and still others debated the labels. One curator said, "I had to fight for years to include a few of our precious musok artifacts in the public display. The museum director would have preferred that they stay in storage and be used for research purposes only." I will not detail these disputes, out of respect for my informants' desire for confidentiality. What all the interviewees repeated was that curators were well aware of the power that lies in a museum exhibit's design. Thirty years of museum critique have shown that curators are not value neutral (Karp and Lavine 1991). However, all curators involved in these disputes related their intention to treat the exhibits "objectively," which for them meant without religious bias. They viewed their long-term educational purpose as an important task and genuinely wanted to be scholarly and impartial.

As will be discussed, biased curatorial agendas have been criticized in relation to colonial conditions worldwide. In Korea, folklore museums are curated by Koreans, and one might assume that there should not be such issues. However, I noticed that the ideology of each curator could be traced in the form of musok presentation that they espoused. Are they fond of musok practices or not—for example, if they are Christian? Do they want the museum's visitors to understand religious meanings or only to enjoy the aestheticism of musok? Do they respect the efficacious, mystical aspect of musok or view it as a harmful superstition? Of the curators I met, only one is a practicing mansin (Mansin Sin, whose work is discussed later in this chapter), but many have researched kut rituals and are very knowledgeable about musok norms and practices. Their ability to produce displays that are similar to musok activity is beyond question. Therefore, when they make curatorial choices—for example, to display musok items in a way that is visually similar to the original context or to decontextualize them, or to provide an artistic design or educational labels—they take a stance.

Crispin Paine states that "as Western Europe becomes an increasingly 'religious supermarket' society, with a pick'n'mix spirituality, perhaps museums have an increased duty to present religion straight. They are, after all, one of the ways—and not an unimportant one—in which society reflects itself, celebrates its beliefs and attitudes, and seeks to pass on its understanding of the world" (2000, xiii). In Korea, however, this "pick'n'mix spirituality" is not new. Before the advent of Christianity in the seventeenth and eighteenth centuries, there was little religious exclusivity. Many people practiced Buddhism, Confucianism, Daoism, and vernacular religions such as musok simultaneously. When Protestant Christianity was introduced on a large scale toward the end of the nineteenth century, more Koreans had to choose between the new belief and the vernacular and local traditions (described in chap. 2 in relation to the film *Munyŏdo*). However, Christianity did not become the most common religion in Korea. Even now, when 30 percent of the population is Christian, a person outside Christian communities can practice musok together with Buddhism and other religious practices without being criticized by religious experts or other practitioners.[2] This tolerance toward religious syncretism has been noted as one of the reasons for the resilience and visibility of musok through the ages (Grayson 1984, 1998). Moreover, musok is a vernacular religion; it is orally transmitted and varies by region and by the individual preferences of practitioners. Under these relaxed religious conditions, there is little point in figuring out what "straight," using Paine's term, would mean for Korean religion. In the case of musok, there is also a problem of tracing historical processes from the fragmented knowledge of such an oral folk tradition. Such lacunae result in individual interpretations by scholars and curators.

Still, musok can be included in or excluded from museum exhibits, and it can take center stage or be marginalized. Nevertheless, visitors expect folklore museums to provide authoritative, scholarly mediation between themselves and the vast knowledge available in Korea's "religious supermarket." The tension between presumed objectivity and the agency that lies within knowledge production is more significant in this realm than in films. Museums are supposed to be curated by scholars who conduct research and are tied by ethical responsibilities much stricter than those of film directors (Shelton 2000, 159). However, as Paine (2000, xiii) laments, plain mediation is not always offered in such establishments. With regard to musok, Korean museums often fail their "duty to present religion straight." As O'Neill (1996, 188) says more generally, "The most obvious and important thing to be said about making histories of religion in museums is that they don't do it very often." In Korea, museums often fail to offer a concise history of musok and instead reflect the curators' political, cultural, and ideological tendencies. Just as in the case of festival performances and films, the folklorization and aestheticization of musok in museums result in sidelining religious meanings. Instead, nationalism, religious values, and artistic rigor are at the center of the messages delivered to visitors.

In all the museum displays of musok that I surveyed, the only significant misrepresentation that I noted was the absence of replicas of sacrificial animal offerings or animal parts. This is not because offerings are not artistic productions; fruit and sweets are represented in museum recreations of musok altars. As described in the introduction, every private kut ritual that I have seen, and most staged ones included animal offerings, ranging from parts of a cow or pig to an entire animal. The emotional and aesthetic effects of animal sacrificial offerings can be debated; however, their existence in real rituals and their absence from museums and some staged rituals is a clear indication of the politics of inclusion and exclusion. It reflects the choices that curators make when presenting musok to the public.

The exhibit is a mediator between musok and museum visitors, and the mediation is achieved through objects and spaces. Objects in museums are the main agents that produce emotional responses in visitors because, in most museums, there are no human mediators between the exhibits and their observers. The objects' power is their mere existence in an exhibit as objects of affective presence (Armstrong 1981). The museum is a contact zone between people and tangible entities that are rarely encountered in daily life. The visitor's culture and the culture in which the objects were produced connect in a way that produces new understandings and tensions. In the Korean case, visitors are mostly Korean rather than people from different nationalities and cultural affiliations. The museum producers and consumers belong to the same national culture but not necessarily to the same belief system or social status (J. Clifford 1997). Moreover, there is an inherently asymmetrical hierarchy between the presumably knowledgeable curators who plan the exhibits and the consumers of knowledge who visit and learn without much questioning.

Objects and observers are both present at the end of the exhibit production process. Objects encapsulate their internal qualities as well as the intentions and knowledge used to spatialize them in the museum. Observers choose their way across the exhibition halls and yards, and can dedicate differential attention to each object according to their personal interests and predispositions. Rephrasing Robin Boast (2011, 58) in relation to contemporary views of museums, objects embody knowledge; moreover, objects mediate knowledge. As discussed in the introduction, Arjun Appadurai's (2015) idea of the "mediant" can serve in theorizing the various layers of affect production in museums. The experience of the museum visitor is shaped by interaction with objects, with little human mediation during the visit. The objects are active in the visitor's contemplation of ideas, historical events, and folklore. During the exhibit's production, there is also interaction between objects and humans. Curators, designers, and exhibit producers work closely with objects, absorbing their aestheticism and meaning. We have already discussed how films and other technologies influence the production of musok's image, and now museums broaden our exploration.

In discussing museums, I add to the already established idea of object agency (see, e.g., Brown 2004; Douglas and Isherwood 1979; Gell 1998; Graves-Brown 2000; Mitchell 2005), the importance of spatial positioning (see, e.g., Oppenheim 2008), and the social power structures of object-centered establishments such as museums (see, e.g., J. Clifford 1997; Kirshenblatt-Gimblett 1998; Paine 2000; Pearce 1994). The case of Korean folklore museums demonstrates that in such an object-centered discourse, strife is negotiated through material representations of culture. Examining this recontextualization process reveals diversity of forms and types of museum displays. These differences reveal the tension between antecedent forms and practices, such as musok, and new cultural–historical conditions.

Mansin rarely participate in planning museum displays, even if they are consulted during the collection of objects. Although the cultural sphere of mansin (i.e., musok) is represented through these artifacts, they often perceive the exhibit as an affect-laden discourse between curators and observers—a one-directional opinion exchange that happens without personal encounter. In this ongoing process, "groups are 'constantly' being performed and . . . agencies are 'ceaselessly' debated" (Latour 2005, 64). My conclusion in this respect is that the way exhibits are planned and executed creates an image of musok.

When musok artifacts are displayed in folklore museums, it is possible to contextualize them and understand their uses and meanings beyond their aesthetic appeal. Collections owned by institutions and people other than practicing mansin are new contexts in which sacred objects are used outside religious sites and for nonreligious purposes, such as education and the creation of a unique national identity (Bauman and Briggs 2003). To ground these politics of identity in data collected at contemporary museum displays, I analyze three significant aspects of the recontextualizing process in which ritual artifacts are arranged into museum displays. At these three points, choices about the use of space and content shape the image of musok and are fixed into the exhibit.

The first stage of museum display production is the removal of artifacts from vernacular ritual contexts into a scholarly, sanctioned museum exhibit, placing them in a display case, and labeling them. This process relates to the placement of the musok exhibit within the larger museum complex. I will discuss this step in the context of two kinds of museums: large, national institutions (focusing on the National Folk Museum) and municipal or regional museums (focusing on the Andong Folk Museum).

The second phase relates to arranging the artifacts vis-à-vis each other and choosing how to enliven musok and communicate some of its qualities to museum visitors. The examples discussed will be from for-profit museums, including corporate museums (focusing on the Lotte World Folk Museum) and regional, tourist-oriented museums (focusing on the Cheju Folk Village). Different kinds of museums demonstrate varying concerns in the process of recontextualizing musok as material displays outside religious contexts.

The third phase relates to how individuals who have accumulated extensive musok collections have tried to enter the saturated scene of folklore museums, to establish a permanent musok exhibition, and to attract visitors. In the case of a large institution, such as the National Folk Museum, this is not a concern related to musok display choices. However, for small, topic-specific museums, legitimization is a central concern. Their controversial appreciation by the Korean authorities and the local scholarly community serves as yet another demonstration of musok-related identity politics in the making. These private collections also demonstrate the gaps in how curators, mansin, and the public think about musok.

This somewhat artificial division between the various official and private museums that display musok is used to analyze why Korean museums present musok in such contradictory ways. I do not discuss each museum as a specific articulation of musok. Instead, I follow James Clifford's manner of comparing four displays of Northwest Coast cultures. In this book, I also explore examples discussed "as variants within a unified field of representations.... [as] continuations of indigenous traditions of storytelling, collection, and display.... [to] stress entanglement and relationship rather than independence or an experience significantly outside the national culture" (J. Clifford 1991, 110–111). In Korea, visiting folklore museums has become such a mainstream activity that many people visit several establishments each year. The role of museums in creating the public image of musok should be explored not through singular experiences afforded by each establishment but as a cumulative experience to which multiple museums contribute. Before I discuss the museums specifically, I provide a brief introduction to the history of Korea's religious folklore in museums.

KOREAN RELIGIOUS FOLKLORE AND MUSEUMS

Musok is an ancient practice. Archeological findings suggest possible traces a few thousand years old (Pai 2000). Pictures of bears, human figurines, and other objects are perceived as indications of shamanic cults on the Korean peninsula. However, there are few written texts from that period to shed light on the belief system that inspired these images. Historical records of shamanistic practices exist from the Samhan period (first century BCE to third century CE, before there was a Korean nation as such), but these sources are fragmentary. The documented practices for the various tribes living in Korea around this time are not uniform. We cannot determine with assurance the ethnic identity of these tribes, but it is likely that they included proto-Manchus, proto-Mongols, and even proto-Japanese (Clark Sorensen, pers. comm., June 2015). Richard McBride (2006) complicates the notion that shamanism was the main religion of ancient Korea, stating that it is a legacy of the colonial and dictatorship eras. By analyzing data from the first millennium, he asserts that there were clear differentiations among animistic worship of objects, ancestor rituals, rulers' appeals to the powers of nature, and the work of local shamans. Moreover, each of the three kingdoms practiced different forms of rituals. In all cases, he found descriptions of sacrifices to spirits and gods but few descriptions of possession-based dialogic communication with the supernatural, such as the musok rituals today. Lee Jung Young (J. Lee 1981, 21–22) ascribes Japanese and Chinese roots to the ancient Korean religion. In contrast, Ch'oe Kil-sŏng (K. Ch'oe 1999) does not see continuity between Silla and Koguryŏ customs of the early centuries of the Common Era and contemporary shamanism.

However, when the history of Koreans is depicted in museums, it is usually assumed that shamanism was the ancient practice of Korea in general. At the same time, Buddhism, which was introduced in the fourth century CE through China, is celebrated in its artistic manifestation in Korea rather than as folklore. This tendency can be spotted, for example, in the display of bronze figurines of Buddhas in the National Museum but not in the National Folk Museum. The distinction between Buddhist art as "high art" and musok art as folk art has taken strong roots in Korean museum culture.

Buddhism was adopted extensively in the Korean peninsula in the fourth century and became important to the elites in the three-kingdom period because it introduced more sophisticated technologies, arts, and literacy. The designation of Koguryŏ, Paekche, and later also Silla as Buddhist kingdoms placed them in a cosmopolitan culture that spanned India and China (McBride 2008). Some scholars debate a further slow decline in the status of mudang when women took over this practice in the early Koryŏ period (tenth century), in contrast to Silla's shaman-kings (McBride 2008, 128). However, in Silla, there were also queens who practiced spiritual communication and divinations, most notably Queen Sŏndŏk (Shin 2012, app. 2, 141–142). From the eleventh century on, mansin were regarded as the impure, the lowest social stratum of the neo-Confucian hierarchy (Deuchler 1992, 12–13). Women traditionally predominated in charismatic spirit communication, whereas men dominated Korean politics, official scholarship, and neo-Confucian ritual life—and this division reinforced and reified the low status of mudang (K. Ch'oe 1982, 1984, 1998; E. Kim and Choi 1997, 1–9).[3] This distinction is still visible in the attitude that Buddhist material culture is art that should be displayed in art museums, whereas musok material culture is craft that should be displayed in museums of anthropology and folklore.

The division between Buddhist and musok art ignores the syncretism of both vernacular Buddhist and musok practice. Many mansin venerate Buddhist entities, and most Buddhist temples venerate musok entities, such as *sansin* (the mountain god) (Grayson 1984, 1996). I have not seen this syncretism mentioned in any musok museum display. The distinction also implies that musok is not a living tradition. Many publications by the Korean government state that musok is almost extinct in contemporary South Korea, despite the fact that kut are widely practiced in contemporary South Korea, even within Buddhist complexes (Baker 2001; K. Ch'oe 2003; Sarfati 2010).

Because of the lower status granted to musok art, early exhibitions were limited to paintings of gods (*musindo*). Paintings used by mansin during rituals have been described as "functional...simple...and naïve" (Korean Overseas Information Service 1995, 3) and the artists as "nameless artisans, following prescribed compositions" (Covell 1984, 24). Other genres of musok objects, such as costumes, cut-paper adornments, and brassware, are not even considered art forms. In Korea and elsewhere, collections of items that are categorized as folk art often challenge existing genres in the definitions of art, aesthetics, and values. Folk art has often been treated as inferior to more historically acknowledged forms of material artistry because of the objects' utilitarian value (Glassie 1989, 61–64). Consequently, unlike Buddhist art, musok artifacts have not featured significantly in museum exhibits of Korean art and history, such as the National Museum of Korea. Their artistic value has been appreciated only recently, mainly by folk art collectors and some folklore museums (Kendall and Yang 2014).

In the 1970s, the Onyang Folk Museum featured the first exhibition of Korean musindo. The curators chose "paintings as artifacts of folk belief—but also paintings that 'looked good to them' (*choahage poinda*), that 'caught the eye' (*nunettŭinŭngŏt*)" (Kendall and Yang 2014, 12). Later, in the 1980s, the short-lived Kŏndŭlbawi Museum in Taegu also exhibited musindo. The trendiness of this art peaked only after the 1988 Seoul Olympics, as a part of the search for a unique national identity and as a consequence of the improved economy (Kendall and Yang 2014). Dr. Yang Chong-sŭng (who was introduced in chap. 1 and will be discussed later in this chapter) told me that in the 1980s and 1990s, he could buy such paintings cheaply at downtown galleries, even when they were old, exquisite samples. By now, musindo have become so expensive that he allows himself to purchase new ones only when he gets them directly from a deceased mansin's family that wishes to discard all the musok paraphernalia fast. Although musok art has been displayed out of ritual context for almost fifty years, categories of musindo were not clearly set. These paintings, some crude and some sophisticated in technique and style, have often challenged normative boundaries among art, efficacious objects, and crafts.

Beyond musindo, other musok artifacts also began to be included in exhibits more regularly. Korean folklore museums play an important part in fostering nostalgia for a premodern, rural culture, which contemporary urbanites often perceive as happier, more moral, and more group-oriented (Mun 1997). This view of the "olden" countryside has been labeled *furusato* in the Japanese context and was shown to be connected with the display and consumption of objects that are related to an imagined, glorified past (Creighton 1997; Ivy 1995). In Korea, the minjung movement of the 1980s saw musok as a part of such an idealized past, and this feeling has lingered in various sites of contemporary culture, such as films, as explained in chapter 2 (Kendall 2009; Tangherlini 1994). Many Koreans of the urban middle classes began to use traditional outfits and similar commodities for nostalgic purposes (Mun 1997). Korean art lovers of that time began to see the artifacts of musok as interesting and worth collecting, and museums increasingly featured musok objects (Kendall and Yang 2015).

Some museums continue to treat musok as a shadow of Korea's cultural past, although all my observations suggest it is a living tradition that is continuously transmitted and current with technological innovations and other cultural and societal changes (see also Kendall 2009, xix). Allocating musok to the past might be an ongoing echo of Japanese attempts to portray Korea's culture as primitive through the emphasis on spiritual practices and shamanistic rituals, even when similar ones existed in Japan (Averbuch 1995; Blacker 1986). The first organized collection and exhibition of Korean folklore was curated by Japanese folklore scholars of the colonial period. Their legacy as tools in the imperial project of assimilating Korea to Japanese culture has not been overlooked by Korean curators, who sometimes discuss this issue in their displays. In this respect, the persistence of Korean culture is discussed as proof of its uniqueness and beauty but not necessarily of its fitting the contemporary world, as was thought in many other contexts of evaluating premodern art (e.g., Boas 1955).

The culture of "the people," known as *minsok* (folklore), relates to some imagined premodern rural folk. The Hanja character used for *min* represents commoners or peasants. Accordingly, minsok might not be perceived as a culture that is suitable for sophisticated, contemporary urbanites. Poetic detachment usually serves as the basic guideline for modern museum exhibitions, folklore performances, and festivals (Kirshenblatt-Gimblett 1998, 50). However, Korean curators work to represent their own culture and thus cannot entirely alienate themselves from it, as colonizing curators in imperial situations could (Shelton 2000). They can choose whether to represent musok as belonging within contemporary, urban, educated Korean culture or to situate it as belonging to rural, uneducated people of premodern Korea, remote in time and space. These broad choices take the form of specific decisions about space and content as curators recontextualize musok objects within museum exhibits.

RECONTEXTUALIZING MUSOK FROM VERNACULAR RITUALS TO FORMAL MUSEUM EXHIBITS

Objects of musok are meant to be displayed. As discussed in chapter 1, in their primary context, they are manipulated to please gods and to appease their rage; objects are organized neatly for ritual audiences to observe and enjoy; and they serve as proof of the knowledge and attentiveness of the performing team. Belief in these objects' performance efficacy and supernatural effect is unquestioned in ritual; however, museums can present the objects in ways that are either similar to or different from their ritual use. Altering the actual objects is seen as unprofessional in the ethos of museum curating; spatial arrangement and interpretive texts are more negotiable.

The recontextualization of the artifacts in formal displays opens many options. Some museums choose to present the artifacts within an imitation of a ritual. Others sever the items from their ritual context and from each other, showing them as itemized visual lists of ritual props, for example, "shaman's bells," "Mountain god statue," or "printed amulets." My analysis of the process of recontextualizing ritual artifacts in museums focuses on two large museums—the National Folk Museum in Seoul and the Andong Folk Musesum. In both venues, musok constitutes only one part of a broad display of folklore artifacts and customs.

The National Folk Museum in Seoul is located inside the royal palace (Kyŏngbokkung) under a soaring, five-story pagoda modeled after a legendary ancient structure (KCIS 2009, 97). The musok exhibit is located in one of the central halls, which is dedicated to the Korean life cycle, and more specifically at the end of a narrow corridor that leads only to that display (fig. 3.1). This particular corridor is unique in the museum's design, which consists mostly of open halls and broad walkways with large exhibits located within view of others exhibits. Most visitors, distracted by the many colorful exhibits located in clear sight, overlook the entrance to this corridor and never enter the narrow passage to the musok display. Several museum staff members have suggested to me that this location was an intentional choice to leave superstition and magic outside the main museum halls—as some management executives thought would be appropriate for Korea in general.

The entrance to the hallway has a bamboo pole with a red-and-white flag, just like many musok practitioners' divination places. Within one case, a doll dressed in *hanbok* (traditional Korean dress) and holding an open fan represents the mansin. A low table features a few folded clothes and a red mountain-god hat. On the floor lie pairs of ritual knives, brass bells, and half-rolled silk divination flags. An outstanding item is a pair of chaktu blades that stand together in a very uncommon position, not bound with white cloth, as is common in ritual, and not on the altar. This item is decontextualized here, and its central role in the ritual for chaktu General is not expressed. A set of brass mirrors hangs on a red silk ribbon and white streamers. There are some metal weapons, two paintings of gods, and a small altar with imitation fruit and candies as well as a vase of paper flowers. This re-created offering altar is much more modest than any of the sumptuous ones that I have observed in actual rituals (see fig. 0.1). It resembles what the stories of senior mansin suggest about altars in olden times. Because of the slow economy, until the 1980s, most offering altars were meager compared with contemporary altars.

The label confirms this impression, because musok is discussed as belonging to a past culture that used to be common but no longer is: "Smallpox and measles were among the most dreaded illnesses during Joseon [Chosŏn dynasty 1392–1910] when there were no remedies for them. Shamans were often invited to perform rites to appease the spirits governing these fatal diseases in the hopes of preventing or curing them. These rites were called byeolsang-gut (pyŏlsang kut) or hogu-gut (hogu kut). Shown here is a reconstructed scene of a hogu-gut (hogu kut), in which a female shaman is conducting this particular

Fig. 3.1 Musok display in the National Folk Museum, 2014. Credit: Author.

rite with a folding fan and a set of rattles in her hands." This label situates musok as a practice belonging entirely to the past, as the Chosŏn period ended in the early twentieth century. The Korean text is very similar to the English and does not reveal anything about contemporary musok. Another glass case on the adjacent wall displays objects used for divination and fortune-telling. No label tells who produced or owned these items in their original context.

Labels are an important part of how objects are presented and meaning is communicated in museum exhibits. When labeling became common practice in museums, during the nineteenth century, "the written label in an exhibition was the surrogate for the words of an absent lecturer, with the added advantage that the exhibited objects, rather than appear briefly to illustrate a lecture, could be seen by a large public for a longer period of time" (Kirshenblatt-Gimblett 1998, 32). Accordingly, postmodern ethics of formal museum display deem curators as teachers rather than mere collectors, organizers, and preservationists. Curatorial work is based on "the central task of disseminating knowledge to the public" (Kurin 1997, 82).

Labeling musok as an extinct activity misinforms museum visitors about the estimated two hundred thousand active mansin practicing in South Korea today. This exhibit is another example of how, as Laurel Kendall says, "modernity preserves its disdain of 'superstition' while embracing 'tradition' and rendering it safely in the past tense" (2001, 33). This tendency to place musok in the past is also apparent in a few short documentary films of mansin that are played on loop on a medium-sized flat screen along the same hallway. All the films shown are black and white, although some are contemporary with color digitally deleted to lend them a more historical appearance. As discussed in chapter 2, black-and-white footage resembles rare documentation of ancient practices, and erasing the color presents musok as a vanishing tradition.[4]

The marginalization of contested traditions evident in the curatorial choices at the National Folk Museum is not unique to Korea. In museum displays of Native American ethnography in the United States, this practice has attracted fierce criticism. James Nason suggests that to overcome such biased displays, museums should consult representatives of the cultures on display during the planning stages, or at least employ an expert in that culture. He insists that curators should include contemporary objects and label them with the names of owners or producers to prevent the viewer from assuming that such objects are no longer in use (Nason 2000, 37–41). In the National Folk Museum of Korea, a musok expert was on the curatorial team from the 1990s to 2013, but his input on the musok exhibit was not fully accepted.

Interestingly, an earlier exhibit of musok at the same venue in 2005 was located in a central hall, along the path of all visitors. The display was inside a clear glass case that was visible from two sides and three times larger than the current exhibition case. Within it were several dolls designed to imitate a kut ritual. Along the wall outside the glass box was a series of framed paintings of ancient musok outfits. With the arrival of a new director who was an art historian and had different aesthetic and value-related considerations, the positioning of musok within the museum changed drastically. The stark difference between the earlier exhibit and the newer one demonstrates how personnel changes and staff members' individual agendas can affect the ideological stance of a museum.[5]

In contrast to this musok exhibit in Seoul, the rural Andong Folk Museum displays musok as an important part of Korean culture. A large space is allocated to it, at the center of the second-floor hall, clearly visible to any passing visitor. The musok exhibit includes a glass-case diorama of an initiation ritual (*sin naerim kut*). In the diorama, a newly initiated mansin stands by her spirit mother, the former clad in full musok attire of the spirit of the Big Dipper (*ch'ilsŏng*) and the latter in the attire of the mountain god (*sansin*). Behind them, an altar holds an abundance of imitation food offerings, paper flowers, and other ornaments. On the side, two drummers are positioned in a drumming posture (fig. 3.2). For several years, an image of this diorama was

Fig. 3.2 The Andong folklore museum's diorama of a kut ritual, 2007. Credit: Author.

the first photograph of the indoor exhibit on the museum's official website (Andong Museum 2017).

The exhibit's central location matches the respect with which the labels describe musok. A second glass case holds items such as brass cymbals, knives, an ancient musok handbook, talismans, tools, a god painting, and divination flags, all arranged in rows. Each item is labeled by name and use, some only in Korean. A large label, "Andong Shamans and Their Rituals," introduces this part of the exhibit as follows:

> One may attempt to define a shaman as a ritual specialist who attempts to mediate with spirits or to appease them, thus preventing natural disasters and curing illnesses. Some people believe that all potential shamans experience Sinbyung [sinbyŏng] (possession sickness) of varying length, during which time they may behave in ways that may cause them to be mislabeled as insane. Moreover, they believe that recruits can become crazy if shamans officiating at their initiation rite fail. If recruits are successfully initiated they become full-fledged practitioners through training and practice. There is another type of shamans who inherit the family business of professional shamanism. Andong shamans are recruited by initiation rite, after experiencing possession sickness. Koreans do not think of a shaman performance (kut) as a pure religious ceremony but more of an event that combines strong theatrical dramas with music and dance. A Korean mudang

(shaman) is a magician, a priestess, an actress, a dancer, and an acrobat all in one. It depends upon the nature of rites but local shamans perform their duties seated most of the time.

This English text, which appears alongside Korean and Japanese versions, discusses musok in the present tense, not as a disappearing tradition. It also extends the roles of musok in society to include its economic function as a family business and its entertainment function as a theatrical spectacle. The label refers to recruiting methods and mentions the diversity of ritual styles. By including technical, organizational, and performative aspects of musok in the label, the Andong Folk Museum helps visitors to understand musok as belonging in the here-and-now. Through word choices such as "ritual specialist" and "full-fledged practitioners," labels in this exhibit frame musok as a vernacular religion, an integral part of Korean belief and practice, an art, and an existing folk performance.

The contrast between how musok is recontextualized in the National Folk Museum and in the Andong Folk Museum shows that by following an object through such alterations—or in the words of Appadurai (1986), writing the social life of things—we learn a lot about people, including curators, mansin, and the public. However, doing this kind of close inspection is not always possible in museums. For example, when rituals are over, food offerings are usually distributed among audience members and participants to be consumed at home, outside the sacred ritual context. In this manner, musok objects can enter and exit states of holiness. This stage in the life of the offerings is not possible in museums because showcase displays are prepared with plastic or wax imitations to prevent decay. Museum food offering imitations are frozen in time, always in the same form and role. Could the spirits be upset by the plastic offerings? Do curators, museum visitors, and mansin have the same stances on the matter? By choosing to represent musok with imitation offerings, the curators make an aesthetic choice, even if it does not match most actual ritual situations. Plastic fruits look like real ones but cannot be consumed.

We might conclude that in this choice, curators might cause a religious concern. In fact, the use of fake offerings has been observed in recent staged performances, for which real fruit could not be easily transported and stored (K. Howard 2006, 148). Practical choices in museum presentations are part of an overall contemporary reassessment of meanings and uses of ritual artifacts in which both practitioners and curators participate. In interviews, some curators expressed worries that if musok artifacts are disrespected, some unexpected misfortune might happen. "We must respect the spirits represented in the paintings," said Kim, a young curator who had just begun his work in a large museum. "Even if we do not believe that spirits exit, some museum visitors believe that they are actual beings. It is a difficult task to respect the spirits without actually saying that they exist. On the other hand, if something bad happens, people might think that it is the curator's fault." Mansin hold diverse opinions on this issue. In interviews, several warned against the use of gods' representations in nonreligious settings. Others said that casual kut performances on museum stages are enough to placate the spirits represented in the museum displays and that the spirits are glad to be shown in a respectable museum. Many mansin believe that gods and spirits understand new display contexts better than we might think. Mansin Sin told me, "As long as they are kept from damage and shown in respectable venues like these, the spirits are happy. They do not need the museum in order to be real." Indeed, Sin had created a musok museum herself.

Museums are based on Western philosophies of rationalization, representation, and recontextualization (Arthur 2000, 20–22). Accordingly, they raise many contested issues in various locations and cultures. The sacredness of items in museum displays has often caused uneasiness among people of the origin cultures. Vietnamese villagers were concerned about the display of their one-eyed god in a controversial location, and some museum staff were reluctant to handle the object for fear that it was still animated and efficacious (Nguyen and Phan 2008, 202–203). The different attitudes of practitioners and curators toward sacred objects is particularly evident in the case of god paintings. The favorable stance of art dealers toward musindo since the 1980s has affected some mansin, who use them in rituals even if they do not fit their professed style of practice. Similarly, many rental shrines have a large variety of musindo attached to the altar to suit a broad variety of renters' pantheons. However, museums do not often display such paintings because most curators dislike mixing regional styles within a single museum exhibit. If mansin donate paintings that the curators view as "fusion style," the artifacts probably will not be exhibited.

In the museums displays discussed, we clearly see that the criteria for determining an object's worth differ between curators and mansin. For curators, rarity and uniqueness often determine value. Rarity applies to older musok items because such artifacts are often destroyed during rituals, after a practitioner dies, or through intensive use. Uniqueness pertains when an item is loaded with meaning and symbolism but is not beautifully crafted. For example, straw shoes, used to symbolically facilitate spirits' journey to the afterlife, are often displayed despite their low cost and simple preparation.[6]

The evaluation of religious meanings is based on scholarly analysis of musok belief systems and worship patterns, but sometimes the research findings do not match practitioners' emic interpretation. For example, in the eyes of a mansin, an object that belonged to her spirit mother (*sinŏmŏni*) has more value than an older item of unknown origin, whereas the museum curator often deems the older item more precious. Furthermore, most mansin do not care how well preserved a painting is, as long as it maintains its efficacy. For the museum curator, the ability to restore such a work to a presentable condition and to preserve it for the future are major concerns. Several curators in the National Folk Museum proudly showed me old paintings that they were working to preserve, as evidence of the importance of their work in the museum. In contrast, no mansin that I know has attempted to preserve a painting that she cannot use. Sometimes they store old samples that were used by their sinŏmŏni and that are no longer on display in rituals; the spiritual daughter has her own pantheon of venerated entities, one that does not necessarily overlap with that of her spiritual mother.

Another gap between museum staff and mansin is related to the identity of musok artists and artisans. Unlike some Western religious art producers, musok artisans are not acknowledged as artists in the National and Andong Folk Museums, and their names are not mentioned on labels or in the museums' collections, although some are well known within the community of musok practitioners. The virtuosity and talent of artifact producers have not been major considerations in the choice of museum musok artifacts. However, in mansin's home shrine displays, works prepared by famous musok painters or costume makers are often pointed out with pride, even though they are not signed. In the folk museums discussed, such objects are displayed to demonstrate mythological, folkloric, and religious aspects of folklore rather that the mastery of individual producers.

The tension between a religious, efficacy-based collection and an artistic, educational assemblage is intensified in the case of musok by the controversial nature of this tradition, which often results in providing little detail about the veneration process. Moreover, a generic label such as "shaman's tool" often flattens the complex preparation process and the rich religious meanings of ritual artifacts, and the objects are often stripped of related accessories. Such reductionist displays are also common in the use of mansin images in brochures about Korean culture, the placement of a framed talisman among folk paintings of various kinds, or a standing *sansin* (mountain god) statue in the Andong Folk Museum's courtyard. Stripping religious meanings from artifacts is not unique to musok; it is also seen in displays of Buddhist art (Saeji 2014) and in exhibits outside Korea. In the next section, I explore two museum exhibits that try to offer a livelier depiction of musok as a performative practice of supernatural veneration.

CONTEXTUALIZING MUSOK BY BRINGING THE EXHIBIT TO LIFE

Despite the respectful language of some labels and the inclusion of three-dimensional imitations of real rituals, museum displays like the ones in the National Folk Museum and the Andong Folk Museum lack many of the semiotic and sensuous elements of an actual event. There is no religious purpose. There is no participating audience. The display is usually motionless, and there are no real offerings with smell and taste. Furthermore, in most such displays, artifacts are placed inside a glass box or behind ropes. This presentation removes them from direct contact with museum visitors and thus precludes close, sensory appreciation of the items presented. Preparation of museum dioramas requires more than just moving a ritual set to a different location. It is a completely different mode of presenting kut artifacts and lacks most of the performative aspects of kut. Some folk museums seek to overcome this impediment by staging free, live ritual performances by mansin several times every year. Other museums have experimented with different strategies to overcome the static nature of a diorama. I will consider two such attempts by the Lotte World Folk Museum and the Cheju Folk Village. Both museums attract many visitors to the rich folklore displays, of which musok is only one section. In addition, both are for-profit venues with entry costs of $5 to $10. Perhaps the curators in these nonofficial places had more freedom to experiment with musok as a religion than those in the national and regional museums discussed earlier.

The Lotte World Folk Museum is a private museum located within a huge recreational and shopping center in south Seoul. Much of the folklore section is made up of miniature dioramas of daily life in a premodern Korean village. The farmers are represented by cute, round-faced dolls that are not realistic in form. The musok exhibit is located next to the exit sign, symbolically placing musok outside other Korean folk practices, as an outcast. This location is analogous to the actual location of most musok shrines outside villages and towns. The musok exhibit consists of a life-sized doll of a mansin standing in front of an altar loaded with plastic food offerings and decorated with cut-paper flowers. Many god paintings and brass mirrors line the back and side walls of the re-created shrine. A hanging line holds several musok outfits. This exhibit resembles contemporary kut scenes but lacks representations of musicians,

Fig. 3.3 The Lotte World Folk Museum kut diorama, 2012. Credit: Author.

assistants, and clients (fig. 3.3). A button outside the exhibit initiates the doll's motion and the sound system.

On my first visit to that museum in 2005, the cord connecting the button to the wall was unplugged. An elderly museum staff member insisted that I could not reconnect it because the mansin's dance was a "bad thing to hear, a shameful display of superstitious practices (*misin*)." When I asked another staff member about the musok exhibit, she insisted that there was no such exhibit in the museum. Clearly, the intentions of the curators did not correspond with the values and intentions of some staff members. Two years later, no one stood next to the exhibit, and I quickly plugged in the cord and saw the doll jump and shiver as if it were a mansin performing kut. Loud kut music played while the doll moved. In this exhibit, the decontextualization and recontextualization of musok as a ritual and practice was emphasized over its artistic craft—it did not include all the musok paraphernalia, but only one ritual re-creation. In the official folk museums, objects that are not necessarily used together in reality are positioned together for the sake of convenience. Such arrangements create alienation between the observers and musok, but sometimes they reflect a more academic atmosphere than that of the moving display in the Lotte.

Fig. 3.4 Cheju Folk village: old shaman's house, 2007.
Credit: Author.

The most distinctly lively musok display is located in the Cheju Folk Village. This large re-creation of a premodern Korean village dedicates an entire section, called "Shamanism Village," to musok.[7] The structures are said to have been collected from various locations in Cheju, moved to the folk village, and then restored for display. In such an open-air museum, the visitor walks on dirt paths between traditionally designed huts divided into themed sections, such as Fishermen Village and Noble House. The Shamanism Village huts are labeled with typological identifiers, such as Witch House, Maiden Shrine, and Fortune-teller's House. Inside the huts are neatly arranged displays of items such as talismans, divination flags, and god paintings (fig. 3.4). Between the huts are many rocks that were sculpted by wind and water to create unique shapes. These have been used in Cheju as musok symbols of the spirits of the earth; others are more graphic, such as a phallus that was used as a fertility icon. Cheju people worshipped these natural sculptures; therefore, they were placed in the Shamanism Village section of the museum. Inside the compound, labels on carved wood explain the original use of each structure, the musok belief system, and the various kinds of musok practitioners. One smaller wooden signboard stands at the entrance to the village. It reads, "A Place Where Divination Is Done." The particular wording, which focuses on the act of divination, directs people to participate in shamanic practice and shows that the museum considers this practice an important and attractive part of the display.

A visitor walking into the Divination Hut is lavished with sensory impressions. Chanting voices emerge from a sound system, colorful cushions line the wooden floor, store-bought paper lotus flowers line the roof, the smell of incense fills the air, and the offerings on the small altar are real, unlike the wax fruit set on altars inside the rest of the huts. It all seems too real to be a museum display. During one of my visits, the presiding diviner fiercely blocked us from entering the hut, stating (in Korean), "Unlike the other displays, this is the real house of a grandmother [a female ancestor spirit of a deceased mansin]. You cannot go inside. If you want divination done, wait outside." The diviner showed us to the small divination porch, where clients could sit on cushions while divination was in progress. A small sign stated that the fee for each divination session was ten thousand won. During another visit, I saw two elderly women and a man sitting on the cushions while the fortune-teller explained at length what they would encounter in the following year. Because the diviner spoke only Korean and was the only staff member present at the Shamanism Village during my two visits, I guessed that her clients were mostly Korean tourists. Encouraging visitors to take part in such an activity legitimizes its existence within Korea's contemporary culture and society. It also differs from many folk villages in the West, where actors play artisans or historical figures. In Cheju, a practicing diviner regularly performs her religious rituals within the museum. This representation of musok in the Cheju Folk Village is as real as it gets in such a Western-style, contemporary context.

This choice contrasts with the government statements in an online explanation of Cheju Island's shamanic ritual: "The ritual's designation as an important intangible cultural heritage paved the way for its survival" (CHA 2005). It is true that some musok practices, like the Cheju tradition of *ponp'uri* (myth recitation), are increasingly giving way to charismatic musok (with possession trance practices). Still, the local museum is more accurate than official government publications in its depiction of musok as a living tradition. It seems that, among government employees and museum staff, the two attitudes that Kim

Chongho (C. Kim 2003) calls "cultural paradox" coexist. In some cases, musok is perceived as an inappropriate practice involving superstition, wastefulness, and bad influence—one that should be hidden beyond a narrow corridor. In other cases, musok is seen as an important part of Korean culture that should be displayed at the museum's center. It is interesting to see what happens when a mansin wants to display her musok artifact collection. Do the state or regional government support her efforts? The sad answer to this question will be discussed in the next section, along with the happier case of another private collection-turned-museum.

STRUGGLING TO GET OFFICIAL RECOGNITION IN PRIVATE MUSOK MUSEUMS

So far, I have discussed four museums that are large venues sponsored by government agencies or wealthy private organizations. They reflect official or mainstream attitudes toward musok and do not struggle for legitimacy. However, there is no institutional museum in Korea dedicated to musok. Instead, several collectors have attempted to offer the public an organized display of their musok artifacts.

The museums that I have discussed are large, hierarchical establishments. In contrast, private collections are the product of individuals' interest and delight in collecting certain kinds of items. Their intentions and actions are not monitored by bureaucracies, and they might have different evaluation criteria than museum curators (Baudrillard 1994; Danet and Katriel 1994). In some cases, private collectors who promote their own preferred items, even when these are ignored categorically by specialists, have increased art experts' recognition of new genres of human creativity (K. Brandt 2007, 11–20; Kendall and Yang 2014). This is the case with musindo, as described earlier.

Musok collectors include scholars who study Korean folklore and mansin who view their collections as part of their occupational practice. Other collectors of Korean folk art in general include musok items in their collections but do not usually dedicate themselves solely to musok, as Korean crafts of other kinds are also prominent in such assemblages. Sometimes a collector who is fond of musok crafts keeps a broad range of objects for the sake of a more balanced presentation of the collection or as proof of their knowledge of the field.

Unlike museum exhibits, which are intentionally prepared for public consumption and exposure, private collections are not always presented to viewers. Sometimes collectors fear that their collection is not well arranged for viewers. Others have indexed the items for research purposes and fear disruption of

Fig. 3.5 Mansin Sin Myŏng-gi's musok museum, 2007. Credit: Author.

their order.[8] Some collectors show their assemblages to only a few people, hoping one day to be able to produce a full-scale museum, and others have managed to achieve that dream. I explored two private collections that were arranged in recent years as publicly available displays. In some respects, they functioned like small museums, but they had not gained significant official recognition or sponsorship. Since my first encounter with them in 2005, one has closed, and the other has gained partial official recognition and a better exhibition venue. I discuss them here to further explore the politics of inclusion and exclusion that mark musok displays in Korea.

Most mansin show their collected items in their home shrines and during rituals, but Mansin Sin Myŏng-gi, a famous spiritual mediator in her sixties, took her collection one step further and installed a private museum called *musindo kaelleri* (gallery) in her country house, a two-hour drive south of Seoul. The exhibition filled the second floor of her house (fig. 3.5). Mansin Sin inherited some of the items displayed in her museum from mansin that she had worked with. Others she purchased during the years of her musok activity or received during festivals in which she performed. Her collection contained mainly artifacts representing the Hwanghae-do style of kut that she performs.

Fig. 3.6 Painted fans and a pair of divination knives displayed in a glass case at Mansin Sin Myŏng-gi's musok museum, 2007. Credit: Author.

Mansin Sin took care to display these items in the style of modern anthropological museums. Paintings were protected with glass and hung on the walls. Accessories such as fans, bells, and hats were grouped in large glass cases, and some outfits were set on life-sized mannequins. Labels in Korean and English stated the name and purpose of each artifact (fig. 3.6).

This display mode is different from the common home shrine, where paintings are rarely framed, accessories are packed in white paper inside boxes, and costumes are either folded in drawers and suitcases or hung on racks. The only part of the museum that looked much like a mansin's house was a pair of large metal racks that held the many costumes and outfits that could not fit on mannequins. This form of display was the result of space limitations, not an intentional aesthetic choice. Sin was proud of her costume collection and hoped to arrange it in a glass case in the future. When I asked to record an interview with her on video, she chose the costume racks as the background.

Visitors to the museum entered the house through a yard with several human-sized stone and bronze statues of gods and spirits. A small shrine in the corner marked the place as a musok worship venue. Visitors ascended a flight of stairs to the second story of the house, where they were allowed to wander on their own in the display area and take photographs. They could also purchase Sin's books, colorful postcards featuring items from the museum, and some artistic, black-and-white photographs of kut rituals. A wooden box near the visitors' book accepted monetary donations. Such a setting created a professional museum atmosphere. When clients of Sin's religious services came, she took them directly to the third floor, where her home shrine and her personal residence were located.

The home shrine was a smaller room where a long shelf served as an offering altar. The paintings on the walls were not framed and were positioned above wooden statues of gods. The altar contained many offerings, some of which had to be replaced each day, such as cooked rice, fruit, and water. Others, such as candy, cigarettes, and liquors, were kept for longer periods. This part of the house was arranged like many other musok worship sites, with much attention to the needs and wishes of the supernatural entities venerated there, and thus had different rules. Photography was not allowed, and Sin or a helper escorted visitors at all times. The home shrine offered abundant locations on and beside statues of gods and spirits where clients could leave money and checks.[9] The different treatment of that part of the house marked it as a sacred site, unlike the artistic, educational display downstairs.

When a kut was planned in Sin's house, the open space of the museum, which was usually empty, was transformed from an exhibition hall to a sacred locus, a bustling center of activity. On such occasions, a wooden bench was fixed below the framed paintings along the wall as an altar, and the usual kut paraphernalia was set up for the ritual. Clients had to walk through parts of the museum to reach the ritual space, which was at the farthest end of the floor. Then they stayed more or less confined to the ritual area while the rest of the museum remained dark. Under these circumstances, objects of worship helped to transform the space into a sacred place of meeting with the gods, as did the actions of the people who set the altar, prayed, and performed inside the decorated room.

Many Korean musok scholars thought that Sin was risking her musok career for an unachievable personal impulse to become a scholar. When I told people of my interest in Sin's collection, I was often warned that she was not a reliable informant, despite her respectable spiritual lineage as the apprentice of Kim Un-sun, who was herself the successor of a famous mansin, Pang Su-dŏk. Such a reputation usually ensures scholars' legitimation of the mansin's qualifications. Indeed, Mansin Sin has performed on respected stages, such as the National Folk Museum of Seoul, and on various television programs; prepared special talismans (*pujŏk*) in several large-scale festivals, such as the *Tanoje* (held in the fifth lunar month); participated in educational programs about Korean culture and religion; and was interviewed by newspapers.[10] Still, no Korean scholar ever suggested that elaborate exhibition to me as a research site. I asked Sin if Korean scholars were aware of her museum, and she answered bitterly that they all knew and ignored it: "It was all my work and money. No one wants to help a mansin progress with technology.... People do not think that mansin should do these things. They would rather keep us uneducated and tame." The mansin's bitterness was perhaps justified by what a famous Korean scholar told me: "You should not keep Mansin Sin Myŏng-gi as an informant, because she is no longer a good source for real musok. When she was young she learned from a good sinŏmŏni, but now she is trying to become a scholar.... Furthermore, she puts so much effort in her website that her veneration practice was cast aside." The resentment that this scholar expressed corresponds with a disdain for mansin that still exists in contemporary Korea, despite their increased education.

After she published a book, *Mudang Naeryŏk*, in 2001, several scholars shunned her and talked about her with harsh disdain. This situation intensified a few years later, when Sin opened her musok museum. At the time, hers was the only exhibit in Korea devoted entirely to musok. A scholar who criticized Sin said that she "extended her professional horizons to a point where she cannot be taken seriously anymore." That phrase struck me as contradictory to the general agenda of the person who said it—a folklorist devoted to the preservation of Korean heritage. Another famous Korean scholar told me, "She thinks she can be both a mansin and a scholar, but this is impossible. Mansin Sin has become an amateur in both ways." Crossing a social status boundary that had been accepted in Korea for many hundreds of years proved a risky undertaking. Conventionally, mansin belong to the lowest social class, whereas scholars belong at the other end of the hierarchy. I know of no case where a mansin was also an accepted scholar, but Sin did not let this norm hinder her from producing a professional-quality museum.

Although trained in the standard manner, Mansin Sin is perceived by some as striving too hard to gain a "sophisticated image." Indeed, she takes pride in her book, her museum, her sophisticated website, and the master's degree in business administration that she earned long after becoming a practicing mansin. Although she is controversial among scholars, she enjoys many loyal clients and has plenty of work. However, the combination of Confucian perspectives on female subordination, bias against musok practitioners, and professional exclusivity of legitimized scholarly knowledge has left Sin an outsider in the male-dominated sphere where museum work is usually carried out in Korea.

Nevertheless, several scholars supported Mansin Sin in her endeavors to open a museum and publish her pujŏk book. Eventually, in 2015, she closed her museum, rented out the lower section of her house, and maintained only her home shrine and divination office on the upper floor. A new outdoor metal staircase now leads to the third floor, bypassing the areas that used to be the first extensive musok museum in Korea.

A remarkable collector of musok items, Dr. Yang Chong-sŭng, has also crossed the line between scholarly work and religious performance and shares with Mansin Sin an ambivalent and somewhat liminal position. However, whereas Mansin Sin is a spiritual mediator who also engages in some scholarly work, Dr. Yang is a full-fledged scholar who can also perform parts of kut. He completed his doctorate in folklore and ethnomusicology in the United States in 1994 and worked for many years as a senior curator for the National Folk Museum in Seoul. Before becoming a graduate student, Dr. Yang was an apprentice to a mask dance artist and a famous mansin. He learned both arts and, according to him and his acquaintances, was a talented performer.

In our conversations, Dr. Yang often mentioned his devotion to his spirit mother. "She fell ill at the same time that my birth mother was hospitalized. I was scheduled to perform the initiation ritual to become a legitimized mansin when the old mansin was ill, and while I was torn between visiting her and my mother, I was exhausted and tortured." His problem became even more complicated when his mask dance teacher pressed him to leave the practice of musok: "My mask dance teacher was against the initiation, as it could mark a breach between us. If I became a mansin, I likely would have abandoned my mask dance art in favor of the spirits." Mansin often earn more and dedicate more time to their trade than mask dance performers. Eventually, Dr. Yang decided not to go through with the initiation, despite his spiritual mother's pleadings, and changed his life course. He chose to become neither a professional performer of mask dance nor a mansin. Instead, he traveled to the United States and became a scholar of musok.[11] He has published books and essays and organized several international conferences and professional gatherings on musok.

Dr. Yang's extensive firsthand knowledge of and abilities in musok arts single him out within the mansin community as a scholar who is also "one of them." Mansin consult with him on professional matters such as the planning of a staged performance and the authenticity of some songs and dance moves, and often tease him, saying, "We know you can do it, why don't you put on a spirit costume and dance with us?" Dr. Yang rarely agrees to perform during rituals, even when other guests join in the *mugam* dance (see Kendall 1977), although he does perform in secular, scholarly contexts, such as talks and workshops.

Dr. Yang has worked hard to maintain the boundary between his status as a scholar and his former status as a performer, knowing that agreeing to perform during religious rituals might damage his image as a serious researcher. I have heard several people mention that his past as a mansin's apprentice might be the reason that he was not employed as a full-time professor in a Korean university on his return from the United States with a prestigious degree.

In 2007, Dr. Yang produced a new association for the research of musok, called the Association for Study of Korean Spirit Worship (Han'guk kwisinhak), in which many mansin were also members. At the association's first annual meeting, at the National Folk Museum, many scholars and mansin were present. In contrast, several weeks earlier, I did not see any mansin in the audience at the meeting of the older Association for the Research of Korean Shamanism. Dr. Yang contends that because mansin are the main sources of knowledge that musok researchers use in their academic endeavor, they should be present and contribute when their arts are being presented and discussed at academic conferences. This fresh approach marks a difference between Dr. Yang and his colleagues. His view is supported by the high level of education of contemporary mansin, which enables them to understand academic discourse on musok. They want their opinions about musok to be heard in academic meetings, but they are not often welcome there.

His close relationships with many mansin have helped Dr. Yang to accumulate an impressive collection of musok objects. His first valuable collection, inherited from his sinŏmŏni when he was an undergraduate student, was lost when he stored it at a friend's house; the friend's family, fearing that these objects might attract harmful spirits to their home, discarded the whole collection. Dr. Yang resumed his collecting efforts on returning to Korea in the early 1990s and has managed to accumulate thousands of items. He purchased or received them from retired mansin, the relatives of mansin who had passed away, and musok artists who conducted workshops at the museum where he worked. Sometimes he asked for items that were bound to be destroyed after a kut, such as straw and paper ornaments. This made collecting more affordable than buying such items at the antiques stores that he frequents but rarely patronizes. Dr. Yang's private collection is the successful outcome of personal interest, extensive networking, persistence, and broad knowledge.[12]

During his work as a curator at the National Folk Museum, Dr. Yang had limited free time to prepare his collection for display. For a long time, his artifacts were stored in a shed behind his home, exposed to winter cold, summer heat, and humidity. By 2007, he was able to purchase a small house adjacent to his home. He fortified the large windows with iron bars, hired a surveillance company, and equipped the place with systems for humidity and temperature control. In the main room, wooden shelves lined the walls, displaying some of the items. However, most of the collection was still densely packed in boxes. Although several famous mansin offered generous donations to his project, he refused. He feared that their financial support would be accompanied by pressure to represent them in certain ways, which he viewed as unprofessional. He donated parts of his collection to the National Folk Museum and loaned several pieces to a traditional art gallery so that they could be publicly displayed.

When Dr. Yang retired from his museum job, he devoted his efforts to the private collection. He expanded and remodeled the storage house and moved his own residence elsewhere. Mr. Chang Chin-su, a former graduate student of his, joined the work, and together they created a beautiful and extensive display of various musok styles in Yang's ex-home. The Museum of Shamanism opened in 2013. Many mansin and scholars attended the opening ceremony, and the museum's brochure included the commendation of several Western scholars.

The museum featured a re-created altar in the Hwanghae-do kut style, a re-created shrine in the Ch'unch'ŏn musok style, framed musindo, Siberian shamanic outfits on mannequins, assorted fans, statues, and ancient musok textbooks in glass cases.[13] Photographs of Dr. Yang's sinŏmŏni performing kut in the 1980s decorated one wall. The storage building housed a library and an archive of Yang's several hundred videos of kut from the last twenty years. A third small building featured many musok statues made of wood, straw, metal, or plastic. In the yard was a display of traditional earthenware pots and plates. In 2016, the Museum of Shamanism was relocated to the newly restored ancient shamanic shrine called Kŭmsŏngdang, in the northern suburbs of Seoul.[14] For the first time, the museum gained formal recognition and some sponsorship, as Dr. Yang had dreamed of for many years (fig. 3.7). Dr. Yang states that the most frequent visitors are mansin, for whom the presence of musok artifacts in a formally sanctioned place is a source of personal pride and evidence of supernatural blessing (Kendall, Yang, and Yoon 2015, 130). Every year, the museum's yard hosts a large public kut for the spirits of the place, allowing the mansin who worship them to appease their supernatural guardians.

Even before a religious artifact is displayed in a new context, transferring sacred objects from their original location to museum exhibitions can be a complex process with unexpected results. Donors to secular establishments, such as national festivals and museums, are not always aware of the process that the objects might undergo as part of their preparation for display. Preservation and

Fig. 3.7 Dr. Yang Chong-sŭng in the new Shamanism Museum, 2018. Credit: Author.

other actions deemed necessary by professional curators might cause anxiety and even prompt requests to return a donated item to its original, sacred location (Keappler 1992, 462–463; Kendall 2007, 182–183). However, in the case of Dr. Yang, the mansin who donate objects to his collection trust that he knows enough about musok to maintain the artifacts' dignity and the spirits' blessings. Some mansin think that the gods leave their painted image once it is given to a museum, whereas others consider the picture as still inspired and connected to the supernatural (Kendall, Yang, aand Yoon 2015, 123–125). To avoid religious sacrilege or criticism by mansin, the Museum of Shamanism in Seoul held a special kut when it was opened, separately from the official opening event. In the kut, all the spirits represented in the altars and other exhibits were asked for their blessing and approval of the new arrangement of the artifacts.

When an exhibition is focused on displaying a religion, it is not obvious how to "approach this tension between words, images, objects, and an apparently incommunicable core? . . . how do you picture the unpictureable?" (Arthur 2000, 2). Museum visitors tend to overlook this tension and to treat religious artifacts in museums as sacred, regardless of the secular setting. For them, it is not always clear where the museum ends and the religion begins. In the Museum of Shamanism, visiting mansin and believers prostrate themselves, bow, and pray in front of recontextualized assemblages, because they were constructed with musok items that had been used in rituals. Several times I have seen visitors place a ten-thousand-won bill on a museum re-creation of a musok altar as an offering to the spirits, but this kind of gesture is not possible in other kinds of displays, such as those in the National Folk Museum or Andong Folk Museum, where the artifacts are behind glass.

South Korea's government invests a lot in protecting and exhibiting the indigenous culture of the nation. Therefore, the two collectors discussed could reasonably hope to receive official acknowledgement and sponsorship for their private museums. Being recognized by the authorities as owners, planners, and producers of permanent exhibitions of musok art was not just a professional goal for each; it was also a personal yearning for confirmation of their merits. That kind of materially visible, official confirmation would reward their long and difficult struggles. Such hopes were also based on an understanding that their deep knowledge of the extensive paraphernalia of musok and its meanings was uncommon. Usually, an ethnographer or museum curator seeking to reconnect ritual objects with their original use and significance "is a detective who toils long and hard to decipher material clues . . . compet[ing] both with the native informants and with other ethnographers . . . for the facts that comprise his descriptions" (Kirshenblatt-Gimblett 1998, 33). In contrast, Mansin Sin and Dr. Yang serve as collectors, curators, and informants. Nevertheless, their firsthand knowledge achieved little acknowledgment and support from other Korean scholars, especially in the case of the mansin-turned-scholar Sin Myŏng-gi.

The differential academic response of Korean scholars to the two collections represents the politics of inclusion and exclusion in relation to musok in Korea's society. The sincere effort of Mansin Sin to give her collection a standard museum appearance was not enough to overcome the cultural bias against a musok practitioner and a woman. Conversely, Dr. Yang's collection was considered a serious manifestation of knowledge and expertise even before it opened to the public. Unfortunately, personal and other considerations make it unlikely that these two impressively rich and diverse collections will be incorporated into one legitimate, academically acknowledged, government-sponsored educational exhibit of musok.

DIVERSE MESSAGES IN DIFFERENT KINDS OF MUSEUMS

Currently, there is no government-sponsored musok museum, and the musok exhibits in folklore museums offer a glimpse into the same politics that affected Dr. Yang and Mansin Sin. Musok exhibits in large Korean museums are contextualized within structures influenced by Western perceptions and incorporate conventions such as glass cases and labels. However, this formal conventionality does not imply uniform intentions. The many ways that musok is recontextualized demonstrate that this supposedly objective medium conveys contradictory narratives. These complex, three-dimensional spaces—full of materiality and textuality—may shape visitors' perception of Korea's spiritual traditions and vernacular religions. Hidden in a narrow corridor, central in a main hall, or covering a full section within an outdoor museum, musok in Korean museums has become an agent in the national process of identity construction.

In this chapter, I discussed the value and meaning of such displays in terms of several criteria. Where are the items displayed within the museum space? How are they arranged? How are they recontextualized through labels? Analyzing these criteria sheds light on how musok is positioned within the world, within the general culture, and within the moral and aesthetic conventions of the time. In the examples presented, labels reinforce the spatial choices of the curators. It is not a coincidence that large, easily accessible exhibits of musok carry comprehensive labels that reflect positive attitudes, whereas venues with smaller, less centrally located exhibits choose a more distancing approach. This is the direct outcome of the still-existing dualistic attitude toward musok in general. Museum planners, curators, and policy makers are mediators between mansin and the public, and their intentions are transmitted through artifacts and create the agency of the displays.

As can be seen, in many institutional museums, there is little attempt to create a dialogue with the represented people—in this case, the mansin. Unlike many other anthropological museums in the world discussed by Boast (2011), where the represented culture is increasingly involved in the museum preparation, large museums in Korea are detached from the musok world. Moreover, when a mansin attempted to produce her own version of a museum exhibit, she could not receive sponsorship for her project, although she mostly planned her project along broadly accepted Western museum norms.

The material aspects that museums display in a static manner play a central role also in screen-mediated representation, such as the films discussed in chapter 2. Whereas films are mostly constrained in length and format, television programs provide more options to represent the materiality, textuality, and meaning of musok. In chapter 4, I analyze the differences between television drama series that depict Korean culture of at least two hundred years ago and those that depict the present. I also discuss the new and intriguing phenomenon of incorporating mansin into talk shows, reality programs, and the news, which has increased the visibility of this religious practice in Korea and abroad. Viewers watching mansin on television gain a sense of familiarity with musok and its practitioners that they cannot achieve in museums or even by meeting a practitioner in real life.

NOTES

1. In Korea, folklore museums are more common than anthropology museums as a result of the distinct paths that these two academic disciplines have taken, as discussed in chap. 2. See also Kim Kwang-ok (K. Kim 2000) and Roger Janelli (1986).

2. Official numbers supplied by the US Department of State (2008) include "Buddhist, 22.8 percent; Protestant, 18.3 percent; and Roman Catholic, 10.9 percent." This leaves almost half of the population unaccounted for, suggesting that many people practice vernacular religions not mentioned in the survey, such as Confucian rites, animism, and shamanism. Similar figures from 1995, by the National Statistical Office (cited by A. E. Kim 2002, 293), include several new religions and Confucians but not the vernacular beliefs, which might be prominent in about half of the population that asserts "No Religion." Musok is generally not viewed as a religion in the modern interpretation of the term because it is not organized or bound by clear laws and community life (Guillemoz 1992, 116). Moreover, as discussed, many Koreans use the services of mudang only in times of crisis, in contrast to the expected ongoing engagement with Christian practices. Therefore, they might not consider themselves as adherents of musok, even if such a category existed in statistical questionnaires.

3. There are records in Koryŏ of both male and female mudang and of shaman-advisers to the royal court, but by Chosŏn (in the late fourteenth century), there are not nearly as many records of male mudang (Michael Pettid, pers. comm., May 2012).

4. Shai Sarfati, an experienced film editor, noticed this detail and brought it to my attention in a personal communication (2007).

5. Musok was given a much more central role in this venue for a few months in 2011–2012, when the museum arranged a special exhibition of more than five hundred shamanic artifacts from the Himalayas, Russia, Mongolia, Japan, and Korea. However, this was not a display of Korean culture, as musok was only a small part of the exhibition. In 2013, the museum honored the famous musok researcher Ha Hyo-gil, who had served as director of the museum in the 1980s, by showcasing some of the thousands of artifacts he had recently donated in small niches at the end of the children's section. It was advertised but was small and unimpressive and thus attracted little attention from visitors (Suh 2013).

6. The Kyŏngsan Museum near Taegu (Daegu) took a similar stance when, in 2015, it dedicated two halls to a special exhibition of musok practices and artifacts in which there were mostly hundred-year-old musok paintings. For a paper musok artifact, achieving such age is rare.

7. See Kyoim Yun (2006) for a discussion of Cheju's transformation from a remote fishing island into a tourist attraction.

8. Some other collections of musok to consider include a legendary accumulation by the deceased scholar Kim T'ae-gon, which was donated to the National Folk Museum in 2015. Moreover, Japanese colonial anthropologists, who studied musok in the early twentieth century, allegedly assembled another collection, which I have tried to locate in Japan with the help of several scholars, to no avail.

9. In South Korea, checks are used for sums greater than $50, because there are no regular bills over fifty thousand won.

10. Sin's extensive public performance record was listed on her now discontinued website (formerly http://www.chunbokhwa.com) and in her book, *Mudang Naeryŏk* (Sin 2001).

11. More details about his interesting life and research can be read in an interview published in *Folklore Forum* (S. Kim et al. 2012).

12. Several of Dr. Yang's collected outfits were analyzed in a book by Kim Ŭn-jŏng (U. Kim 2004, 58–63).

13. Many Korean scholars perceive Siberian shamanism as closely related, or even the source of Korea's vernacular rituals that involve trance. Therefore, Korean scholars conduct extensive research about Siberian practices.

14. I discuss the struggle by Dr. Yang and a local nongovernmental organization to save Kŭmsŏngdang from demolition and, subsequently, to restore the shrine elsewhere (Sarfati 2010, 2017).

FOUR

Getting to Know a Korean Shaman through Television Representations

WE ARE INSIDE A MUSOK shrine. The altar is decorated with paper flowers and loaded with fruit, drinks, and rice cakes. Behind it is a row of god paintings (*musindo*) and statues (*sinsang*). A young woman wears a beautifully embroidered silk hanbok and shakes two fans in all directions. She jumps onto the rim of a large clay jar and continues to dance. Between her jumping and talking, she announces the names of the spirits who possess her, and other women wearing hanbok stand around her and welcome those supernatural entities by offering bows and greetings. Seated on the floor, dressed in modern skirts and jackets, two women move uncomfortably and dry their tears. They seem suspicious, particularly an older woman who is constantly scolded by the mansin for her greed.

Such a sight can be observed almost every day at various mountain shrines around South Korea. As accurate as it is, this initiation kut is not real but rather a reperformance produced in a scene from episode 126 of the television drama *Lotus Flower Fairy* (*Wangkkot sŏnnyŏnim*, 2004–2005, directed by Yi Chin-yŏng). The mansin and audience members are all actors, and the setting is a television studio. Nevertheless, viewers learn a lot from watching this reperformance. They observe the forms and procedures of kut, the services rendered by the mansin, the artistic manifestations within the rituals, and the sociopsychological effects that the rituals might have. They understand musok better and become more aware of its prominence in Korea.

Many Koreans perceive musok as occult, outlandish, distant, and impossible to understand. Only a few relatives and close clients and friends can sincerely say that they know a mansin, and even they rarely claim to understand her. Whether participating as an audience member or client in a kut, watching a film, or visiting museum displays, none of these interactions allow people to know a mansin.

Television programs add a unique dimension to the other representation venues discussed in previous chapters. For the past ten years, Korean television has depicted musok in a manner that brings the mansin's worldview and activities closer to many viewers. This chapter discusses television representations of musok as agents that work toward improving the public image of mansin, both emotionally and intellectually. We can ask whether empathy is the vehicle we need to broadly appreciate the mansin's life and work, and whether television does more than make the mansin banal in the familiar form of a suffering woman in a soap opera. A partial answer to these concerns is offered by the positive view that most mansin that I interviewed expressed toward such depictions. They like to watch talk shows and reality programs about musok and to upload links to those representations into their personal internet web pages.[1] The online forums, blogs, and social networking pages of mansin reveal many discussions of television depictions of musok. Practitioners debate how well the mansin and actors performed and whether the interviewer or screenplay writer really understood musok.

Mansin Kim Nam-sun, whom I have known for fifteen years, likes watching television dramas and watched several chapters depicting mansin together with me. In summer 2014, after we watched a reperformed kut that did not match her own knowledge of the performance, she said,

> We cannot expect television directors to really understand what we do. They are not mansin, and the actress has not experienced *sin naerim* [the descending of spirits into her body]. But I think that they nicely captured the struggles that the life of a mansin presents. The actress is good in understanding the suffering of the character and, because she is a good actress, the audience can sympathize with her. This is important, because instead of looking down at her as a haunted person, they see what she has to go through and learn of the benefits that mansin bring to the community. This is why I like these kinds of television shows.

Soon after this interview, I happened to meet several Korean executive office staff in Seoul. They were surprised to hear about my interest in musok, and expressed the common statements regarding it. "Musok contains the beautiful dance and music of our ancestors," said a thirty-year-old secretary and college graduate. "It used to be common when I was a child, and would hear the mansin beat the drum in my village," said the office manager, who was in her seventies. When I asked if they thought that musok was common in our time, they seemed a bit embarrassed and inquired if I had really met mansin and how I knew where to find them. Was I not scared of the spirits, they wanted to know, and did the mansin treat me nicely? I continued to say that the kut I watched in the *Lotus Flower Fairy* drama were quite similar to the ones I observed in my research. Soon we began chatting about the drama's plot, which they knew well. I also learned that one of them had had her fortune told by a mansin as a teenager, and another decided her wedding date after a mansin consulted with spirits of the natural elements. Their knowledge of mansin in real life was much narrower than what they learned from watching the drama.

This was how I came to think of television representations of musok as more than entertaining reperformances of musok. After interviewing ten well-educated Korean friends, I was surprised to learn that even those interviewees who usually mocked musok and commented sarcastically about my frequent participation in kut knew much about it from televised reperformances that they watched. I conducted ten more in-depth interviews with male and female residents of Seoul aged twenty to sixty years, only to find similar results. All my interviewees had watched more than one mansin on television. However, the television genres that each liked to watch varied, as did the representations of mansin to which they were exposed. This discovery led me to dedicate particular attention to each television genre in this chapter. It turns out that different qualities of musok take center stage in each genre. Some delve into the personal consequences of becoming a mansin, others represent musok practices, and still others use mansin for practical purposes, such as deciphering unsolved murder cases or advising celebrities about the new year.

This chapter demonstrates the complex relationship between the agency of television as a structure and television as a product of human work. As Renato Rosaldo (1993, 104–106) states, the agency of the structure and the human factor are not mutually exclusive; rather, in each ethnographic case, complex relationships between the two construct the culture in question. Moreover, media technology should be discussed at both the macro and micro levels as a game changer and as a conduit of content (Meyrowitz 1994, 61). Accordingly, televised depictions of musok are unique in their production strategies and dissemination patterns and serve as options for constructing new modes of knowledge about this tradition.

Although this research is not quantitative in nature and does not aim to measure the exact effect of television programs on the public image of musok, as an ethnographer, I noticed that popular television programs affected mansin, clients, and other Koreans that I met throughout my fieldwork. Television can achieve goals that are unique to this medium's features, including its broad distribution, rich content production facilities, and popularity. However, if the medium is the message, as stated by McLuhan (1964), then why were mansin depicted only sparsely until about ten years ago? Why were most earlier television programs about musok based on documentary film conventions? Why did this practice change recently? And more generally, why do new genres emerge without technological innovations to spur them?

Of all the venues for representation discussed in this book, television is the most universal. The general availability of many television channels requires constant content production, which makes showing nonmainstream topics such as musok plausible. Moreover, some television genres that deal with current affairs, such as news and talk shows, are often less tightly planned and executed than film, which makes it easier to work with the chaotic lifestyle of some mansin. The mansin that I know are usually very busy, and their plans are made only a few days in advance. Still, they do their best to accommodate any invitation to appear on television because such an appearance greatly boosts their clientele. Several of my mansin interlocutors framed screenshots of their television appearances and hung them in their offices and shrines. Most list their television appearances in their curriculum vitae, which appears in promotional brochures and websites. The mass distribution of television appearances contributes to their popularity among mansin. For some, this medium changed their career trajectory when televised interviews made them celebrity mansin in an instant. This path to becoming famous has been added to the governmental designation that was discussed in the 1980s (Choi 1987), except that the contemporary, screen-mediated stardom reaches much more diverse audiences than sponsored religious rituals. Television, as a technology, encapsulates many new possibilities, most of which materialized for musok only in the past decade, when other cultural shifts took place, as discussed in previous chapters. As we will see in this chapter, there was little televised musok representation until the 2000s, and this in itself demonstrates that the scope of musok representations was not produced by the medium but rather in relation to other cultural processes. One thing that is clear from this exploration is that, through television programs, people can get to know diverse aspects of musok that would rarely be available to them otherwise.

Television audiences get to know mansin in three ways, each of which will be discussed below. The first aspect is what mansin do, which is mostly addressed in reality shows, documentaries, and talk shows. The second aspect that interests television viewers is what mansin feel and think. This is a bit trickier to tackle in talk shows, because people tend to be suspicious about the sincerity of interviewed mansin. It turns out that emotional identification is achieved more efficiently while watching multichapter dramas, where the life story of a mansin protagonist is revealed slowly and in detail. The third aspect that television audiences learn is how mansin can help others—what the benefit of meeting a real mansin can be. This is elaborated in programs where mansin serve as professional consultants on topics ranging from new year's divination to personal makeovers to unsolved crimes.

These three aspects that television teaches its viewers follow the conventional three dimensions of attitudes, which include thoughts, feelings, and actions (as accepted in classical psychology; e.g., Katz 1960). Koreans who might have viewed mansin as strange before the mediated television encounters feel more familiar with them in all dimensions of attitudes, which is crucial to forming a stable public opinion (Katz 1960, 168–169). In fact, several of my Korean friends told me that the drama *Lotus Flower Fairy*, discussed earlier, changed their perspective on musok because it was the first time that they sympathized with a mansin and understood how harsh her life can be. Pak, a recent graduate of the history master's degree program at a prestigious university, told me in an interview in summer 2016,

> I could not believe how much I identified with the protagonist [of *Lotus Flower Fairy*]. Think about it, I am a graduate of Seoul National University and she is a mudang. We are the same age, but other than that, there is no real similarity. I have a loving mother, and she had so much complexity in her relationship with her biological mother. What are her prospects in life? I can get a good job now. Who will hire her? I have a loving boyfriend and we are about to get married. She has difficulties with this too, because she is a mudang. And still, I felt so much pain when she was suffering. This is what dramas are meant to do. They want you to cry so that you will wait for the next episode.

The participation of mansin in television programs, such as talk shows, melodramas, and documentary series, is a new and intriguing phenomenon that increases the visibility of this religious practice in Korea and abroad. However, unlike real-life interaction, this process of acquaintance is unidirectional. Most television viewers do not expose their own lives to the mansin (unless they seek her out as new clients), as their televised acquaintance with her is mediated through electronic devices of mass communication.

The names and designs of the television programs discussed below, which often include Koreanized English terms, intentionally align their content with a modern, global culture that most viewers espouse in their daily lives. This global–local exchange of images and ideas adds another fresh connotation to musok. Television representations of this indigenous, vernacular belief system come full circle when their accentuation of this practice as a local trait is mediated by global technology and in global program formats. The colorful, traditional aesthetic of musok practitioners often contrasts with the programs' presenters, who wear fashionable, Western-style outfits. The intriguing combination of contemporary living conditions and ancient ideas and customs has contributed to the increased volume of musok representation in television shows.

This chapter combines textual and visual analysis of television programs, along with participant observations and interviews with friends and informants in Seoul who have watched such television shows. This investigation of musok's representation on television expands on the issues discussed in previous chapters and includes new options for acquiring knowledge about musok that television avails. Other topics discussed in previous chapters will also be examined: how do mansin mediate between people and the supernatural? How is technology used and emphasized in representations of musok rituals? How has musok's image changed over the past half century? How have the politics of cultural exclusion and inclusion manifested through musok representations? I first address the theoretical question about television's effect on society and television as a reflection of society. This will illuminate why televised representations of musok are so important for understanding the place and roles of mansin in contemporary Korea.

TELEVISION'S EFFECT ON SOCIETY

Television contributes to public knowledge about musok not just by capturing and broadcasting representations of extreme ritual activities. Other media, such as festivals, films, newspapers, and practitioners' promotional websites, depict these activities too. Rather, televised depictions of musok offer a unique opportunity for viewers to learn about the private lives and emotional experiences of musok practitioners. These aspects are less accessible to most people in real life, even to mansin clients. Moreover, television representations of musok cultivate an increasingly homogenized perception of mansin in the Korean public and position musok within acceptable, mainstream cultural trends. This is another case in which folklore is being preserved, disseminated, and articulated in diverse manners through this mass medium.

Televised depictions of society have been proven to have significant effects on public discourse and norms and on personal perceptions of the world. Greg Philo (1990) demonstrates that television audiences tend to believe what they see on television, especially in the case of news reports. Richard Sparks (1992) argues that watching popular cop shows increases the intensity of fear related to crime. Television has been identified as a factor in producing negative body images in women and increasing eating disorders (Thompson and Heinberg 1999).

Others note that media create different interpretations in each person and public they encounter (e.g., Hall 1980). Such theorists see the personal agency of television viewers as central to the production of media effect. To discuss the influence of media on people, George Gerbner and colleagues (1986) use the term *cultivation* instead of *effects* to include the reaction of diverse audiences to the content of television programs. They state, "Television neither simply creates, nor reflects images, opinions, and beliefs. Rather, it is an integral aspect of a dynamic process" (23). Complex interactions between messages produced by media experts and contexts of audience reception result in alterations of sentiments and worldviews in viewers. Eventually, such messages shape group identities. The analysis continues, "Institutional needs and objectives influence the creation and distribution of mass-produced messages which create, fit into, exploit, and sustain the needs, values, and ideologies of mass publics. These publics, in turn, acquire distinct identities as publics, partly through exposure to the ongoing flow of messages" (Gerbner et al. 1986, 23).

Ideologies and needs of institutions are interrelated with the perspectives held by their audiences. The media messages that institutions produce have to fit existing norms to some extent, even while attempting to create change. Philo and Miller (2001) criticize the idea that audience interpretations determine the messages of television programs, because it downplays the importance of influence by television and emphasizes the viewers' active role. They argue that although there are reasons to focus on reception and interpretation, researchers must realize that there is an objectively available media representation that can be analyzed. In his previous research, Philo (1990, 1996) shows that responses to media output by diverse audiences have common features. Philo and Miller conclude that most viewers understand the intended message in a similar fashion; therefore, the effect of media can be quite homogeneous.

My interviews with many television viewers in Korea suggest that, in the case of musok, the relevant reception model is dynamic. My interviewees in Seoul articulated a shared understanding of television programs' topics and statements and of what mansin believe and do. When mansin were shown to suffer because of their vocation, most of my interviewees, regardless of their age, gender, or religious affiliation, felt sorry for the mansin and related to the mansin's life as a pitiable result of uncontrollable conditions. None of my informants questioned the accuracy of television depictions of musok. Moreover, mansin take pride in their own televised appearances.

Nevertheless, acceptance of the religious messages conveyed in the televised reperformances of musok varied, as message encoding was influenced by the viewers' previous experiences, cultural histories, and worldviews. Television programs convey to the Korean audiences that musok is interesting and worth understanding, but judgment of the spiritual credibility and implications of the content shown were tightly correlated with people's preexisting ideological stances. I found that Buddhists and people with no precise religious affiliation viewed mansin as potential consultants and believed that musok practice might be beneficial at times. "I think that if a mansin could help my friend overcome the suicide of her brother, she should be congratulated for it," said a twenty-five-year-old computer programmer who shared with me the sad story of a friend whose brother suffered severe depression. The friend felt guilty for not supporting him enough because she was studying in another city, but after a mansin assured her that the brother is now happy and peaceful, she could go on with her life. In contrast, Christians who watch programs about musok tend to treat this belief system as nonsense and blasphemy, and several Christian interviewees stated that musok was a satanic plot to lure innocent people away from the path of real faith. "When I watch those crazy women jump up and down for a fee, I think that as a Christian, I must put more effort into convincing people of the true god. People are easily tempted by the agents of Satan," said a fifty-year-old Methodist pastor. My Christian interviewees mostly understood the televised representations as a part of that wrong worldview, and they interpreted these digital texts as part of a reality that they strive to alter. Notably, all the interviewees, regardless of their ideological stance, reported strong emotions toward the mansin depicted in television programs. Their iterations ranged from "so sad to see her [the mansin's] hard life," "amazed how wonderfully she danced and sang," "really liked the beautiful decorations on the altar, especially the paper flowers," to "angry that he convinced the poor old lady that his fake gods are protecting her deceased husband," "afraid of such contact with ghosts," and "shocked that people in my country are willing to pay so much for this nonsense." In this way, television representations produce affect and (somewhat disputed) knowledge of musok in a manner similar to daily processes of getting to know people and practices. The medium is readily available, entices in its various formats, and creates emotional and intellectual engagement with the material, textual, and behavioral folkways of musok.

The influence of television on opinions related to musok is amplified by the fact that, for many Koreans, communication with the supernatural is a taboo topic. It is discussed very little in public or in front of children. Philo (1996) shows that children in particular are heavily influenced by television when there is little face-to-face discussion of an issue, as is the case with topics such as mental illness. Such lacunae in general discourse are filled in by televised depictions, which become the main representation of such taboo topics. Korean television denotes musok's taboo status by showing a slide before the program begins advising parents that the content to follow does not suit children younger than fifteen.[2] Such warnings appear even when the program does not depict any violence or visually disturbing scenes. The very idea of musok and spiritual communication is the problematic content that justifies an age restriction. Protecting children from harmful content is, in the case of musok, the result of a moral stance that doubts the musok world. Some staged reperformances, such as the one discussed in chapter 1, host whole families in the audience; however, televised representations might reach children of families who are Christian or otherwise against musok. The age limit demonstrates the debated status of musok for some families and the state's support of the parents' right to determine the religious experiences of their children.[3] However, such programs are still broadcast in the afternoon and primetime evening hours.

Accordingly, I agree with Philo and Miller's (2001) criticism of the tendency to analyze the effects of televised representations on audience perceptions out of context, as if the program had no grounded existence (Philo and Miller 2001; Philo 2001). In my research, I looked for the relationships between the ambient culture and the television shows that were produced and consumed. Korean culture has reached the stage that it can embrace its vernacular religion not only as an art form but also as a constructed way to tackle issues of supernatural intervention in people's lives. South Korea's youth nationalism has moved away from an ethnic all-encompassing identity construction toward more practical, self-centered perspectives (Campbell 2006). Contemporary young Koreans enjoy watching musok in the media for entertainment purposes, as a means to help them rethink their personal concerns, and for personal spiritual interest.

Televised depictions have changed to match these new interests and now are rarely narrated by an authoritative male voice discussing musok as "our unique national heritage." Instead, many television programs use interviews with mansin as a soundtrack behind visuals of musok altars and rituals, and more programs focus on the mansin's emotions and personal lives than on ritual texts and mythology. A culture that increasingly encourages an individualistic view of life—in which personal benefit and success are no less important than the nation's development—has learned to treat musok not merely as a tradition that deserves preservation but also as a functional therapeutic option, accompanied by performative expertise. Moreover, the subversive aspects of kut rituals, such as gender crossing and vulgarity, have become less disturbing to Koreans. People have grown used to such traits in other popular culture and music performances, as part of the *Hallyu* phenomenon. This term relates to the global cultural influx of Korean popular culture. Among the more international popular culture trends, depictions of supernatural interventions such as the British book series *Harry Potter* (1997–2007, by J. K. Rowling), and the American television series *Charmed* (1998–2006, produced by Aaron Spelling) have probably contributed to the general acceptance of narratives that discuss spiritual mediation in musok.

Even when viewers refuse to accept the ideology of musok, their exposure to such ideas creates a new and different discourse that rests on common knowledge that has been created by watching similar television representations of musok.

GENRES OF TELEVISED MUSOK REPRESENTATION

I collected data about several television programs that provided the bases for this analysis of representation modes and ways of manipulating audience emotion to gain high television viewer ratings. Nancy Abelmann and Kathleen McHugh (2005) observed, in relation to Korea's golden age film melodramas of the 1960 and 1970s, that there was no need to dramatize reality in order to create suspense in movie plots because the reality of postwar South Korea was truly dramatic. In contrast to Hollywood's melodramatic depictions of extreme cases, which are rare in real life, "South Korean cinema construes melodrama as the most efficacious mode of realism" (Abelmann and McHugh 2005, 4). Similarly, I suggest that the lives and ritual practices of mansin are extraordinary, to the extent that little exaggeration is needed when transforming them into televised representations. The genres analyzed include scripted melodramas, reality shows, talk shows, documentary series, and the news.

I chose the romantic drama *49 Days* (*49 il*, 2011, directed by Cho Yŏng-gwang and Pak Yong-sun) because its narrative is based on musok ideas such as spirit possession. This drama was very well received in Korea. It reached a viewer rating of almost 19.9 percent in its final episode (TNmS 2011). Another romantic drama, *Lotus Flower Fairy* (*Wangkkot sŏnnyŏnim* [also called *Heaven's Fate*], 2004–2005, directed by Yi Chin-yŏng), tells of a mansin's life throughout the initiation process. This drama revolves around the influence of fate on the lives of the protagonists and their difficulties in finding romantic love. The drama aired daily on the MBC network. It was well received, and the lead actor, Yi Ta-hae, won the 2004 MBC Drama Award for best new actress. The historical drama *The Moon Embracing the Sun* (*Haerŭl p'umŭn tal*, 2012, directed by Kim To-hun and Yi Song-jun), based on the novel *Haerŭl p'umŭn tal* by Chŏng Ŭn-gwŏl (Ŭ. Chŏng 2005), depicts mudang and their practices around the fictitious King Yi-hwŏn in the Chosŏn era. This show peaked at a 42 percent rating in its final episode (TNmS 2012). It also received various awards, including two Paeksang Arts Awards and eight MBC Drama Awards. *Chumong* (also called *Prince of Legend*, 2006, directed by Kim Kŭn-hong and Yi Chu-hwan) is a drama about prehistorical Korea that discusses spirituality and spirit mediums as parts of court culture.[4] It was one of the most profitable dramas in Korea, with a viewer rating of 52 percent at its peak in 2006 (Mickler 2009). It was also shown in many other countries, including Japan.

The talk shows I analyze are those that have dedicated much time to mansin. These include *I Am All for Life* (*Taech'an insaeng*, 2013, TV Chosŏn), in which mansin were asked about their initiation and the impact it had on their lives, and *Job Stories* (*Sŭt'ori chapsŭ*, 2011–2013, TV Chosŏn), which related mainly to professional aspects of musok.

I chose television documentary series according to their uniqueness and popularity in order to discuss television productions that ignited public discourse on musok. These are *Shamanic Journeys in Life* (*Musok kihaeng salm*, 2011, ETN), *Interview Documentary* (*Int'ŏpyu tak'yument'ari inyongwi kkŭn*, 2011, Living TV), *Why?* (*Wai kunggŭmhan iyagi*, 2009–present, SBS), *Leakage of the Sky's Mysteries* (*Ch'ŏn'gi nusŏl*, 2013–present, MBN), *Insight People* (*Insait'ŭ p'ip'ŭl*, 2011, Insite TV), *Exorcist* (*Eksosisŭt'ŭ*, 2008–2009, tvN), *Mystery Reportage: Black Hole 2* (*Misŭt'eri rŭp'o pŭllaekhol*, 2012, tvN), *Yi Sŭng-yŏn with a Hundred Women* (*Yi Sŭng-yŏn kwa 100 inŭi yŏja*, 2011–2013, StoryonTV), and *24-Hour Observation Camera* (*Kwanch'al k'amera 24 sigan*, 2012–2017, Channel A).

To complete the scope of televised engagement with musok, I discuss a few news items that depicted shamanic rituals, including the ritual held at the Namdaemun gate in 2008 after its destruction by arson. As will be demonstrated, genre is closely related to how musok rituals, worldview, and usability are represented and to the public image that each televised representation fosters.

AMAZING ACTS: WHAT DO MANSIN DO?

The impressive control that mansin might have over the supernatural is depicted on television differently when representing historical and contemporary practitioners. Each genre—contemporary and historical drama—creates a distinct image of musok. In contemporary romantic drama shows, the mansin are mostly sensitive people who help others. They are not involved in politics or in black magic, which my mansin interlocutors say is forbidden in musok. In contrast, historical dramas emphasize the political power of mansin's activities and depict them in spiritual acts meant to harm others. Mansin Kim Nam-sun said that "directors of dramas cannot show us as malicious and bewitching because many people know that we are all for helping others." As discussed in chapter 2 in relation to film, directors of feature movies in the 1970s had no such reservations. But times have changed, and the public image of musok has improved significantly. As Kim noted, "black magic can be shown now only in historical drama because people like it, it sells well, and is not taken as part of what we do these days, just like flogging, concubinage, and other things that they show in such productions."

The shamanic priestess of two thousand years ago in *Chumong* is an aide to the mythical Puyŏ kingdom ruler before the emergence of the Koguryŏ kingdom in 37 BCE (S. Song 1974). She often works to eliminate his enemies using her spiritual capacities. Several contemporary musok realities and images are reflected in the drama, among them that mansin are needed at certain times and are otherwise scorned. Some practitioners are accused of faking their divinations for material gain, just as suggested in rumors that are common in contemporary Korean public discourse. The drama also shows mainly female practitioners. The male rulers, who notice the main diviner's increasing power, try to diminish her influence over official matters.

The first episode includes a scene that reminds one of politicians in colonial Korea who were accused of adhering to mansin's advice on political issues (Hwang 2009, 93). The king of Puyŏ stops an important meeting when the head shamanic priestess summons him. He leaves his office in haste to hear her vision, in which, instead of the two-legged bird that symbolizes the king and the crown prince, she sees a three-legged bird. The king chokes with surprise and exchange worried glances with his advisers. In the next episode, the priestess wants to meet the crown prince, and he immediately goes to her room and follows her advice about freeing a female prisoner. She asks the crown prince boldly if he has fallen in love with that prisoner, and he confesses. Later, the mansin advises the rulers of Puyŏ to prevent war with the mighty Han, and they agree. In episode 3, the diviner prepares an offering altar, and the king kneels and offers thanks to the gods of heaven, wind, and earth. These four scenes show how the drama's narrative empowers the female diviner. Through her predictions of the future, she controls the king's schedule, intervenes in the prince's love life, inserts doubt regarding a declared war, and causes the king to humble himself. The mansin is depicted as majestic and calm. She is always dressed in a fancy silk gown, has a personal maid, lives in the palace compound, and does not exhibit uncontrolled or unusual behavior in her daily encounters.

Similarly, in *The Moon Embracing the Sun*, mansin are at the center of power. Inside the palace, they have a school and religious facility from which they do the queen's bidding. Such a narrative choice is not backed by significant historical data, but the scriptwriters took some liberties in imagining musok in Korea five hundred years ago.[5] The older queen is mostly a malicious character who works to eliminate anyone who might threaten the kingship of her favorite heir to the throne. In episode 5, she asks the head mansin to perform a ritual that will suffocate a girl that the older queen fears might become the new queen. Black smoke rises from the altar and up through the roof, travels some distance, and crawls under the girl's door. The smoke forms snake shapes and presses on the girl's throat like human hands. She is strangled by it, not suffocated by breathing it. As the smoke disappears from the girl's room, the mansin is shown again, telling her sponsor that the mission has been completed. She is thus depicted as seeing beyond walls and physical barriers. The mansin tells the king's mother that causing death is beyond her abilities, but she has made the girl so sick that she cannot disturb the plan to prevent her from becoming the next queen. The mansin trembles and has a strange facial expression to demonstrate her trance state of consciousness. The ritual employs elements that are common in musok, such as using pieces of paper with a person's date of birth and burning paper for good luck, but harnesses those features of prosocial spiritual activity to depict evil.

In contrast to the evil historical mudang, television dramas depict contemporary mansin mostly as well-intentioned, dedicated religious practitioners. Their life is complicated, as is also shown in the feature films discussed in chapter 2, *Fortune Saloon* and *Man on the Edge*, but they mean no harm. I could not find television dramas with mansin as protagonists before the 2000s, perhaps pointing to the fact that there was little interest in representing them as full characters. Just like films from the early 2000s, contemporary dramas depict mansin holistically and focus on their lives and feelings.

The few television programs depicting musok in the 1980s and 1990s were documentaries. These depicted star mansin dancing and singing and scholars talking about musok as an important heritage, just as documentary movies of the time did. Clearly, even documentary conventions have changed. In the 2000s, mansin have been documented differently in Korean television. The series *Why?* dedicated an episode in 2013 to a young mother who tells how she discovered that she was destined to become a mansin when spirits possessed her and caused her to behave strangely. The filming crew documented her discussions with her husband on the topic, the hardship that she experienced for not wanting to become a musok practitioner, and her fear that the spirits might harm her family if she declined this supernatural demand.

In watching television-mediated private conversations and behaviors by mansin whom I have never met, I recalled moments in my own fieldwork. The special feeling I had when participating in events such as initiation kut stemmed from knowing that it was a rare and precious event. Most Koreans cannot observe an initiation kut, let alone participate in moments of professional and emotional coaching. Because it is likely not possible to hold these noisy performances in dense urban environments, there are slight chances of incidental encounters with a kut, unless one knows of a scheduled ritual and travels specially to attend it. Watching such rare events on television mediates emotion sharing and a mutual understanding that did not exist before. In some programs, viewers can follow the daily routines of mansin and feel closer to them as people and as religious leaders, without ever meeting them.

The documentary series *24-Hour Observation Camera* films one site over twenty-four hours and then edits the raw footage into an hour-long program.[6] In the program, subtitles appear on the screen to emphasize and explain what is going on in the filmed footage. In a dramatic voice, a narrator tells details about the people and activities shown. The fourth episode introduced mansin from Suwon. Eight cameras were located along one alley, each showing a different house. The episode begins with footage taken in the early morning, of an old mansin seated on the floor of her home shrine. She is chanting while beating a brass gong. Then the camera follows a younger mansin to the kitchen, where she fills white porcelain bowls with fresh tap water and carries them on a plastic tray to her shrine's altar. She tells the camera people about her daily routine. We see a consultation session with the mansin. A male client, whose face is digitally blurred to prevent recognition, explains the reasons for his visit to the mansin. The mansin shakes a bunch of brass bells and waves a painted fan to receive inspiration and response from supernatural entities. At 2:00 p.m., the shrine is filled with the sound of cymbals, drums, and gongs. A kut ritual has begun. Some of the male clients' faces are digitally blurred, although the face of the ritual's sponsor is shown clearly. An edited sequence of various kut scenes follows. The episode reveals to the audience the daily routines and various religious practices of mansin. It enters the private space of their home shrines and allows close inspection of objects and behavior of which most Koreans have little knowledge.

In episode 87, aired in January 2014, a male practitioner (*paksu*) reveals his profession, which he says was a secret before the filming. The opening scene shows the television crew waiting in the paksu's reception room. When he arrives, the audience sees him dressed as an ordinary person—allowing a glance into his personality beyond musok practice. In the next shot, the paksu is shown putting on makeup using a hand-held mirror, and then he is in a full musok outfit and bells performing a divination. Other ritual preparations follow. Costumes and accessories are arranged and cleaned throughout these activities, and in between, the paksu is interviewed. He talks about his initiation into the musok world. He explains why he needs the makeup, saying, "You see, when I wear this white makeup and paint my lips dark red, *uri halmŏni* ['our grandmother,' referring to his main venerated spirit] is happy." He refers to the common situation in which the spirit guardians (*momjusin*) of male practitioners are often female and like their mansin dressed and cropped as women, whereas female practitioners have male guardian spirits who like to smoke, drink alcohol, and fling knives, as discussed in chapter 1. While the man talks, his words are subtitled.

Next, the television crew films female clients seated in the waiting room. Their faces are blurred digitally. The paksu enters the shrine, bangs on the drum, shakes some bells, and then explains to the interviewer what it means to receive a spirit into his body. When the interviewer seems to misunderstand, the surprised paksu asks him, "Have you never seen people who receive spirits into them?" He points at paintings of spirits on the walls (a red arrow is added in the editing to emphasize his motion) and explains the process of consultation with the spirits. He elaborates on blessing by supernatural entities as a means to heal people and to help them to get married. In another sequence, the paksu goes to a mountain shrine while a camera follows him on the rough path. He explains, "A tiger spirit that needed the good mountain *ki* [energy] asked me to take this trip." A kut ritual, including the preparation, is documented. The photographer asks why bananas and bell peppers, which are not Korean fruit, have been placed on the altar, and the paksu explains that they are tasty and beautiful (on imported ritual goods, see Kendall 2008). The presentation is augmented by adding red circles around objects that the paksu discusses and yellow sunshine beams around items on the offering table.

A detailed initiation to become a mansin, mentioned in the introduction to this book, is shown in an episode of *Exorcist* that aired on September 9, 2009. In the episode after the paksu announced to the woman that she was destined to be a mansin, the film crew interviews the woman in her home. She shows them strange marks on her arms and a wrecked closet and curtain that she says she destroyed while ecstatically possessed. A senior mansin is interviewed saying that a sin-naerim kut has to be performed. Sequences of the possession dance from the initiation kut are intercut with conversations between the novice and more experienced practitioners. The older mansin offer sympathy and support to the reluctant young woman and tell her about their own similar experiences. As the drums and cymbals play faster, she begins to dance, jump, and convulse uncontrollably. The supervising mansin hold her and help her to the floor, where she lies with her hands and feet spread out, motionless. The first ritual is not successful enough to make her an independent practitioner, however, and the second ritual is also difficult to control. The mansin has a serious talk with the initiate, demanding that she make up her mind one way or another—in a manner reminiscent of Chini's filmed initiation some thirty years earlier, discussed in chapter 2 (Kendall 1991). The woman laments her fate, and the mansin hugs and caresses her. The camera zooms in and shows the two women hugging and swaying. Next the initiate is shown praying before the altar, and the initiation kut is rescheduled. While the two women shop for the event, the presiding mansin declares, based on the initiate's reaction to various god statues (*sinsang*), that her personal momjusin is *tongja*, the spirit of a child. The initiate becomes possessed by it while at a store and finally believes that she can manage to talk the spirits' words. The sin-naerim kut day arrives, and the film crew follows the performers closely. The novice manages to stand balanced on a clay jar and speak the words of the spirit helper *taesin halmŏni* (great spirit grandmother). She is very happy and hugs her supervising mansin. The program ends with a slow-motion shot of her jumping up and down while the American song "Knockin' on Heaven's Door," by Bob Dylan, plays. Other than the Western music, the story resembles many initiation kut that I have observed.

These examples of television documentaries about mansin's daily and ritual activities differ markedly from the older documentaries, which focused on the tradition as an object of inquiry rather than on the people who perform it. Like the documentary film *Sai-esŏ*, discussed in chapter 2, in which the director documented the initiation of several mansin over several months, this new convention of following mansin in daily life enables better understanding of them. In this manner, it becomes clear to the viewer that, beyond the amazing supernatural acts, the mansin is an ordinary person.

News items that include mansin or musok often appear when public events feature a kut ritual, such as the European Union Chamber of Commerce convention held in Seoul in February 2012 or when a new shopping mall is inaugurated with kut. Entertainment news may discuss musok when it is relevant to Korea's media stars—for example, in the new year's special to forecast how the coming year will affect pop stars and actors. Famous people who turn to the musok path and become mansin might become a news item. The story about model Yim Chi-yong becoming a mansin was featured in *Star News* of Ystar Channel in October 2011. Cultural news sometimes run items on musok as a part of the general quest to report on the current situation of Korean traditions. When the Seoul monument Namdaemun burned down in 2008, it was a major news item. This old city gate was built about six hundred years ago, and its burning was considered a devastating loss of an important piece of cultural heritage.[7] Several mansin cooperated to perform a large kut ritual to appease the angry spirits of the place and related ancestors. The ritual was attended by hundreds of spectators and featured unique sequences, such as running over sharp blades fixed to the floor. The ritual's public effect was enhanced because it was broadcast in local and international news as part of the discussion of the disaster and the cultural response to it (e.g., ODE 2008). Musok is thus becoming an acceptable part of contemporary Korea's culture, and gradually, it is becoming acceptable to show it to international visitors as well.[8]

In 2007, one of the largest television stations in Korea broadcast a special documentary that depicted the internationalization of musok (May 13, 2007, SBS Channel). It showed Andrea Kalff, a German woman who became a mansin after apprenticing with Mansin Kim Kŭm-hwa (the protagonist of the documentary *Mansin*, discussed in depth in chap. 2). The new Western mansin could not speak Korean and was not knowledgeable about Korean culture before she met Mansin Kim in a public performance. This story intrigued Korean viewers, and I heard many comments on it. To the best of my knowledge, this documentary was neither translated nor aired outside Korea. For Korean viewers, this and other televised renderings of mansin who do not fit the stereotype of rural uneducated female practitioner create a more complex perspective of the vernacular religion. Without such television shows, many would not be aware that musok is so widespread. Even people who visit some mansin for healing or fortune-telling would not necessarily know that musok is practiced by such a variety of initiated mansin. Television representations of mansin show Korean audiences what mansin do and entice them to understand also how mansin think.

STRANGE THOUGHTS: WHAT DO MANSIN FEEL?

The belief that spirits wander in the human world before entering the afterworld is common in Korea's vernacular religions. Several rituals—among them, the famous Ssitkim kut, Tari kut, and Chinogi kut—are performed in several regional styles to help the spirit in its path to the underworld and prevent its lingering in the vicinity of its living family and acquaintances (Bruno 2007a). In the drama *49 Days*, the protagonist, a successful young woman named Chi-hyŏn, is in critical condition after a car crash—unconscious and hanging between life and death. She is told by a messenger from the afterworld that her life will be spared if she manages, within seven weeks, to collect three teardrops from people who really love her but are not her family members. Chi-hyŏn's soul must separate from her disabled body and find another body through which to execute her task. She possesses the body of a lonely and depressed woman, and the behavior of that hosting body changes significantly while possessed. Showing spirits penetrating and leaving people's bodies at will makes the basic assumptions behind musok more believable. Viewers vividly learn the director's understanding of what mansin think and feel when they say that spirits enter their bodies.

My mansin interlocutors had contradictory opinions about the possession moment in the show. Some said that the drama reflects more or less what they feel. They said that they have a moment when, as in the drama, they feel as if they were becoming transparent before the spirit penetrates their bodies. For others, the drama's depiction of possession was far from their own experience. Paksu Yi Sŏng-jae said, "During possession, I am like a double person, both myself and the spirit at the same time. I can see through both of them and even conduct a dialogue between them." In contrast, in the drama, the possessed woman's consciousness is suspended, and she does not remember what happened while she was possessed. Most mansin that I interviewed found it difficult to explain their possession experiences in words. The visual, dramatized version in the show was an alienating representation for some. For others, it was an entertaining demonstration of the unique quality of their spiritual experience, the aspect that William James (1902) calls "ineffability." For viewers, observing spirit possession as a daily occurrence played by popular actors increases their ability to identify with mansin or, at least, to appreciate their difficult religious quest. The drama emphasizes the risk of having a spirit linger, which makes the need to perform shamanic rituals after funerals more understandable.

The characters in *49 Days* treat mansin with respect and deep belief. Chi-hyŏn's best friend, who has been plotting to alienate the unconscious girl from her loved ones, visits a mansin in episode 16. The scene's establishing shot wanders through the mansin's office and shows close-ups of a golden Buddha statue, food offerings, and other musok materials. The mansin shakes a bunch of bells and shrieks. The bells are instrumental in calling for the spirits' attention and asking for their help. The mansin tells the best friend that the injured girl's spirit is still around and that she, the friend, should be thankful for being alive because she has done many bad things. The mansin speaks the words of the spirit, and the friend asks the mansin for advice. She believes that the diviner really knows what she has done and that the spirit of Chi-hyŏn is haunting her. We see her memories of strange events that have happened to her, such as an official stamp that suddenly disappeared before her eyes, to strengthen the credibility of the spirit's existence in the girlfriend's life. This particular scene affirmed the belief in supernatural mediation for some of my interviewees, whereas others thought it ridiculous.

The persona of one mansin is more closely examined in *Lotus Flower Fairy*, in which Yun Ch'o-wŏn, a successful graduate student engaged to a wealthy, young man, finds her peaceful life abruptly disrupted when she learns the spirits are demanding that she serve them as a mansin. The woman is featured as loving and kind and produces only good deeds in her work. No official sanctioning of the practice is depicted in this contemporary story, and most of the series is dedicated to the woman's personal life. Like *49 Days*, *Lotus Flower Fairy* portrays its protagonist as a victim of circumstance, not as a plotting holder of supernatural powers. On hearing of her new vocation, Ch'o-wŏn's grandfather decides that she must live away from her family. He is afraid that the family's image will suffer otherwise and that his position in legal research will be jeopardized. Her fiancé's family breaks off the engagement, and Ch'o-wŏn almost loses her will to live. The drama follows her life as she begins to practice musok and is initiated as a full-fledged spiritual healer and diviner. Her difficult initiation process ends with some relief and prosperity.

The drama affects the emotions of viewers through content and form. Yun Ch'o-wŏn's story begins with a normal life. She has loving parents and grandparents, a dream fiancé, and a nice house. After creating a sense of identification with her character, the drama turns to musok topics. Viewers are drawn to feel compassion toward the senior mansin and her young initiate through emotional events, full of close-ups on tearing eyes and desperate hugs. Most of my interviewees reported that hoping to see the mansin protagonists united with their forbidden loves resulted in viewers' confrontation with the traditional social assumption that mansin are not favorable marriage partners (Sarfati 2010, 85).

Comparing contemporary and historical dramas shows that the producers allow themselves more freedom of imagination when they portray events that might have happened in the remote past. Depictions of contemporary South Korea demand more factual accuracy and less exaggerated cinematic effects. Nevertheless, one point of resemblance is that the mansin's male partners (in politics or romance) hold higher social status than the female practitioners. This kind of relationship has long been a favorite theme of many Korean folktales, *p'ansori* (traditional musical storytelling) performances, films, and television dramas. The most well-known is *The Story of Ch'unhyang*, which has been performed in all these genres (Chan 2003). However, in folklore productions, few mansin manage to win the hearts of their beloved. Television dramas allow such happy endings.

Talk shows also enable viewers to learn about the feelings of real mansin. *I Am All for Life* is a program that tells the stories of hardship.[9] In this talk show, a person who had an eventful life—a female spy who was left alone in North Korea, an actor who went bankrupt—is interviewed by the actress and model Pak Mi-sŏn. Across the interviewer's table sit men and women of various ages. The interviewer can ask questions, and the interviewees are shown expressing their emotions while their tragic story is told. Subtitles emphasize important points in the story, and the main idea is projected onto the floor. In episode 44, a famous model, Pang Ŭn-mi, tells how her successful career was destroyed when she began hearing voices calling her to be a mansin. "I became partially paralyzed until I could barely move my fingers or utter comprehensible phrases. I understood that I was being summoned by the spirits to serve as a mansin, and began to see ghosts everywhere, and even thought that my husband was a ghost." She tried to commit suicide, but her husband found her and called an ambulance. Later, she bore a son. Her sinbyŏng improved for a while, but after one hundred days, her leg became paralyzed. When her son was two, she began to see ominous signs predicting her son's death. At that point, she made up her mind to be a mansin and began a divorce process. While training to be a mansin, she could meet her son only twice a month. Sometimes she would hallucinate for as long as four days. She began performing rituals for new models, which led to their success.

Throughout Pang's televised story, short sequences of music, bells, and amplified audience gasps and sighs were added to the soundtrack to lend a more dramatic effect to her spoken words. Such artificial constructions are meant to intrigue viewers and create an emotional effect that will draw them in to watch the show and improve its ratings. This televised setting enables the interviewer to ask the mansin provocative questions and maybe drives the mansin to answer frankly because she knows that this is her role in the situation. A real-life consultation with a mansin can hardly produce such a detailed version of her life story and internal state because such consultation sessions are focused on the client. Detailed life stories of mansin have appeared in research publications (e.g., Kendall 1988) but never had such broad viewership as the televised stories.

There is much similarity between my and others' ethnographic findings in the musok world and how Korean television represents musok. These stories offer television producers a dramatic base that can be helpful in achieving high viewer ratings. There is no need to exaggerate or add false information to create an intriguing interview or scene with a mansin. Most are expressive and practiced performers who know how to entice audiences and tell unusual stories.

PROFESSIONALS NEEDED: HOW CAN MANSIN HELP?

The participation of mansin as professional advisers in television programs has increased in the early twenty-first century, in accordance with their growing social legitimacy and in parallel to their more holistic depiction in television dramas and in films. This phenomenon ranges from short sequences of divination before the new year—a traditional time for divination that is still widely practiced in contemporary Korea—to entire programs in which mansin advise audience members seated in the television studio. Audiences for these televised performances include famous actors and singers. Audience members are invited to go onstage and receive advice from various guests, among them mansin, on their love affairs, relationships with family, and work stress. Mansin also help solve enigmatic crimes.

Advanced editing technologies help to spur insights and convey emotions when responses by studio audience members (e.g., exclamations or sighs) are amplified and heard clearly by viewers at home. Moreover, the camera often zooms in on faces of expressive audience members. Postproduction graphics, such as subtitles, animated figures, and infographics, direct the viewers' attention to certain parts of the program's content, strengthening their impressions. These additions and audiovisual manipulations increase effect.

A very successful series that used the supernatural insights of mansin to solve mysteries was the *Exorcist* (2008–2009). In episode 66 (September 2009), host Paek Chong-hak, a famous film actor and producer, set out to discover the "real facts" about the death of a seventy-seven-year-old woman a year earlier. The coroner's report says that she was poisoned from drinking herbicide, but it makes no sense that she did this. One possibility explored is that she was mugged and killed by intruders. Paek interviews her children and visits her house, which has remained intact since her death. He brings along two exorcists. The male practitioner identifies the place where the murder was committed. The female mansin suddenly begins speaking as the spirit of the grandmother. She hugs her daughter, cries, and beats her own chest with a folded fan. Suddenly, she goes into a small storage area with a low door and begins talking of how she liked to eat corn on the cob; the daughter confirms this. The daughter asks her who entered into the house on the day she died, but she says, through the spirit mediator, that she does not know. Later, the mansin says that there was a curse on the village because the people had cut down some old trees and angered the spirits. The mansin and the crew prepare a kut ritual for the spirit of the grandmother. During that event, they also appease the spirits of the place to bring peace to the grieving family members and the whole village. The ritual is edited as a sequence of short moments in which close-ups of the mansin, the daughter, and the village people convey the ritual's emotional effects.

Another program that demonstrated musok practitioners as professionals is *Job Stories* (2012–2013).[10] A different profession was highlighted each week, from singers and aircrew to beauty experts and even criminals. The professionals participating in the program told their stories and interacted with the studio audience. The second episode (November 22, 2012) was dedicated to practitioners of divination and musok. In this show, twelve spiritual mediators, including *musogin* (practitioners of musok), answered questions from the audience and told about their own work and lives. Nine practitioners were male, in contrast to the predominance of female musok practitioners. Some diviners were not mansin but rather other kinds of spiritual mediators. A series of sequences from films and television dramas depicting mudang introduces the audience to the theme of the program.

In response to a question from the audience, the practitioners clarified the different titles *mudang, paksu, yŏksurin,* and *posal* while a traditional-style painting of mudang in ritual appeared onscreen, along with an explanation of the term. One practitioner stated that his income was more than $100,000 a year, extracting loud exclamations from the audience. He explained that mudang do not choose to become spiritual mediators, and that, from the moment the spirits choose them, they have no peace. Their high wages cannot really compensate for the hardship of their lives. Another practitioner said that she had received a payment equivalent to $100 million for her first-ever divination. As the story unfolded, it turned out that a modest sum was invested based on her vision decades earlier and yielded that incredible profit over time. Several of the diviners described their careers before becoming musok practitioners; one was a model (I discuss her story earlier), another was a stylist, and a third was a violinist. They explained that only following many illnesses and life-threatening situations did they agree to become mansin. After the former violinist played a short piece, an audience member, shown weeping during the violin playing, said that she never thought of the lives and careers that mudang had to give up when they were forced to become musok practitioners. The hosts presented a survey showing that 78 percent of respondents have had at least one divination session in their life. An audience member who grew up in North Korea said that divination was very common there and that her own grandmother was a famous diviner. The practitioners invited the audience to have divination sessions. Throughout these, there were sound effects of gongs and visual graphics such as fire, lightning, and fireworks around the clients' faces to emphasize their responses to the professionals' predictions. The show ended with one of the senior diviners predicting three good years for South Korea.

Extensive representations of mansin's abilities and stories might convince audience members that musok can be a viable resource for people in need. If so many clients pay large sums for their services, television programs use their services to solve mysterious deaths, and they were really chosen by the spirits in spite of successful careers, then mansin might be true spiritual mediators. This is the message these programs convey.

TELEVISION DEPICTIONS OF MUSOK AS BRIDGES BETWEEN MANSIN AND ORDINARY PEOPLE

My interviewees in Seoul articulated various ideological responses to television programs about musok, although their general understanding of the programs was similar. Television programs convey to Korean audiences that musok is interesting and worth understanding. Personal interpretations varied when I asked about spiritual credibility and the implications of the content shown. As discussed, some people who viewed television representations of musok thought that it was a false belief; however, none of my informants stated that television depicted musok inaccurately.

Television representations of musok have made it more difficult to ignore the vernacular spiritual traditions of Korea. Television producers and mansin use the mediation of technology for diverse reasons. Producers seek captivating moments that will broaden the prospective audience and announce the program as a success. In return, the mansin are given a platform to become famous, to acquire new clients, and to abate stigma toward their trade that some parts of the Korean audience maintain. The television genres discussed disseminate the idea that musok is all around in contemporary Korea.

While watching programs for enjoyment, Koreans learn about the practices of musok more than they might have intentionally sought to do. Each genre's depiction of musok serves a different role in the overall creation of bridges between mansin and television viewers. Drama series such as *Lotus Flower Fairy* and documentary series such as *24-Hour Observational Camera*, which depict mansin's personal lives, bridge the emotional gap between ordinary people and spiritual practitioners. Talk shows such as *Yi Sŭng-yŏn with a Hundred Women* and *Exorcist*, which show mansin offering personal advice and solving crimes, narrow the gap between the beliefs that musok is important and musok is vain superstition. Presenting mudang alongside other, more respected professions, as in the program *Job Stories*, bridges the gap between the stigma of mansin as phony practitioners and their attempts to be perceived as caring professionals.

Genre norms are related to their different purposes. Dramas offer scripted, fictional events that lack credibility but create empathy and identification. The typical audience for daily dramas with hundreds of episodes includes housewives and retired people. Talk shows, news, and documentary programs are designed to create a feeling of engagement with real people and real stories but are also enhanced with sophisticated editing techniques to attract a diverse viewership.

Jason Mittell asserts that "hierarchies between programs and genres are one of the primary ways in which television viewers situate themselves among media texts and their social locations" (2003, 36). Some viewers do not trust "reality" programs and talk shows content and believe that they are scripted. Others think that dramas are unrealistic. However, even among audiences that dislike the religious or ritualistic aspects of musok, constant visibility increases knowledge and understanding. In the years 2002 to 2008, talk shows presented mansin in a somewhat mocking manner. In particular, I recall a new year divination session with Paksu Yi To-ryŏng, who was interviewed in his shrine. The film crew emphasized the colorful lights that he had in his shrine, making it look more like a bar than a professional advising facility. Rituals were often depicted at fast speed, which created a humorous effect. Few top-rated talk shows dedicated time to a serious interview with a mansin. The penetration of musok into the various genres of television talk shows and drama series around 2010 testifies that musok practitioners are no longer considered a marginal social category or a topic relevant only to morning dramas targeting women and elderly people. Furthermore, in many talk shows where mansin appear, the mansin are now seated alongside other professionals. In the talk show *Yi Sŭng-yŏn with a Hundred Women*, the mansin are part of an advisory panel that includes interior decorators, *p'ungsu* (geomancy, feng shui) specialists, and psychologists. In *Job Stories*, diviners who see through astrology and retinas, and who are considered learned masters, are positioned alongside mansin, which seemed to annoy some of the older masters. For audiences, such parallelism demonstrates that musok is an important profession and an acceptable advising method.

Another noteworthy recurring norm is the introduction of real musok practitioners in television programs—including the episode of *Job Stories* discussed earlier—by first showing several scenes from feature films. Paradoxically, the actors in *Fortune Saloon* and *Man on the Edge* are considered the best musok representation for a general audience. Their reperformances, which include scripted acting instead of spiritual invocations, are often shown before real mansin are introduced in talk shows and documentary television programs. Such intertextual references also reveal that films about mansin have become well known in Korea, and editors think they will focus viewers' attention on the topic.

The use of fictional films as symbolic links to real mansin's stories demonstrates how powerfully media affect public opinion and knowledge. This editing choice also demonstrates that for the producers of television programs, the boundary between fictional and real-life practitioners is blurred. Real mansin are not necessarily favored as more authentic or worth showing than their reflected images in dramas and films. Furthermore, there is no reference to the actors playing imagined characters when using these images as an introduction to the topic of musok. Reperformances can replace the actual ritual in these cases because there is no need for religious efficacy. However, when advice to real people or other help is sought, even television programs use full-fledged mansin. This feature employs an experimental approach that uses the performance skills of mansin to turn them into screen actors, and the acting skills of entertainers to turn them into representations of mansin. This approach is also used in the short film *Night Fishing*, discussed in chapter 2, in which real mansin and actors participate side by side in several scenes.

The intertexuality between traditional folk performances and filmed reperformances that is used in television shows accords with David Morley's assertion that media representations can serve as "common references" (1986, 32) during personal interactions. Television products take that idea further from daily interaction and back into the production of new media texts about musok. By using fictitious practitioners as "eye candy" to present a talk show's topic, television producers reenact the importance of films in Korean society and demonstrate that cinematic musok representation is effective in conveying knowledge of musok to the public. A multilayered digital and real depiction of musok is created for viewers, who are not necessarily aware of the transitions between documentary and scripted product. This is especially so if they do not recognize the film shown and if the scene is realistic. Another possible explanation for this fluid transition between film actors who play mansin and real spiritual practitioners might be that television producers are aware that the representations prepared by them are, to some degree, fictitious even when portraying real practitioners. Maybe by blurring the boundaries between real and scripted scenes, these producers manifest their awareness that television production distorts reality in various ways.

In the examples discussed, television programs were shown to produce new emotions in viewers not only by representing a shift in social norms but also by allowing viewers to know mansin in a substituted relationship mediated through technology. Watching mansin talk, interact with others, and perform spiritual rituals on television has offered Korean audiences an opportunity to experience an imitation of a personal acquaintance with a mansin. Televised reperformed rituals allow viewers a peek into events that are out of their reach in the real world. The effect of Korean dramas' knowledge construction in relation to musok does not end in the Korean sphere because these shows are aired in other countries as part of the Korean Wave.[11] Several of my students felt that they were knowledgeable about musok themes from watching these series, and their understanding of that belief system was surprisingly close to my ethnographic understanding of it. Exporting these depictions of musok around the globe spreads knowledge of this cultural trait beyond Korea. Various reasons for international Korean drama fandom have been mentioned in research, including the assertion that each country finds a different appeal in them (Jang and Paik 2012, 198). Comparative research of international television audiences is beyond the scope of this book, but it is likely that local norms and traditions lead to even more diverse reactions to musok in different cultures than among Korean viewers.

This chapter analyzed Korean dramas, talk shows, and documentary series about shamanic beliefs and practices as an embodiment—and an agent—of the shift in social perception toward greater appreciation and understanding of musok. Mansin have become practitioners of a legitimate cultural trait that is discussed publicly. Mass media help reduce negative views of musok and have been an important agent in the mainstreaming of this practice, to use a term offered by Gerbner and colleagues (1986, 30). If television often produces the boundaries of what can be termed a "mainstream" culture, then the inclusion of musok as a legitimate topic to broadcast makes it an accepted part of Korea's culture. This shift from the culture of premodern and early modern Korea, which tended to exclude musok from accepted norms, is significant. This change resembles a similar trend we have seen in films.

This mainstreaming is even more evident in the internet culture of Korea. The next chapter analyzes how the internet allows mansin to join the pulse of contemporary Korean life with less mediation by professional producers and directors than in television and film and more agency for the practitioners. As Korea has become a world leader in information technology and usage, mansin work hard to keep pace with this new venue for promotion and communication. They have successfully harnessed this new technology to extend their client base and to improve their public image.

NOTES

1. An example can be found on the blog "Exsosisŭt'ŭ Musokin Yun Mi-yŏng" [Exorcist Musok Practitioner Yun Mi-yŏng], http://blog.naver.com/PostView.nhn?blogId=whwlvkf&logNo=178514985.

2. Korean newborns are considered one year old; thus, fifteen in "Korean age" is equivalent to fourteen in the Western age calculation.

3. Likewise, in Korean schools there is almost no religious content.

4. The ancient period in which the story is located does not prevent the drama from delving into modern cultural debates about belief and religion, power and politics. The show's story of fighting against an oppressive foreign invader echoes Korean resentment of Japanese colonization in the early twentieth century (Dudden 2005; Duus 1995; Schmid 2002). Personal matters such as love and family control over individuals are also prominent themes in this drama. Michael Mickler (2009) suggests that the success of this drama stems from its discussion of current ideas about personal and communal transformation that are similar to the nation-building processes of modern Korea.

5. A few stories in Chinese documents suggest that shamans laid curses and cast spells (McBride 2006, 26–27).

6. The show was produced by Kim Chŏng-jung and aired weekly on Channel A (a nationwide cable channel), reaching about one hundred episodes in 2014. The second season aired in 2017.

7. The news reported that Ch'ae Chong-gi, a sixty-nine-year-old man, set the fire as a protest for not being compensated well for land he had sold to government developers. After the fire was extinguished, the municipality covered the remains with a large sheet of polyester, on which a full-scale photograph of the gate was printed, until the gate was fully restored and opened to the public in May 2013.

8. Some countries, such as Bali, have used shamanic rituals as a tourist attraction. However, in Korea, musok has been mostly excluded from the national image of contemporary culture (as discussed in chap. 3 in relation to museums).

9. The program has been aired since January 2013 on Chosŏn TV every Friday at 11:10 p.m.

10. The male host, Yim Sŏng-hun, is a famous television persona who has been hosting talk shows since the early 1990s. The female host, Pak Chi-yun, is a famous K-pop singer and actress. The popular show's website asserts that it got rating of more than 15 ("Job Stories" 2011–2013).

11. The Korean Wave (*Hallyu*) is a term describing the increased popularity of Korean pop genres including music, film, and television dramas outside Korea (Y. Kim 2013).

FIVE

Shamans Online
Internet Promotion of Musok Practitioners

THIS BOOK BEGAN WITH A ritual reperformance of an ancient Korean tradition and ends with the representation of that tradition on the internet. In the staged ritual discussed in chapter 1, practitioners introduced various changes to enable a vernacular tradition from earlier village settings to continue in contemporary Seoul. Although I considered these technological innovations and mediations, that chapter was centered on the ritual itself and on the practitioners' actions. In subsequent chapters, I discussed the representation of such practitioners in mass culture genres: films, museums, and television. The focus on mediated representations of musok reflects Theodor Adorno's comment in the 1950s that "people no longer 'live together' and know each other directly, but are related to each other through intermediary objectified social processes" (Adorno 1994/2002, 36). This observation is even more relevant since the development of television and the internet. Popular culture can be the heading for the genres discussed in this book. The representations analyzed in chapters 2–4 are more or less static, commoditized ontologies compared with the ever-changing nature of face-to-face, living experiences, such as the staged kut described in chapter 1. This is one of the main distinctions between the actual ritual and its mediated reperformances in museums and on screens.

Screen culture has changed significantly with the introduction of internet platforms. People can communicate in real time through the internet, respond to the content presented on the screen, and upload new content easily whenever they wish. In these respects, the experience of internet users is closer to face-to-face encounters than other media. In several other respects, however, the internet resembles other screened representations of events. For example, its two-dimensionality and reliance on electricity and digital technology provide a less sensuous experience than tangible, off-screen events. Nevertheless, the internet presents a unique analytic opportunity within the discussion of mediatized representations of musok. As an interactive technology, it offers possibilities that were unavailable in previous screen-mediated communications. In this chapter, I explore how this interactive technology determines the ways in which mansin and their clients use the internet and how societal and cultural changes have contributed to the message conveyed online about musok.

I frame this discussion using Adorno's (1994/2002, 34–127) terminology about the impact of media on people's beliefs and actions, although Adorno offers little empirical evidence for his ideas. I discuss musok here through the ethnography of the World Wide Web, which has become essential in studying contemporary urban culture and religion (see R. G. Howard 2006, 2011; Miller 2003; Miller and Slater 2000; Turkle 1995). By combining on-site fieldwork with mansin and their clients and textual and visual analysis of the websites they produce and consume, I depict the internet holistically as a cultural arena both within and outside musok practice. My interviews produce evidence that complicates Adorno's theory. I argue that in Korea and elsewhere, audiences in any medium are not monolithic but formed by various personal and social situations and inclinations. In previous chapters, I established that reception of mediated representations in films and television products depends on individual values and perspectives. I analyze the texts as artifacts, as Adorno does, and consider how they might affect people reading them; however, my observations of many mansin and their clients inform a richer audience-response assessment. The multilayered online arena of musok-related representations and opinions is less amenable than other media to a coherent theory. Nevertheless, it more readily allows us to understand reality as it is in twenty-first-century, urban, hypertechnologized societies such as Korea.

Digital media, especially the internet, feature inexpensive production compared with film and television. Content is easy to change as the need arises, and the technology allows faster, cheaper distribution of amateur content. Mistakes are more easily forgiven because the rate of technological change makes products age fast. As a result, analyzing websites of mansin and mansin associations is more similar to on-site ethnography than to the analysis of films and television. Images and text are ever-evolving—there is no final product. A multiplicity of factors interplay to change the field constantly. Many of the websites I cite no longer even exist.

Another, more important result is that a simple interface and anonymous audience response enable many more clients to contact a mansin without fear of being mocked by their acquaintances. Many interviewees attested that the musok online community includes people who would not venture into a mansin's office or attend a ritual. Kim Ch'ae-in (not his real name), a thirty-year-old television reporter, attended a ritual after a few months of online communication with the mansin and told me,

> I would never think to visit a mudang's office in Seoul. Many people know me and might recognize my face. Paparazzi are everywhere in Korea. When I was young, my father used to ask my mother to go visit a diviner discreetly before his business ventures. I am not married, and even if I were, my wife might not be into such beliefs. So I went online and found this woman who communicated with me in a chat room. When she was serious about holding a ritual, she chose a small shrine in the middle of the week, so that no one might see me. This is also why I asked you not to photograph me or use my real name in your research.... I agreed to come here only because she insisted that a previous ritual that I did not attend failed because of my absence.

Kim's career was slowing down when he first contacted the mansin, and she assured him that the spirit of his grandmother was interfering in his life, causing him to become less popular. He was so frustrated that he decided to give her a chance to change his fortune. He attests that since he began chatting with her, his producers said that he was much more lively and edgy in his media appearances, and they gave him a larger role in the program he was hosting. Although we cannot judge the mechanism that changed Kim's career progress, his story demonstrates the main point of this chapter—the unique characteristics of the internet enable mansin to reach a more diverse and dispersed audience. Their services are appreciated by many who are not their regular sponsors and followers.

This chapter reveals that mansin and their clients are not weak, easily influenced consumers of media, as Adorno (1994/2002, 38, 44–45) suggests of modern urbanites, or at least readers of astrology newspaper columns. The internet has enabled many mansin to produce their own public image, to control and direct their screened representation, and to become leaders for other mansin. It also has enabled musok clients to virtually meet many practitioners, read their messages, and decide whether they want to use their services. Nearly everyone is empowered in this process.

Adorno (1994/2002) projects a homogenizing process of culture; however, musok's entry into mainstream media such as film, television, and the internet demonstrates the dynamic character of cultural processes. It also attests to the importance of the sociocultural context of medium use in establishing meanings and religious messages. In terms of content choices and topics handled, the internet has replicated many traditional characteristics of musok. It emphasizes the roles of mansin as healers and leaders, and it maintains much of the material and spiritual messages and characteristics of the creed.

Internet platforms for musok are handled through networks of electronic tools that, although "high-tech," are no less tangible than a shrine or a statue. Devices for filming, distributing, and watching musok performances online and for communicating with clients over the internet have become necessities in the offices of most mansin. Instead of creating "a crisis of boundaries between the real and the virtual, between time zones and between spaces, near and distant" (Shields 1996, 7), in Korea, the internet enables real spaces and people to enter into dialogue. This would not have been possible without the mediation of elaborate technology. Mansin use the internet to contact potential clients, bridging cultural biases and geographic distances.

In rural and semiurban conditions, which existed in Korea until the 1970s, mansin conducted long kut rituals in clients' homes. Such events, with their festival atmosphere, attracted large audiences (K. Ch'oe 1989; Kendall 1985). As discussed in previous chapters, in contemporary Korean cities, the mediation of kut rituals through screened depictions has allowed musok to remain visible, beginning with the profusion of television sets in Korea in the 1970s. The internet has sped up this process. More than 85 percent of South Korean households were connected to the internet in 2001, and Korea has been considered the most internet-connected nation in the world (C. Taylor 2006; Na 2001; Young 2004). Digital media have become the main venue for publicity, advertising, public discourse, and culture construction.

During my ethnographic fieldwork, I documented my informants' personal websites (homp'eiji) and the manners in which they created and maintained them. I extended my analysis to include ten more home pages of mansin that I watched during kut but who were not my main informants. I also included various musok portals produced by associations of mansin. There are many online "instant divination" portals in Korea, where there is only brief personal communication between diviner and client. My analysis focuses mainly on websites that offer a more extensive engagement with musok, including explanations, photographs, videos, and long personal statements by the mansin. The extensive use of the internet as a platform to conduct self-promotion, professional discussion, and virtual veneration of the spirits provides firm evidence of the new type of mansin—no longer an uneducated woman of low social status, as in the early days of South Korea. Twenty-first-century mansin have gained sophistication, knowledge of technology and media, and often high levels of education. In the hypertechnologized life of South Korea, healers and diviners exert new forms of social power and personal agency.

An internet portal produced and maintained by Kyŏngsin yŏnhap (the Federation of Associations for the Respect of Beliefs) represents the professionalization of musok and the increasing education level of mansin.[1] The website offers its visitors an image of musok as a tradition with an international business style. The welcome screen shows layered mountains in shades of blue and gray, evoking the hour of dusk. From the craggy peaks and forested valleys, an animated drawing of a yellow lotus flower rises like the sun. Inside the yellow shape is the Sino-Korean ideogram *kyŏng* 敬, which means *to venerate*. Korean text below the sun announces that this website belongs to the three hundred thousand musok practitioners of South Korea. One click on the screen brings the visitor to a landing page, with a banner photograph of countless people, mostly in casual hiking clothes, at worship on a rocky shore. Some hold their hands together in prayer, and others squat by the water. Before one can fully grasp the full scope of activity in the scene, the banner changes to a photograph of several dozen mansin clad in kut attire, apparently in a festival setting. Again, the photograph changes quickly. This time it is a formal, staged photograph of many men in black suits and a few women in traditional hanbok. In the background, the Blue House (Ch'ŏnghwadae), the house of the president of South Korea, can be seen. These introductory images demonstrate the various aspects of contemporary musok, including pilgrimage to holy sites, ritual performances, and formal (male) acknowledgment. Below these changing images (which have been updated now and then) are announcements of upcoming events and hyperlinks to photo galleries, information about musok, and a bulletin board with advertisements of rental shrines and mansin offices. Many mansin and their clients report that they use this website daily and find it a useful tool. It is textually laden and requires knowledge of how to use the internet, which has become a given for most Koreans.

The internet has become inseparable from Korea's cultural and practical activities. The increasing levels of education in Korea and the contributions of individual mansin have combined with the broad availability of technology to form an extensive online presence of musok. Accordingly, my inquiry begins with how modernization has affected the education of mansin. Next I discuss how several mansin embraced the internet as early as the mid-1990s and, by producing personal websites, introduced an online presence as the new norm in musok professionalism. After establishing the societal and cultural context of musok representations online, I turn to a detailed analysis of the websites' content. I show how the new technology has affected the image of musok but only in accordance with the personal choices of individuals involved in its production.

MODERNIZATION AND MANSIN'S EDUCATION

In August 2007, Sin Myŏng-gi, whose work was introduced in chapter 3, invited me to visit her country house. In the entrance hall of the spacious white structure, she hung her framed diploma for a master's degree in business administration from a well-known university. Sin explained, "As a young woman I was so glad to have such a famous and experienced *sinŏmŏni* [spirit-mother]. I did not think about my options in life. I just felt lucky to learn the ways of musok." Busy learning the new profession, she did not plan beyond that spiritual quest. But in her late forties, after gaining financial stability, she began to study business administration. She said, "I am so proud of my grades. With all these young students around me, I still made it." While looking at the diploma, she reflected, "Had my sinŏmŏni been alive, she would surely be surprised by my educational aspirations."

Growing up in Korea of the early twentieth century, the mansin was socialized to accept male dominance of formal education. The spirit daughter gained access to new mechanisms of social status formation, such as a merit-based education system. She learned to manipulate this resource, just as she learned to wield mass media, the internet, and other publicity venues. Mansin Sin said about her website, "I fight to change the negative social image of mansin and musok. I use online publications and appeals because in our country, the younger generation can see these more easily than coming to meet me in person." Her work in shaping the public image of musok has reached from ritual, through museum production, to the internet.

I met Mansin Sin during a public new year's blessing kut that she performed in February 2007. The ritual was held at Unhyŏn'gung, a small palace in downtown Seoul that also serves as a museum. The event was advertised on a bulletin board next to the entrance gate, and I simply walked in. Before the ritual began, the mansin sat in the palace yard and prepared talismans (*pujŏk*) based on a special elaborate use of complicated *hancha* (the Korean version of Chinese ideograms) for visitors (C. Kim 2004; M. Kim 2007). I watched as she artistically crafted red ink characters on thin yellow paper. From my reading of ethnographies about Korea, I learned that most mansin were illiterate. I was surprised to see a mansin draw Chinese characters, which are mostly absent from contemporary South Korea's press and education system (in favor of the indigenous *han'gŭl* phonetic script). However, the data for most of the research that I could read in the early 2000s had been gathered in the 1970s and 1980s. Although I met some elderly practitioners who could not even sign their names, most Koreans are now fully literate. Some mansin that I met during my fieldwork bought professional pujŏk prepared by men in specialized stores. All of them could draw at least some basic ones on the spot, according to their clients' needs. Some could copy patterns that they learned from books, but not with Sin's unique brush stroke and sophistication. She had acquired the ability to write complex ideograms in artistic calligraphy by reading calligraphy books and taking some private classes. In 2001, she published a book about her life and practices. In the mid-2000s (as discussed in chap. 3), she opened a museum of musok paintings and ritual artifacts in her country house. In 2010, she wrote and published a book of about three hundred pages featuring colorful photographs of many pujŏk to help others looking for guidance (Sin 2010). Calligraphy used to be the main marker of a scholar in traditional Korea, but modernization has enabled women from lower social ranks to venture into this discipline. This was not the only way Mansin Sin crossed the social boundaries between spirit mediator and scholar.

Sin's case is only one example of the new educational possibilities for contemporary spiritual mediators. In the past seventy years, Korea has undergone deep social changes. From a premodern, agrarian, annexed territory of Japan and then a war zone, Korea has turned into a postindustrial, divided, but independent nation that is influential in the world economy and essential to global security. This political change occurred alongside substantial cultural alterations, including the emergence of social mobility (Abelmann 2003). With the introduction of capitalist values into this Confucian culture, success as business owners increasingly allows even mansin to achieve social prestige and advanced education. Women have taken on more significant and respected roles and learned ritual texts in the case of Confucian ancestral rites (Janelli and Janelli 2002).

Literacy rates in Korea have reached almost 100 percent, and large parts of Korean society have shifted from inherited to merit-based social status. Today's mansin are not only avid readers of literature and research about musok but also authors of books published by respected presses (e.g., K. Kim 1995; Sin 2001). This situation contradicts the prevailing assumption of mansin being uneducated. As Laurel Kendall wrote, "Scholars value shamans and their rituals as evidence of ancient and enduring national traditions, while the observers maintain their intellectual distance, as learned men and modern progressives, from the unlettered and superstitious-seeming women who maintain these practices in the twentieth century" (2001, 33). Kendall criticized scholars who still viewed mansin as unlettered when she conducted her initial fieldwork in the 1970s, a period when this social marker was becoming obsolete.

As Sin's case demonstrates, the education of mansin extends beyond formal institutional learning. In a world characterized by a free flow of knowledge, mansin have become experts not only in musok but also in Korea's traditional arts more generally. They gather such knowledge through various channels of communication. Historical film and television melodramas about Korea's past contribute to a general awareness of life in premodern Korea. They increase the general public's acquaintance with the clothing and accessories of famous kings and queens who often possess mansin during kut. A few decades ago, a mansin who was possessed by Queen Min—who was allegedly murdered by Japanese soldiers in 1895 as part of an international palace intrigue (Simbirtseva 1996)—had little access to historical paintings, texts, or photographs; she had to imagine the costumes and headpieces she would need for a kut. A contemporary mansin's imagination is fed by viewing pop culture products such as television dramas, visiting specialized stores for musok outfits, and even attending academic conferences (Sarfati 2010, 274). Relevant academic and pseudo-academic books are sold quite often in musok goods stores (e.g., Kwŏn 1998). Information about Korea's history is also readily available online, and photographs of famous practitioners dressed as the queen during rituals are uploaded regularly to personal websites. In a recent visit to a musok goods store, I observed the store owner browsing a famous paksu's home page to show a client what kinds of elaborate ritual costumes can be ordered. Extensive musok knowledge has become easy to find in contemporary Korea if one can read and use the internet.

INTERNET REPRESENTATION AS A NORM OF MUSOK PROFESSIONALISM

In view of these recent changes in how musok knowledge flows in contemporary Korea, it is only natural that the prestige and public recognition of mansin are no longer achieved primarily through word of mouth. Their reputations increasingly rest on participation in the media. Their use of the internet has become a marker of their professional standing, and their control of it is much greater than in other screened representations.

The internet has changed the asymmetric structure of gender and power that was so prominent in the relationships between mansin and scholars, film directors, and television producers, as discussed in previous chapters. Mansin have seized control of their own publicity and social image. The internet enables them to become professionally active beyond ritual events and within mainstream digital media. They no longer depend on male intellectuals to achieve public exposure and legitimacy through official nominations and academic publications, even if they will never be considered equal to the established elites (Bourdieu 1984). Commercial relations with technology providers have largely replaced cultural and personal relations with male scholars, who might look down on their female mansin informants. Men dominate most internet production companies in Korea, but affluent mansin have more leverage when they become clients of such providers. In this novel situation, power has shifted into the mansin's hands and depends mainly on personal and financial resources.

Some famous and successful practitioners produced individually designed home pages as early as the mid-1990s. Producing a personal website is considered cost-effective. A simple website costs as little as $2,000—similar to a single silk ritual outfit. Such a price can be covered with no more than ten new clients each holding two consultations (at about $100 per meeting). However, not all mansin home pages get intense traffic without other venues of promotion. The cost of operating an online brochure might rise if mansin need to advertise on large musok portals, such as the Kyŏngsin yŏnhap, discussed earlier, or in internet magazines. Less affluent mansin initially sufficed with advertising their services on musok portals or presenting amateur videos of their rituals on YouTube, Naver, and other free video-uploading platforms (e.g., M. Cho 2009). These free platforms granted mansin who were not *k'ŭn mudang* (star shamans) easy promotion and access to potential clients. Public images take time to change, but the new online agency of mansin, who actively seek to bring about new and greater appreciation of their work, can help speed this process.

In chapter 2, I discussed the documentary film *Between* (2006), which features Mansin Yi Hae-gyŏng. During filming, the crew and the mansin kept a blog to promote the film (H. Lee 2006). After the film's release, the mansin took control of the website. In the subsequent eight years, the home page changed form and structure. Until 2016, it was a well-maintained, artistically designed popular internet venue that complemented Yi's Twitter activity and Naver blog. However, as she began to use social networks, including Facebook, more intensely, she has neglected the home page, in accord with the changes in internet usage patterns in Korea, which prioritize online social networks. Mansin Yi, well over sixty years old, remains on the cutting edge of internet promotion in Korea. She often uploads her thoughts and stories to social networks; shows photographs of various mountain pilgrimages, public performances, and other gatherings; and publicizes her staged rituals. She also announces when her large-scale ritual for her guardian spirits will take place, inviting everyone to participate. Both her personal Facebook page and the page named after her new home shrine produce several posts every month and receive dozens of responses and comments. The mansin sponsors her online activity and supervises the work of programmers and designers that she hires for technical assistance. Her Twitter account (@shaman_hk), active since 2010 and written in Korean, has more than five hundred followers and more than one thousand tweets. Such viewership does not make her a celebrity by the standards of actors and pop music stars, but it demonstrates her being of interest to many beyond her close acquaintances and family members. Few Koreans her age even have an active Twitter account.

Yi's spirit mother was the celebrity "National Shaman" Kim Kŭm-hwa, who passed away in February 2019. Kim had also kept an active home page since the 1990s (http://www.gukmu.com, now discontinued), with a long list of public performances and official awards such as Intangible Cultural Asset nominations. Kim's website had many videos and photographs and explanations of her effort to preserve the designated rituals.

Mansin Kim, Sin, Sŏ, and Yi are among the practitioners who developed an internet presence early on and have since become role models for other, less affluent practitioners. Their efforts and active engagement in the online cultural arena do not correspond with the stigma against mansin or with their ages (Chang 2003). It is likely that new technology would not have been used so extensively in the musok sphere had these mansin and their colleagues not grasped the importance and possibilities of the internet.

THE INTERNET AS A MEANS TO INCREASE SOCIAL AWARENESS OF MUSOK

By now, the internet has been adopted by mansin of various ages and levels of success. Financial prosperity, personal taste, and knowledge of digital media are key factors in the choice of internet platform and scope of online activity. In the mid-2000s, my five main informants were over fifty years old, and three of them had been maintaining their home pages since the mid-1990s. My other informants followed suit later on. By 2016, all the mansin that I met, young and old, either had an internet promotion platform or were planning to obtain one soon. After consulting mansin, musok website platform providers, and musok art dealers, I estimate that at least 40 percent of the mansin who practice openly for clients have established a home page (although those who practice secretly for personal reasons rarely keep such websites). This increased visibility has been harnessed by some mansin to actively counter the stigma against their vocation.

Mansin were criticized in modern times by the government and the press and persecuted by the police for disrupting civil order in their noisy, crowded rituals and for extracting large sums of money from their clients (Kendall 2001, 31–32; C. Kim 2004, 63; K. Yun 2013). In the 2016 presidential scandal, the evil character of Ch'oe Sun-sil, who was involved in corruption schemes with President Pak (Park Gun-hye), was often discussed in the media as related to her being a sort of mudang. As discussed in previous chapters, increased media visibility and formal appreciation continue to erode the stigma against mansin in the twenty-first century, but the process is still ongoing. Mansin Sin is aware of this bias and addressed it on her website: "I have been a mudang for better and for worse for 24 years and four months. Still, it seems that although religious leaders of the world relate to us with dignity and pride, prejudice and ignorance about the meaning of musok and [about the fact] that mudang work still exist here. Therefore, I hope that the website chunbokhwa.com (now discontinued) can help us receive affirmation through explaining the meaning of musok, kut, ritual particulars, and teacher-student relationships in musok." Sin thus positions her work as more than spiritual healing. She is also a social activist who works toward a communal goal—to improve the public image of musok in Korea.

The internet also provides mansin with a larger venue for their social criticism as a part of spiritual mediation. Online empowerment can be seen also in Mansin Sŏ Kyŏng-uk's website (http://www.mudang.co.kr) when she incorporates a criticism of modern medicine into her life story by uploading the following narrative: "At the age of seventeen, she suffered from an unknown disease again. The doctor diagnosed her case as 'lovesickness.' There was no reason for her to have such a sickness." This narrative is a repetition of the same story told in a colorful brochure that she hands participants in public rituals (Yang 2005, 7), but online viewership has a much broader potential scope. Many people who never participate in Sŏ's rituals can find this information by searching relevant terms in Korean.

Mansin Sŏ's perception of spiritual healing is also demonstrated in her home page's description of practices and services. She expresses her confidence in the gods' assistance through trance rituals when she explains how her style of traditional healing is effective: "That person [Sŏ] turned into an *excellent* musok practitioner. People who enjoy musok ways emphasize that 'she must dig well into the core of things,' she is a person who 'has original information about problems that are delivered from the dead [*kongsu*],' and who can heal a disease based on accurate examination. She searches thoroughly for the source of malaise and then pulls it from its roots" (Chŏng

Fig. 5.1 Global Shamanic Healing Arts website, 2016. Credit: Hiah Park.

1999). Internet-mediated musok representations, such as this description from a mansin's home page, do not create new religious concepts but instead adapt old texts, perspectives, and activities to new media in Korea and elsewhere.

Several mansin have extended their activities to other countries with the aid of internet advertising. Mansin Hiah Park's (Pak Hŭi-a) web page, Global Shamanic Healing Arts, contains information in English and German about her performances and workshops in Europe and the United States (Park 2004). There is no information in Korean because she lives in Europe and targets international audiences (M. H. Park, pers. comm., 2007). Mansin Park, who was initiated in Korea by Mansin Kim Kŭm-hwa, includes Western elements in her performances, such as modern dance and New Age concepts.[2] On her website, she asserts that Korean mansin "express our true self. . . . by connecting body, mind, and soul into joyous worship of a Higher Power (whom you can name as Spirit, God, Goddess, Life Energy, Almighty) then ultimately, returned to the Self." This discourse resembles New Age terminology and other practices, such as yoga and Buddhist meditation. It demonstrates how recontextualizing musok within a cross-cultural spiritual search has become easier thanks to internet platforms (fig. 5.1).

Mansin Sin had a full Japanese version of her home page when her son was a graduate student in Japan. She traveled there often to visit him and to perform for third- and fourth-generation Japanese Korean immigrants who could not read Korean. That website mediated not only between Mansin Sin and her potential Korean-Japanese clients but also between Korean tradition and a group that did not belong to the Korean-speaking community of musok practitioners and clients. It allowed the Korean minority in Japan to maintain contact with their ancestral identity. The internet allowed Mansin Sin to take on the social role of facilitator of ethnic identity construction and to incorporate her work into the process of historical consciousness formation.

Intercultural encounters are increasingly common within Korea itself as the number of foreign workers and tourists grows. The few kut that are performed with the intention of attracting mainly foreign tourists or residents are promoted primarily through the internet. In October 2013, for example, Mansin Kim Nam-sun held several kut in Insadong and in the National Folk Museum. These events were advertised online in English versions of expatriate magazines and blogs, and English interpretation was sometimes available.

However, not all representations of musok online can be controlled by the practitioners. Internet-mediated interactions also occur when mansin, who rarely speak foreign languages, are presented in English-language blogs and online newsletters by foreigners who speak Korean or Koreans who speak English. The unique qualities of musok make it an interesting topic for written publications accompanied by photographs. Other occasional observers of musok write reports that often suffer from superficial understanding of the performance but still make it internationally visible (Ethlenn 2012; Ladner 2011; Ogedei 2008; Korean Shaman 2012).

When mansin perform for foreign audiences by invitation, they also end up reaching a wider audience. On August 26, 2007, Mansin Yi performed a ritual dance for the annual meeting of an international surgeons association and distributed charms as souvenirs. The association's website described the event and reached an audience that did not attend the performance (CORLAS 2007). Mansin performances have been part of scientific conferences for some time, but the internet has broadened their international visibility. A few years ago, I was glad to see Mansin Sin performing kut in a photograph posted on the Facebook page of a colleague visiting Seoul for an international conference. The photograph was labeled "With a Korean Shaman." The scholar's Facebook friends now know that there are shamans in Korea and that they perform at honorable venues such as academic gatherings.

Online representations that are initiated by observers rather than the mansin themselves raise questions of agency, gender, and human–object relations. Mansin Sin's hard-won online visibility in this Facebook post encapsulates all of these issues. The mansin clearly wanted to perform and to be photographed, hoping that the owner of this selfie would tell all his friends that there were mansin in South Korea who performed in respectable venues; however, she was little more than an exotic anecdote for the conference scholars. My male colleague photographed her and wrote about the performance on Facebook, but when asked about the woman next to him in the picture, he was unsure. He just posted the picture to document his visit and show off his beautiful and exotic adventures.

In a late-modern, globalizing world, individuals can sometimes choose how to represent themselves and thus create new identities. In other cases, internet representations are created outside the control of the individual depicted (Agre 1999; Appadurai 1996; Giddens 1991). Mansin Park and Sin can target audiences of other nationalities with the help of the internet and become mediators not only between humans and spirits but also between cultural aspects of Korea and other world cultures. Their internet activity has curated their identities as international cultural figures.

A VIRTUAL MUSOK COMMUNITY

The process of creating shared musok norms began before the advent of new media. Associations of musok practitioners were established during the 1970s and had bulletins and newsletters. Television and film contributed to the standardization of rituals and objects. The internet added many new options for participation in the musok community and significantly augmented the speed of these ongoing changes.

One of the first musok portals, called *Mudang Dat Com*, was established in 1999 and has become a supplier of ready-made musok home pages (Neomudang 2014, now discontinued). The portal also features an interactive map of South Korea that provides contact information for mansin from any given area. It costs little to be included in this list, and even beginner mansin can afford this form of promotion. This portal represents the professionalization of musok, and other agencies have followed its example. Such portals also enable communication and knowledge transfer between practitioners, creating a broad musok community. This kind of a dynamic entity did not exist before the mediation of this virtual space.

Mansin who surf musok portals become part of a large interest group. They absorb the image of musok as it is presented by organizations and producers of relevant portals. Kim Un-a, a novice mansin in her early thirties, told me, "In the musok forum I receive daily news of other performers, view artifacts that I have not seen before, and watch videos of famous mansin that I admire." Through the internet, mansin become an imagined community, based on textual representations of mutual interest and joined over large areas through a common imagery (B. Anderson 1991; Chattarjee 1991). This community engages in online, open-forum discussions of musok norms and is exposed to the same visual content that the website advertisers and administrators (mostly men who are not mansin) decide to upload to their platform. Famous mansin add links to their filmed performances, which are studied carefully by others in the community and are often imitated in rituals of less acknowledged practitioners, regardless of their original performance style training. In this way, the internet, together with television and other mass media products, has transformed this diverse local vernacular religion into a somewhat homogenized cultural construction.

REPRESENTATIONS OF MUSOK IN NONRELIGIOUS CONTEXTS

Many mansin are keen researchers when it comes to the historical fashions they want to use when personifying spirits of royalty. Mansin Sŏ, for example, presents herself on her home page as a traditional art performer by wearing outfits that are taken from contexts beyond musok rituals. In the first image, shown as a banner, she wears a headpiece with a flat golden panel adorned with strings with beads. This hat is often used by an elderly man who plays the central part in television recreations of court rites in the Confucian style.[3] The labels on links to further readings on her website are presented in vertical writing that is considered more traditional than left-to-right writing. The background of the links and the colorful pattern on top feature lotus petal shapes common in decoration of Buddhist temples. The knowledgeable visitor can immediately deduce that this website is related to traditional secular performance arts or to Buddhism, as there is no image related uniquely to musok in the first encounter with Mansin Sŏ's home page. To accentuate the scholarly background behind her practice, Mansin Sŏ includes articles written by Dr. Yang Chong-sŭng of the National Folk Museum on her website. These texts describe musok in general and analyze the main rite that Mansin Sŏ holds, the commemoration kut for General Ch'oe Yŏng, as an important artistic tradition. In this manner, mansin websites project the image of knowledgeable, well-read professionals rather than the hysterical, illiterate spiritual mediators that still-current prejudice suggests. Mansin Sŏ views her home page as part of her work with the supernatural but chooses to present herself through the internet mainly with texts and images that depict musok as important cultural heritage rather than religious practice.

As the public perception of musok changes, its imagery increasingly appears in nonreligious, technology-related contexts. In 1998, redirecting the fame of mansin as fighters of evil influences, LG Electronics launched the virtual cyber-shaman Cysha, who would fight viruses and pop-ups. Cysha was a virtual child spirit who had descended from the mountain to help people—in this case, to eliminate viruses from their computers. The service included pujŏk talismans that could be downloaded as screen savers. The project was aborted shortly afterward, as it became apparent that the public was uncomfortable with the manner in which large corporate services were represented through what many perceived as superstition-based imagery (S. Kim 2003, 279–280). The widespread phenomenon of online musok services had not fully convinced the general public, which often dichotomizes modernity and vernacular religion, progress and musok.

Another case of musok imagery in secular, computer-related activities was an advertisement for the computer company Compaq. A series of advertisements featured beautiful young women of various professions, wearing sophisticated clothing and using sophisticated technology. One of the ads presented a model dressed as a mansin—not because musok is an established symbol of peacemaking, healing, and problem solving but because it is a professional option for Korean women.

Watching representations of their practice and profession in such cases can increase the self-confidence of mansin in their lifestyle and legitimize their incorporation into Korean society. Portraying mansin as beautiful and sophisticated in new contexts that used to be closer to the elite, male sphere marks a significant diminution of the prejudice against them. The spread of such images across the internet enhances this process.

THE INTERNET AND SHIFTING AGENCY IN A CHANGING SOCIAL ORDER

As noted, mansin use printed promotional materials such as brochures, advertisements, fliers, and newspaper advertisements to promote their services, and the internet adds possibilities that can be less expensive and more empowering. Mansin negotiate these diverse publicity options that are under their control with a deep understanding of each genre and medium. Printed and online representations often vary in form and content. Being aware of the prevailing negative image of their trade and the wide distribution of online representations, mansin selectively post ideas and images on their websites that are not perceived as too wild or offensive. Mansin Sŏ's home page includes only images that transmit aesthetics related to wealth, professionalism, and harmony. There are no images of kut scenes with a wild-eyed practitioner, animal sacrifice, or anything that might seem less than respectable. However, such images and narratives can be found in her printed leaflets, which she hands out at rituals because the audience watches her perform such extreme acts anyway. Likewise, autobiographical details such as spirit possession sickness (*sinbyŏng*) with symptoms that resemble insanity may take up several paragraphs in the printed brochure of a mansin—even when there are several versions of these brochures—but they are not mentioned in her website. In their promotional materials, mansin use the practical, professional discourse common to many other service and performance sectors in Korea. This includes the norm of promoting themselves by their full names. In ethnographies from the 1970s and 1980s, authors emphasized the use of nicknames related to location, life history, and professional expertise instead of formal names (Kendall 1985, xi–xii; Harvey 1979, 40, 86). This practice has diminished in Korea in general and is used only in the closest social circles of mansin. It is almost absent from both print and internet representations of female mansin, but some paksu still use nicknames that refer to their main venerated deity. Interestingly, although mansin use their full names on their home pages, clients who ask questions in such websites often identify themselves with obvious pseudonyms such as "lonely girl," "worried mother," or "desperate jobless." These clients sometimes prefer not to be associated with musok, whereas mansin are expected to expose their names and be real practitioners, even in a virtual space such as a website. The derogatory public discourse around musok often drives mansin's clients to seek supernatural assistance through the anonymous apparatus of the internet.

These differences between face-to-face interactions and internet-mediated representations are mostly the result of cultural and social trends and are not related specifically to technological innovation. Mansin use mild language and images when targeting audiences that might not visit a mansin in person, although the medium itself could be used to show the most extreme musok practices if these were socially acceptable. Moreover, the internet bestows anonymity on those who wish it, but mansin prefer online promotion with their proper names while clients prefer anonymity. The technology produces distinct messages related to the social positioning of different users and the cultural perceptions of each.

The internet has enabled mansin to gain control over their public image, community life, and business. The emergence of this medium was the climax of an ongoing change in their social options, including education and mobility, brought about by urbanization, democracy, and economic liberalization.

Rob Shields argues that the risk of computer mediation is that "the virtual comes to be seen as more real than the real" (1996, 9), echoing Jean Baudrillard (1983). However, the mansin and their clients demonstrate the ability to distinguish between online and off-line content. Given its abundance of information and opportunities, coupled with its broad use by people of various nationalities, languages, ages, and socioeconomic statuses, it is understandable that the internet provokes new doubts and dire predictions. However, in musok, only simple consultations and sales of generic talismans and divinations have been relocated into virtual interactions. Consumers of internet divination and pujŏk expect the practitioner to exist in reality and to practice off-line. Furthermore, most spiritual consultations that begin as online communication with a mansin eventually lead to an off-line, in-person meeting.

In a six-month sample of correspondence from 2015 in Mansin Yi Haegyŏng's question-and-answer section of her blog, more than half of the questions were related to setting up a meeting with her. Visitors wrote that they found her blog interesting and wanted to consult with her about their personal problems. Clients complained that her address had changed, and they could not find her office. Apprentices wrote to say that her phone line had been busy, and they could not reach her easily. Mansin Yi answered some of the posts individually. In other cases, she wrote a general answer saying that she was very busy lately and asked visitors to try to contact her again over the phone to set up a meeting. Consequently, advanced technologies have added new forms of musok practice but have not substituted for real-life spiritual consultations.

In contrast to this ongoing religious engagement, the South Korean government uses new media to promote awareness of musok as part of its efforts to preserve Korea's indigenous arts and traditions. Its online representations of musok are both less practical and less elaborate than the mansin's home page. The Cultural Properties Preservation Office's website demonstrates the emphasis on preserving aesthetics rather than religious and spiritual activities. It explains, "Because the songs and dances performed during the exorcism have high artistic as well as historic values, the art of exorcism is designated as an important intangible cultural asset" (CPA 2005). Ignoring religious activities that might be perceived as primitive, superstitious, or intimidating fits the official perspective expressed in printed tourist brochures, demonstrating again that the internet does not offer world views contradictory to those of older media. The new technology did not change the message; rather, message makers use the medium in contradictory ways according to their agendas. Both mansin and government officials choose to upload parts of musok that they emphasize according to their particular perspectives.

Mansin home pages and musok association portals are superior to institutional representations online in their sophistication, beauty, complexity, and traffic. Most government websites about musok use lots of text and small images, whereas musok portals offer videos, large images, and personal statements by mansin. The government representations of musok are static and informational, whereas private and commercial representations change frequently and allow two-way communication. They represent a living tradition rather than an attempt to petrify it as a virtual museum item to be explained by experts. In this respect, online governmental representations are closer in their planning and intentions to museums, whereas mansin's usage of the internet extends their religious practice. Consequently, practitioners' personal websites often lead their audiences to intense off-line involvement in the musok scene—as is, of course, intended by the mansin who sponsor such promotional websites.

Scholars and community leaders have expressed concerns that the internet will reduce face-to-face communication and create a virtual world populated by antisocial, alienated, and desolate individuals (Kraut et al. 1998; Nie 2001). Korea's online musok activity reveals a more optimistic view of the internet as a tool for creating larger social networks, a forum for more frequent communication in long-distance relationships, a locus of communication within geographically dispersed communities, a venue for virtual support groups, and a means to build social capital (Bargh and McKenna 2004; Hannerz 1998). Online musok activity helps mansin and their followers to found and find community life that is often difficult to establish in urban settings. Scholars as well as clients and mansin seem to accept the new situation without much resentment. In contemporary Korea, being famous is important, and the internet has become a space where a new kind of fame can be created and maintained. Mansin have learned this new cultural option quickly and have incorporated it as a venue for promoting their spiritual practice. New media have enhanced the social acceptance of vernacular spiritual practices in Korean society generated by other social and cultural changes and the initiatives of individual practitioners.

NOTES

1. This organization had forty-three thousand members in 1983. Its full name was translated as "The Korean Federation of Associations for Victory over Communism and Respect of Religious Faiths" (Guillemoz 1992, 116n4). It was first registered with the Ministry of Culture in 1971 to defend its members against persecution by the authorities. Since then, it broadened its services, which includes an elaborate website (http://www.kyungsin.co.kr/, which is now discontinued, and http://경신연합회.com, which is the current portal).

2. *New Age* is a widely debated term. I use it here as a reference to eclectic practices based on terminology and ideology of spiritual connectedness with nature and the self. For a detailed discussion of the term *New Age* and its various definitions and meanings, see Ruah-Midbar (2006).

3. See Sarfati (2010) for descriptions of musok deities and their corresponding ritual outfits.

Conclusion

From Ritual to the World Wide Web and Back

THE REPRESENTATION OF MUSOK IN print and photography began in the late nineteenth century with the progenitors of academic research on folklore in Korea, who were Japanese and Christian scholars. As I have shown elsewhere (Sarfati 2010), Korean researchers were employed as assistants and translators for Western missionaries and colonial Japanese anthropologists, and they began to produce their own research, even during the colonial period. They were involved in the Japanese research scene and helped fund the first folklore museum in Korea (Janelli 1986; K. Brandt 2007). Social research on musok by Korean scholars was established already in the 1930s. One would expect that the growing interest in musok in Korea and foreign academia would increase the general Korean public's fascination with mansin and ignite the interest of government cultural preservation agencies. However, this did not occur until the 1980s.

Musok rituals have been used to achieve health and fortune for hundreds of years but were not designated as national treasures when the South Korean government system of heritage preservation began to establish a canonical folklore for the Korean nation in the 1960s. At that time, folk music, mask dance, ancestor rituals, and knot making were designated Important Intangible Cultural Heritage. Shamanic rituals were not designated even in the 1970s, when crafts such as furniture making and painting and other festivals and folk performances became parts of officially sponsored Korean culture.

During the 1970s, the government encouraged the persecution of mansin through the New Community Movement (*saemaŭl undong*). It was in response to such persecution that antigovernment movements began to represent musok in films, print media, and museums. Folklore was used by the minjung movement to reconstruct an alternative, nongovernmental nationalism (Abelmann 1996). Protesters seeking democracy for South Korea harnessed musok rituals to their own symbolic purposes to increase the emotional effect of mass demonstrations (C. Sorensen 1995; Tangherlini 1998). Moreover, to avoid persecution, mansin established professional organizations with nationalistic names. These political actions later helped to shape the social placement of musok. Still, most Koreans did not acknowledge the religious aspects of musok as part of modernized Korea. Even when, in the late 1980s, the government included kut rituals in its culture preservation plan, it did so for the traditional arts involved, not for the religious content. These changes were not initiated by any new medium or technologically enhanced venues of representation but by grassroots politics. As shown in chapter 2, the message of film and television in the 1970s through the 1990s was that musok was a dying tradition, unfit for the fast pace of urban Korea.

A significant shift in musok's image in the media and in museums began in the twenty-first century. As shown in chapters 2 and 4, mansin began to be portrayed as sympathetic characters in documentary and feature films and in television programs. The change was not caused by these media, which had existed in Korea since the mid-twentieth century, but rather by the emergence of the internet. This development allowed mansin to control their own messages, as shown in chapter 5. The new medium carried a unique feature—one does not need to be a professional media producer to achieve mass visibility. Interestingly, the new medium did not appeal only to young, media-savvy practitioners, as suggested by Kim Seong-nae (S. Kim 2003). According to my findings, the first personal websites (*homp'eiji*) of musok practitioners were established in the mid-1990s and are still maintained by mansin who are now in their fifties or older. Younger practitioners followed suit and began establishing their own home pages with ready-made platforms that have been marketed by the musok associations and internet portals since the mid-2000s. The structural norms of mansin home pages and their designs have mostly followed those planned in a tailor-made fashion by the senior practitioners in the 1990s.

The globalization of Korea and Korean culture have also been factors in a new kind of appreciation of musok. It became not merely a national heritage but also an individual lifestyle choice—a way in which young urban Koreans can choose to learn about their future through divination, enhance their fortune in business, solve psychological tensions, and get advice about domestic issues. Younger Koreans of the twenty-first century care little if mansin talk rudely in front of older male clients; they are more tolerant toward rumors about the acceptance of homosexuality within the musok community; and they are curious about the loud music and ecstatic dance as performance. In several interviews, I was told by mansin clients that their parents might be against their interest in musok. One woman in her twenties has been trying to bring her mother along to kut ever since she participated in one the year before, but to no avail. The mother grew up in the 1970s developmental ethos and maintained distaste toward anything irrational. Another interviewee, a doctor in his early thirties, said his father was very Confucian and conservative in his views and might be upset to learn that his son visits a mansin to consult about his love life.

The adaptation of musok to twenty-first-century urban settings has been the cumulative product of acts by individual musok practitioners, scholars, producers, and clients. In choosing how to use each new medium, they have established the possibility of enacting an ancient tradition in a manner suited to changing sociocultural structures. In an urban society, museums establish the roles of musok in the general society. Film and television spread knowledge about musok in ever-expanding circles and allow viewers to learn about the lives and aspirations of various mansin. The internet enables practitioners to promote their beliefs and practices themselves, to communicate with other practitioners, to create a virtual community, and to discuss ideas and norms among themselves.

In this process of adaptation, the technological medium was only one "actant," to use a term from Appadurai (2015, 222), within various "mediants," which include human agents and other driving forces behind cultural change. Appadurai proposes that religion, media, and materiality are mutually constitutive systems. This book attests that, in the case of musok, the influence among these three fields is a central explanation for the increased agency of mansin and their continued presence in urban South Korea. The ethnographic and textual evidence added here confirms the richness of the interrelationship among mansin, the objects they use in rituals, and the objects used to represent them in museums and various screen representations of their creed. The material representations mediate between individual beliefs and active religious practice; between mansin and other parts of society; and between contemporary Korea and older perceptions of reality, existence realms, and spiritual entities. This case reaffirms Appadurai's theorization that mediants allow us to foreground the roles of materialities in social processes. This book shows that the behavior of human individuals and the agency of material representations are in ongoing interaction that produces the public image of contemporary musok.

Media representation of musok in the public sphere began with traditional rituals that became increasingly dependent on mediated promotion and coverage, and then expanded to include government-sponsored staged rituals, museums, films, television, and the internet. However, the importance and effect of face-to-face kut rituals has not eroded. Mediated musok practices have not replaced direct human intersubjective exchanges. New musok rental shrines continue to open on every hill around Seoul and elsewhere. Musok goods stores increase the variety of their inventory and their business, including online sales. New mansin are initiated every week. The practice of spiritual mediation is thriving in contemporary Korea. Acceptance of musok as a part of postindustrial Korea is also manifest in the established norm of inviting mansin to perform kut for the success of a new financial venture, such as the opening of a new mall or the inauguration of an office building.

Enduring questions about agency, gender, and the relationship between humans and objects permeate representations of musok in contemporary media. Musok artifacts and practices are colorful and unique, and thus offer attractive photo opportunities for the various media. However, many venues of musok representation are controlled by men of high social standing, which limits the agency of mansin in the production of such representations. Mansin Sin Myŏng-gi's picture on the Facebook page of my colleague, discussed in chapter 5, encapsulates these issues. She was a woman dressed in a unique manner who was willing to be photographed. Although from a traditionally outcast social stratum, she was performing at a respected international venue. Through the internet, she gained international publicity and was treated respectfully as a practitioner of musok. As this example shows, the internet can bridge distances through technology. In Korea, it also bridges differences in social status and cultural biases related to people who practice this vernacular religion.

Any representative medium has intended results, but these can vary according to the ideology and interests of the people that produce specific representations within it. Film has been a common form of entertainment in Korea for almost a century, but mansin were portrayed as evil and scheming until the early twenty-first century. Film and television portrayals of mansin as people with life stories, daily difficulties, and personal charm increased with the advent of more democratized, liberal forms of mass communication, but mostly after mansin began to take an active part in their self-representation online.

Their gender poses less of a hindrance now than fifty years ago, and the growing wealth of many practitioners has also granted them more power. Innovation in medium alone did not suffice to bring about increased agency for mansin; their own doings mattered, as did general shifts in Korean society and culture. Still, most mansin are busy in their daily lives helping clients to appease angry spirits, to heal, and to learn about their futures through divination. The centrality of ritual, interpersonal communication, and face-to-face interaction has not faded but rather increased through the new media that pass along the message: musok is here to stay.

REFERENCES

Note: Korean authors' names are transliterated in the McCune-Reischauer system when the original publication is in Korean. When authors used other transliterations in their English publications, I added the McCune-Reischauer form in brackets if possible.

Abelmann, Nancy. 1993. "Minjung Theory and Practice." In *Cultural Nationalism in East Asia: Representation and Identity*, edited by Harumi Befu, 139–166. Berkeley: University of California Press.

———. 1996. *Echoes of the Past, Epics of Dissent: A South Korean Social Movement*. Berkeley: University of California Press.

———. 2003. *The Melodrama of Mobility: Women, Talk, and Class in Contemporary South Korea*. Honolulu: Hawaii University Press.

Abelmann, Nancy, and Kathleen McHugh, eds. 2005. *South Korean Golden Age Melodrama: Gender, Genre, and National Cinema*. Detroit: Wayne State University Press.

Adorno, Theodor W. (1994) 2002. *Adorno: The Stars Down to Earth and Other Essays on the Irrational in Culture*. London: Routledge.

Agre, Phil. 1999. "Life after Cyberspace." *European Association for the Study of Science and Technology Review* 18 (2): 3–5.

Akamatsu, Chijo, and Akiba Takashi. 1938. *Chōsen Fuzuko no Kenkyū* [Study of Korean Shamanism] Vols. 1, 2. Tokyo: Osakayago Shōten.

Akiba, Takashi. 1957. "A Study of Korean Folkways." *Folklore Studies* 16 (1): 1–106.

Allen, Chizuko T. 1990. "Northeast Asia Centered around Korea: Ch'oe Namsŏn's View of History." *Journal of Asian Studies* 49 (4): 787–806.

An, Chae-hun [Ahn Jae-hun]. 2018. *Munyŏdo* [A Shaman's Story]. Seoul: A Meditation with a Pencil Production. DVD.

An, Sung-t'aek, and Si-jun Yi. 2014. "Iljech'ogi Misinron Yŏn'gu: Mihongtwin Mitŭm Iranŭn Munhwajŏk Nakinŭi Chongch'ihak" [Discourses on Superstition in the Pre- and Postcolonization Years: The Politics of Cultural

Stigma Referring to "Misled Beliefs"]. *Han'guk Minjok Munhwa* [Korean Folk Culture] 51 (5): 295–337.

Anderson, Benedict. 1991. *Imagined Communities: Reflections on the Origin and Spread of Nationalism*. London: Verso.

Anderson, Daniel R., Aletha C. Huston, Kelly L. Schmitt, Deborah Linebarger, and John Wright. 2001. "Early Childhood Television Viewing and Adolescent Behavior." *Monographs of the Society for Research in Child Development* 66 (1): 1–145.

Anderson, Michelle. 1982. "Authentic Voodoo Is Synthetic." *Drama Review* 26 (2): 89–110.

Andong Museum. 2017. "The Andong Folk Museum." Korean Government Tourism Organization. http://english.visitkorea.or.kr/enu/ATR/SI_EN_3_1_1_1.jsp?cid=268130.

Appadurai, Arjun., ed. 1986. *The Social Life of Things: Commodities in Cultural Perspective*. Cambridge: Cambridge University Press.

——. 1996. *Modernity at Large: Cultural Dimensions of Globalization*. Minneapolis: University of Minnesota Press.

——. 2015. "Mediants, Materiality, Normativity." *Public Culture* 27 (2): 221–237. https://doi-org.rproxy.tau.ac.il/10.1215/08992363-2841832

Armstrong, Robert Plant. 1981. *The Powers of Presence: Consciousness, Myth, and Affecting Presence*. Philadelphia: University of Pennsylvania Press.

Arthur, Chris. 2000. "Exhibiting the Sacred." In *Godly Things: Museums, Objects and Religion*, edited by Crispin Paine, 1–27. London: Leicester University Press.

Averbuch, Irit. 1995. *The Gods Come Dancing: A Study of the Japanese Ritual Dance of Yamabushi Kagura*. Ithaca, NY: Cornell University Press.

Baker, Don. 2001. "Looking for God in the Streets of Seoul: The Resurgence of Religion in 20th-Century Korea." *Harvard Asia Quarterly* 4:34–39.

Bargh, John, and Katelyn McKenna. 2004. "The Internet and Social Life." *Annual Review of Psychology* 55:573–590.

Baudrillard, Jean. 1983. *Simulations*, translated by Paul Foss, Paul Patton, and Philip Beitchman. New York: Semiotext(e).

——. 1994. "The System of Collecting," translated by Roger Cardinal. In *The Cultures of Collecting*, edited by John Elsner and Roger Cardinal, 7–24. London: Reaktion.

Bauman, Richard, and Charles L. Briggs. 2003. *Voices of Modernity: Language Ideologies and the Politics of Inequality*. New York: Cambridge University Press.

Bauman, Richard, and Pamela Ritch. 1994. "Informing Performance: Producing the *Coloqio* in Tierra Blanca." *Oral Tradition* 9 (2): 255–280.

Bilu, Yoram. 1997. "Mechkar Hatarbut Haamamit Beidan Hapost Moderny: Sipur Ishi [A Research of Folk Culture in Postmodern Times: A Personal Story]." *Teoria ve Bikoret* [Theory and Criticism] 10:37–54.

Bishop, Angela Bird. (1897) 1970. *Korea and Her Neighbours*. Seoul: Yonsei University Press.
Blacker, Carmen. 1986. *The Catalpa Bow: A Study of Shamanistic Practices in Japan*. London: Allen & Unwin.
Boas, Franz. 1955. *Primitive Art*. New York: Dover.
Boast, Robin. 2011. "Neocolonial Collaboration: Museum as Contact Zone Revisited." *Museum Anthropology* 34 (1): 56–70. https://doi.org/10.1111/j.1548-13 79.2010.01107.x
Boddy, Janice. 1994. "Spirit Possession Revisited: Beyond Instrumentality." *Annual Review of Anthropology* 23:407–434.
Bourdieu, Pierre. 1984. *Distinction: A Social Critique of the Judgement of Taste*. Cambridge, MA: Harvard University Press.
Brandt, Kim. 2007. *Kingdom of Beauty: Mingei and the Politics of Folk Art in Imperial Japan*. Durham, NC: Duke University Press.
Brandt, Vincent S. R. 1971. *A Korean Village between Farm and Sea*. Cambridge, MA: Harvard University Press.
Brennan, Timothy. 1990. "The National Longing for Form." In *Nation and Narrations*, edited by Homi K. Bhabha, 41–70. London: Routledge.
Brown, Bill., ed. 2004. *Things*. Chicago: University of Chicago Press.
Bruno, Antonetta Lucia. 2002. *The Gate of Words: Language in the Rituals of Korean Shamans*. Leiden: University of Leiden Press.
———. 2007a. "A Shamanic Ritual for Sending on the Dead." In *Religions of Korea in Practice*, edited by Robert E. Buswell, 325–352. Princeton, NJ: Princeton University Press.
———. 2007b. "Transactions with the Realm of Spirits in Modern Korea." *Sungkyun Journal of East Asian Studie* 7 (1): 47–67.
Campbell, Emma. 2016. *South Korea's New Nationlism: The End of "One Korea"?* Boulder, CO: First Forum Press.
Cazzaro, Davide. 2006. "2006 Jeonju International Film Festival Report." *Korean Film* (blog). http://www.koreanfilm.org/jiff06.html.
CHA (Korean Cultural Heritage Administration). 2005. "Cheju Shamanism as an Item of Intangible Culture Heritage Preservation." http://jikimi.cha.go.kr/english/world_heritage_new/intangible_treasure_07.jsp?mc=EN_04_02 (now discontinued).
———. 2012. "Heritage Classification." http://jikimi.cha.go.kr/english/search_plaza_new/state.jsp?mc=EN_03_01 (now discontinued).
Chan, Park E. 2003. *Voices from the Straw Mat: Toward an Ethnography of Korean Story Singing*. Honolulu: University of Hawaii Press.
Chang, Pilwha. 2003. "Cyberspace and Sexuality." *Korea Journal* 43 (3): 35–60.
Chattarjee, Partha. 1991. "Whose Imagined Communities?" *Millennium: Journal of International Studies* 20 (3): 521–525. https://doi.org/10.1177/03058298910200030601

Cheon, Mina. 2009. *Shamanism + Cyberspace*. New York: Atropos.
Cho, Chin-gyu. 2013. *Paksu Kŏndal* [Man on the Edge]. Korea: KD Media. DVD.
Cho, Hung-youn (Cho Hŭng-yun). 1983. *Han'guk ŭi Mu* [Korean Shamanism]. Seoul: Chŏngŭmsa.
Cho, Mi-hŭi. 2009. "Shaman of Korea." YouTube video. http://www.youtube.com/watch?v=k_QeO29-MBE (now discontinued).
Cho, Yŏng-gwang, and Pak Yong-sun, dirs. 2011. "*49 il* [49 Days]." Television Series. Written by So Yŏn-gyŏng. Seoul: SBS.
Ch'oe, Kil-sŏng. 1978. *Han'guk Musok ŭi Yŏn'gu* [Research of Korean Shamanism]. Seoul: Asia Munhwasa.
———. 1981. *Han'guk Musongon* [About Korean Shamanism]. Seoul: Hyŏngsŏl Ch'ulp'ansa.
———. 1982. "Community Ritual and Social Structure in Village Korea." *Asian Folklore Studies* 41 (1): 39–48.
———. 1984. "Male and Female in Korean Folk Belief." *Asian Folklore Studies* 43 (2): 227–233.
———.1989. *Han'guk Min'gan Sinang ŭi Yŏn'gu* [A Study of Korean Folk Beliefs]. Taegu: Kyemyong Tehaggyo Ch'ulp'anbu.
———. 1991. *Han'guk Muga 2: Kyŏngbok, Kangwon, Cheju, Sŏul, Hwanghaedo* [Shamanic Texts of Korea 2: *Kyŏngbok, Kangwon, Cheju, Seoul*, and *Hwanghaedo*]. Seoul: Asea Munhwasa.
———. 1998. "Belief in Malevolent Spirits." In *The Anthropology of Korea: East Asian Perspectives*. Senri Ethnological Series No. 49, edited by Mutsuhiko Shima and Roger L. Janelli, 95–110. Osaka: National Museum of Ethnology.
———. 1999. "Shyamanijŭm ŭi Pigyo" [Comparison in Shamanism]. In *Pigyo Minsokhak kwa Pigyomunhwa* [Comparative Folklore and Culture], edited by In-hak Ch'oe, 357–372. Seoul: Minsogwŏn.
———. 2003. "War and Ethnology/Folklore in Colonial Korea: The Case of Akiba Takashi." In *Wartime Japanese Anthropology in Asia and the Pacific*. Senri Ethnological Studies No. 65, edited by Akitoshi Shimizu and Jan van Bremen, 169–187. Osaka: National Museum of Ethnology.
Ch'oe, Nam-sŏn. 1927. *Salman'gyo Tapgi* [Ethnography of Shamanism]. Seoul: Kyemyŏng.
Ch'oi, Ha-wŏn (Choi Ha Won). 1972. *Munyŏdo* [A Shaman's Story]. Korea: Taechang Productions. DVD.
Choe, Sanghun. 2007. "In the Age of the Internet, Korean Shamans Regain Popularity." *New York Times*, July 6, 2007. http://www.nytimes.com/2007/07/07/world/asia/07korea.html?pagewanted=all.
Choi, Chungmoo (Ch'oe Chŏng-mu). 1987. "The Competence of Korean Shamans as Performers of Folklore." PhD diss., Indiana University, Bloomington Indiana.

———. 2003. "The Artistry and Ritual Aesthetics of Urban Korean Shamans." In *Shamanism: A Reader*, edited by Graham Harvey, 170–185. London: Routledge.
Chŏn, Kyŏng-su. 2012. "Musok Yŏn'gu Paengyŏn ŭi Taeganggwa Kulkok: Yi Nŭnghwa ŭihu" [History of Shamanism Studies and its Misunderstanding in Korea: After Yi Nung-Hwa]. *Minsokhak Yŏn'gu* [Korean Folklore Research] 31:5–44.
Chŏng, Hyang-Sa. 1999. "Ch'ŏghyang-sa Tojiam." Mudang. http://www.mudang.co.kr/.
Chong, Kelly H. 2006. "Negotiating Patriarchy: South Korean Evangelical Women and the Politics of Gender." *Gender and Society* 20 (6): 697–724.
Chŏng, Ŭn-gwŏl. 2005. *Haerŭl P'umŭn tal* [The Moon Embracing the Sun]. Seoul: Sigongsa.
Clark, Allen Charles. (1932) 1981. *Religions of Old Korea*. New York: Garland.
Clifford, James. 1991. "Four Northwest Museums: Travel Reflections." In *Exhibiting Cultures: The Poetics and Politics of Museum Display*, edited by Ivan Karp and Steven D. Lavine, 107–125. Washington, DC: Smithsonian Institution Press.
———. 1997. *Routes: Travel and Translation in the Late Twentieth Century*. Cambridge, MA: Harvard University Press.
Clifford, Mark L. 1994. *Troubled Tiger: Businessmen, Bureaucrats, and Generals in South Korea*. New York: Sharpe.
Cooper, Sarah. 2006. *Selfless Cinema? Ethics and French Documentary*. Oxford: Legenda.
CORLAS (Collegium Oto-Rhino-Laryngologicum Amicitiae Sacrum). 2007. "2007 Annual Report." www.corlas.org/Annual%20report%202007_painoversion.doc (now discontinued).
Cosentino, Donald. 2000. "Mounting Controversy: The Sacred Arts of Haitian Vodou." In *Godly Things: Museums, Objects and Religion*, edited by Crispin Paine, 97–106. London: Leicester University Press.
Covell, Alan Carter. 1984. *Shamanist Folk Paintings: Korea's Eternal Spirits*. Seoul: Hollym.
Coulson, Constance J. D. 1910. *Korea: Peeps at Many Lands*. London: Black.
CPA (Korean Cultural Properties Administration). 2005. "Shamanic Arts' Preservation." http://www.ocp.go.kr:9000/ne_dasencgi/full.cgi?v_kw_str =EXORCISM&v_db_query=A1%3a00&v_db=2&v_doc_no=00003042&v _dblist=2&v_start_num=1&v_disp_type=4 (now discontinued)
Creighton, Millie. 1997. "Consuming Rural Japan: The Marketing of Tradition and Nostalgia in the Japanese Travel Industry." *Ethnology* 36 (3): 239–254.
Cruikshank, Julie. 2005. *Do Glaciers Listen? Local Knowledge, Colonial Encounters, and Social Imagination*. Seattle: University of Washington Press.
Danet, Brenda, and Tamar Katriel. 1994. "No Two Alike: Play and Aesthetics in Collecting." In *Interpreting Objects and Collections*, edited by Susan M. Pearce, 220–239. London: Routledge.

Deuchler, Martina. 1992. *The Confucian Transformation of Korea: A Study of Society and Ideology*. Cambridge, MA: Harvard University Press.

Dorson, Richard M. 1973. "Is Folklore a Discipline?" *Folklore* 84 (3): 177–205.

Douglas, Mary. 1966. *Purity and Danger: An Analysis of the Concepts of Pollution and Taboo*. London: Routledge.

Douglas, Mary, and Baron Isherwood. 1979. *The World of Goods: Towards an Anthropology of Consumption*. New York: Basic.

Dudden, Alexis. 2005. *Japan's Colonization of Korea: Discourse and Power*. Honolulu: University of Hawai'i Press.

Duus, Peter. 1995. *The Abacus and the Sword: the Japanese Penetration of Korea, 1895–1910*. Berkeley: University of California Press.

Eliade, Mircea. (1964) 2004. *Shamanism: Archaic Techniques of Ecstasy*. New York: Bollingen Foundation.

Ethlenn. 2012. "Korean Shamanism." *Ethlenn* (blog), November 12, 2012. http://ethlenn.blogspot.co.il/2012/11/korean-shamanism.html.

Exorcist [Eksosisŭt'ŭ]. 2008–2009. Television Program. Seoul: tvN.

"Filmmessenger about the Documentary *Between*." 2006. *Filmmessenger* (blog). http://www.filmmessenger.com/zboard/view.php?id=news2&page=2&sn1=&divpage=1&sn=off&ss=on&sc=on&select_arrange=hit&desc=asc&no=17 (now discontinued).

Gamson, William A., and Andre Modigliani. 1989. "Media Discourse and Public Opinion on Nuclear Power: A Constructionist Approach." *American Journal of Sociology* 95 (1): 1–37.

Garran, Robert. 1998. *Tigers Tamed: The End of the Asian Miracle*. Honolulu: University of Hawaii Press.

Geertz, Clifford. 1973. *The Interpretation of Cultures: Selected Essays*. New York: Basic.

Gell, Alfred. 1998. *Art and Agency: An Anthropological Theory*. Oxford: Clarendon.

Gerbner, George, Larry Gross, Michael Morgan, and Nancy Signorielli. 1986. "Living with Television: The Dynamics of the Cultivation Process." In *Perspectives on Media Effects*, edited by Bryant Jennings and Dolf Zillmann, 17–40. Hillsdale, NJ: Erlbaum.

Giddens, Anthony. 1991. *Modernity and Self Identity: Self and Society in the Late Modern Age*. Palo Alto, CA: Stanford University Press.

Glassie, Henry. 1989. *The Spirit of Folk Art: The Girard Collection at the Museum of International Folk Art*. New York: Abrams.

———. 1995. "Tradition." *Journal of American Folklore* 108 (430): 395–412.

Goffman, Erving. 1959. *The Presentation of Self in Everyday Life*. New York: Anchor Doubleday.

Graves-Brown, Paul M., ed. 2000. *Matter, Materiality and Modern Culture*. London: Routledge.

Grayson, James Huntley. 1984. "Religious Syncretism in the Silla Period: The Relationship between Esoteric Buddhism and Korean Primeval Religion." *Asian Folklore Studies* 43 (2): 185–198.

———. 1996. "Female Mountain Spirits in Korea: A Neglected Tradition." *Asian Folklore Studies* 55:119–134.

———. 1998. "Christianity and Korean Religions: Accommodation as an Aspect of the Emplantation of a World Religion." In *Korean Shamanism Revivals Survivals, and Change*, edited by Keith Howard, 133–152. Seoul: Seoul Press.

Greenfield, Patricia, Dorathea Farrar, and Jessica Beagles-Roos. 1986. "Is the Medium the Message? An Experimental Comparison of the Effects of Radio and Television on Imagination." *Journal of Applied Developmental Psychology* 7:201–218.

Grim, John A. 1984. "Chaesu Kut: A Korean Shamanistic Performance." *Asian Folklore Studies* 43 (2): 235–259.

Guillemoz, Alexandre. 1992. "Seoul, the Widow, and the Mudang: Transformations of Urban Korean Shamanism." *Diogenes* 158:115–127.

Hall, Stuart. 1980. "Encoding/Decoding." In *Culture, Media, Language*, edited by Stuart Hall, Dorothy Hobson, Andrew Love, and Paul Willis, 128–138. London: Hutchinson.

Hancinema. 2013. "Man on the Edge." Korean Movie and Drama Database. https://www.hancinema.net/korean_movie_Man_on_the_Edge.php.

———. 2015. "Mansin: Ten Thousand Spirits." Korean Movie and Drama Database. http://www.hancinema.net/korean_movie_Mansin_2p__Ten_Thousand_Spirits.php.

Handler, Richard, and Jocelyn Linnekin. 1984. "Tradition, Genuine or Spurious." *Journal of American Folklore* 97 (385): 273–290.

Hannerz, Ulf. 1998. "Transnational Research." In *Handbook of Methods in Anthropology*, edited by Bernard H. Russell, 235–256. New York: Altamira.

Happer, Catherine, and Greg Philo. 2013. "The Role of the Media in the Construction of Public Belief and Social Change." *Journal of Social and Political Psychology* 1 (1): 321–336.

Harvey, Youngsook Kim. 1979. *Six Korean Women: The Socialization of Shamans.* St. Paul, MN: West.

Hesselink, Nathan. 2004. "Samul Nori as Traditional: Preservation and Innovation in a South Korean Contemporary Percussion Genre." *Ethnomusicology* 48 (3): 405–439.

Hobsbawm, Eric, and Terence Ranger, eds. 1983. *The Invention of Tradition.* Cambridge: Cambridge University Press.

Hogarth, Hyun-key Kim. 1998. "'Trance' and 'Possession Trance' in the Perspective of Korean Shamanism." In *Korean Shamanism Revivals, Survivals, and Change*, edited by Keith Howard, 45–54. Seoul: Seoul Press.

Hong, T'ae-han. 2006. *Hwanghae-do ŭi Muga* [Shamankic Texts of Hwanghae-do Province]. Seoul: Minsogwŏn.

Howard, Keith. 1998. "Preserving the Spirits? Ritual, State Sponsorship, and Performance." In *Korean Shamanism Revivals, Survivals, and Change*, edited by Keith Howard, 187–217. Seoul: Seoul Press.

———. 2006. *Preserving Korean Music: Intangible Cultural Properties as Icons of Identity*. Aldershot: Ashgate.

Howard, Robert Glen. 2005. "A Theory of Vernacular Rhetoric: The Case of the 'Sinner's Prayer' Online." *Folklore* 116:172–188. https://doi.org/10.1080/00155870500140214

———. 2006. "Sustainability and Narrative Plasticity in Online Apocalyptic Discourse after September 11, 2001." *Journal of Media and Religion* 5 (1): 25–47. https://doi.org/10.1207/s15328415jmr0501_2

———. 2011. *Digital Jesus: The Making of a New Christian Fundamentalist Community on the Internet*. New York: New York University Press.

Humphrey, Caroline. 1999. "Shamans in the Cities." *Anthropology Today* 15 (3): 3–11.

Hwang, Merose. 2009. "The Mudang: Gendered Discourses on Shamanism in Colonial Korea." PhD diss., University of Toronto.

I Am All for Life [Taech'an insaeng]. 2013. Television Program. Seoul: TV Chosŏn.

Im, Chae-hae. 1996. "Meaning of Water in Korean Folk Religion." *Koreana* 10 (3): 32–39.

Im, Kwŏn-t'aek. 1979. *Sin'gung* [The Divine Bow]. Taechang Productions. DVD.

———. 1983. *Pul-ŭi ttal* [Daughter of the Flames]. Korea: Dong-a Productions. DVD.

———. 1993. *Sop'yŏnje*. Korea: Taehung Pictures. DVD.

———. 1996. *Ch'ukje* [Festival]. Korea: Taehung Pictures. DVD.

Im, Sŏk-jae (Yim Suk-jay). 1970. "Han'guk Musok Yŏn'gu Sŏsŏl" [Introduction to Korean Shamanism]. *Asea Yŏsŏng Yŏn'gu* [Journal of Asian Women] 9:73–90, 161–217.

IMDb. 2013. "Man on the Edge." https://www.imdb.com/title/tt2630028/.

Insight People [Insait'ŭ p'ip'ŭl]. 2011. Television Program. Seoul: Insite TV.

Interview Documentary [Int'ŏpyu tak'yument'ari inyongwi kkŭn]. 2011. Television Documemtary Series. Seoul: Living TV.

Ivy, Marilyn. 1995. *Discourses of the Vanishing: Modernity, Phantasm, Japan*. Chicago: University of Chicago Press.

James, David E. 2001. "Im Kwon-Taek: Korean National Cinema and Buddhism." *Film Quarterly* 54 (3): 14–31.

James, William. 1902. *The Varieties of Religious Experience: A Study of Human Nature*. London: Longmans Green.

Janelli, Roger L. 1986. "The Origins of Korean Folklore Scholarship." *Journal of American Folklore* 99 (391): 24–49.

Janelli, Roger L., and Dawnhee Yim Janelli. 1982. *Ancestor Worship and Korean Society*. Palo Alto, CA: Stanford University Press.

———. 2002. "Ancestor Rites and Capitalist Industrialization in a South Korean Village." *Korea Journal* 42 (4): 298–232.
Jang, Gunjoo, and Won K. Paik. 2012. "Korean Wave as Tool for Korea's New Cultural Diplomacy." *Advances in Applied Sociology* 2 (3): 196–202.
Jensen, Klaus Bruhn. 2002. "The Humanities in Media and Communication Research." In *A Handbook of Media and Communication Research: Qualitative and Quantitative Methodologies*, edited by Klaus Bruhn Jensen, 15–32. New York: Routledge.
Job Stories [Sŭt'ori chapsŭ]. 2011–2013. Television Program. TV Chosŏn. http://tv.chosun.com/enter/storyjobs/main/main.html.
Johnston, Keith M. 2009. *Coming Soon: Film Trailers and the Selling of Hollywood Technology*. Jefferson, NC: MacFarland.
Karp, Ivan, and Steven D. Lavine., eds. 1991. *Exhibiting Cultures: The Poetics and Politics of Museum Display*. Washington, DC: Smithsonian Institution Press.
Katz, Daniel. 1960. "The Functional Approach to the Study of Attitude." *Public Opinion Quarterly* 24 (2): 163–204. https://doi.org/10.1086/266945
KCIS (Korean Culture and Information Service). 2009. *Passport to Korean Culture*. Seoul: Ministry of Culture, Sports, and Tourism.
Keappler, Adrienne L. 1992. "Ali'i and Maka'ainana: The Representations of Hawaiians in Museums at Home and Abroad." In *Museums and Communities: The Politics of Public Culture*, edited by Ivan Karp, Christine Mullen Kreamer, and Steven D. Lavine, 458–475. Washington, DC: Smithsonian Institution Press.
Kendall, Laurel. 1977. "Mugam: The Dance in Shaman's Clothing." *Korea Journal* 17 (12): 38–44.
———. 1985. *Shamans, Housewives, and other Restless Spirits: Women in Korean Ritual Life*. Honolulu: University of Hawaii Press.
———. 1988. *The Life and Hard Times of a Korean Shaman: of Tales and the Telling of Tales*. Honolulu: University of Hawaii Press.
———. 1991. *An Initiation Kut for a Korean Shaman*, with filmmaker Diana Lee. Honolulu: University of Hawaii. Videotape.
———. 1996. "Korean Shamans and the Spirits of Capitalism." *American Anthropologist* 98 (3): 512–527. https://doi.org/10.1525/aa.1996.98.3.02a00060.
———. 2001. "The Cultural Politics of 'Superstition' in the Korean Shaman World: Modernity Constructs its Other." In *Healing Powers and Modernity: Traditional Medicine, Shamanism, and Science in Asian Societies*, edited by Linda H. Connor, and Geoffrey Samuel, 25–41. Westport, CT: Bergin & Garvey.
———. 2008. "Of Hungry Ghosts and Other Matters of Consumption in the Republic of Korea: The Commodity Becomes a Ritual Prop." *American Ethnologist* 35 (1): 154–170. https://doi.org/10.1111/j.1548-1425.2008.00011.x.
———. 2009. *Shamans, Nostalgias, and the IMF: South Korean Popular Religion in Motion*. Honolulu: University of Hawaii Press.

———. 2015. "Numinous Dress/Iconic Costume: Korean Shamans Dressed for the Gods and for the Camera." In *Trance Mediums and New Media: Spirit Possession in the Age of Technical Reproduction*, edited by Heike Behrend, Anja Dreschke, and Martin Zillinger, 116–136. New York: Fordham University Press.

Kendall, Laurel, and Mark Peterson, eds. 1983. *Korean Women: View from the Inner Room*. New Haven: East Rock Press.

Kendall, Laurel, and Jongsung Yang. 2014. "Goddess with a Picasso Face: Art Markets, Collectors and Sacred Things in the Circulation of Korean Shaman Paintings." *Journal of Material Culture* 19 (4): 401–423. https://doi.org/10.1177/1359183514551119.

———. 2015. "What Is an Animated Image? Korean Shaman Paintings as Objects of Ambiguity." *HAU: Journal of Ethnographic Theory* 5 (2): 153–175. https://doi.org/10.14318/hau5.2.011.

Kendall, Laurel, Jongsung Yang, and Yul Soo Yoon. 2015. *God Pictures in Korean Contexts: The Ownership and Meaning of Shaman Paintings*. Honolulu: Hawaii University Press.

Kim, Andrew Eungi. 2002. "Characteristics of Religious Life in South Korea: A Sociological Survey." *Review of Religious Research* 43 (4): 291–310.

Kim, Carolyn Hyun-kyung. 2000. "Building the Korean Film Industry Competitiveness: Abolish the Film Quota and Subsidize the Film Industry." *Pacific Rim Law & Policy Journal* 9 (2): 353–378. http://hdl.handle.net/1773.1/811

Kim, Chan-ho. 2004. "Han'guk ŭi Pujŏk Kwanhan Yŏn'gu" [A Study of Korean Talismans]. *Senghwal Munmul Yŏn'gu* [Review of Folk Life and Culture] 3 (12): 53–7.

Kim, Chin-yŏng. 2009. *Ch'ŏngdam Posal* [Fortune Saloon]. Korea: (Chu) P'ŭrijiem. DVD.

Kim, Chongho. 2003. *Korean Shamanism: The Cultural Paradox*. Aldershot: Ashgate.

Kim, Chŏng-jung. 2012–2017. *Twenty Four-Hour Observation Camera* [Kwanch'al k'amera 24 sigan]. Television Program. Seoul: Channel A.

Kim, David. J. 2015. "Visions and Stones: Spirit Matters and the Charm of Small Things in South Korean Shamanic Rock Divination." *Anthropology and Humanism* 40 (1): 1–19. https://doi.org/10.1111/anhu.12065.

Kim, Dong-kyu. 2012. "Looping Effects between Images and Realities: Understanding the Popularity of Korean Shamanism." PhD diss., University of British Columbia, Vancouver.

Kim, Elaine H., and Chungmoo Choi [Ch'oe Chŏng-mu], eds. 1997. *Dangerous Women: Gender and Korean Nationalism*. London: Routledge.

Kim, Hyung-seok. 2014. "[Cine Feature] 2014 Report: *Snowpiercer*, Reaping Good Results Overseas," *Hankyorae*, December 21, 2014. http://www.hani.co.kr/arti/english_edition/e_entertainment/670028.html.

Kim, Ki-hŭng. 2008. "Orinito Orŭnto Sinmyŏngnan Chaesu kut Hanmadang: Kungrip minsok Pangmulgwan Minjok Taemyŏngjil Maja Insaninhae" [Young and Old Participate in a Festive Kut Ritual for Good Fortune: The National Folk Museum Was Bright on This National Day]. *Omainyusŭ* [OhmyNews], June 10, 2008. http://www.ohmynews.com/NWS_Web/view/at_pg.aspx?CNTN_CD=A0000364925&PAGE_CD.
Kim, Ki-yŏng. 1977. *Iŏdo* [Io Island]. Korea: DongAh Exports. DVD.
Kim, Kŭm-hwa. 1995. *Kim Kŭm-hwa ŭi Mugajip: Komunattae Mansin, Huina Paeksong ŭi Norae* [Kim Kŭm-hwa Shamanic Texts and Songs]. Seoul: Munumsa
Kim, Kwang-ok. 1994. "Rituals of Resistance: The Manipulation of Shamanism in Contemporary Korea." In *Asian Visions of Authority: Religion and the Modern States of East and Southeast Asia*, edited by Charles Keyes, Laurel Kendall, and Helen Hardacre, 195–219. Honolulu: University of Hawaii Press.
———. 2000. "History, Power, Culture, and Anthropology in Korea: Toward a New Paradigm for Korean Studies." *Korea Journal* 40 (1): 54–100.
———. 2013. "Colonial Body Indigenous Soul: Religion as a Contested Terrain of Culture." In *Colonial Rule and Social Change in Korea 1910–1945*, edited by Hongyung Lee, Yong-chool Ha, and Clark Sorensen, 264–313. Seattle: University of Washington Press.
Kim, Kyung-hyun. 2004. *The Remasculinization of Korean Cinema*. Durham, NC: Duke University Press.
Kim, Man-tae. 2007. "Pujŏk e Nat'anan Pudu Ch'ilsŏng ŭi Choyŏngsŏng Yŏngu" [A Study on the Plasticity of the Ursa Major in Talisman]. *Han'guk Musokhak* [Korean Shamanism] 15 (8): 203–235.
Kim, Ok-ju. 1993. "Chosŏn Malgi Tuch'ang ŭi Yuhaeng kwa Mingan ŭi Taeŭng" [Smallpox Epidemics and Folk Responses in the Late Chosŏn Period]. *Ŭisahak* [Korean Journal of Medical History] 2 (1): 3–58.
Kim, Sang-jin. *Kwisini Sanda* [Haunted House]. Korea: CJ Entertainment. DVD.
Kim, Seong-nae (Kim Sŏng-nae). 2003. "Korean Shamanic Heritage in Cyber Culture." *Bibliotheca Shamanistica* 11:279–295.
Kim, Seong-nae (Kim Sŏng-nae), Daniel Kister, and Dong-kyu Kim. 2012. "An Interview with Jongsung Yang, Curator of the Exhibition 'Mediator between Heaven and Earth—Shaman.'" *Journal of Korean Religions* 3 (2): 73–88.
Kim, To-hun, and Yi Song-jun. dirs. 2012. *Haerŭl p'umŭn tal* [The Moon Embracing the Sun]. Television Series. Written by Chin Su-hwan. Seoul: MBC.
Kim, Tong-ni. (1936) 2004. "Munyŏdo" [A Shaman's Story]. In *Kim Tong-ni Tanp'yŏnsŏn* [Kim Tong-Ni Short Stories]. Seoul: Munhak kwa Chisŏngsa.
Kim, T'ae-gon. 1966. *Hwangch'ŏn Muga Yŏn'gu* [Research of Shaman Songs of Hwangch'ŏn]. Seoul: Institute for the Study of Indigenous Religion.
———. 1998. "What Is Korean Shamanism?" In *Korean Shamanism Revivals, Survivals, and Change*, edited by Keith Howard, 15–31. Seoul: Seoul Press.

———. 1999. "Definition of Korean Shamanism." In *Culture of Korean Shamanism*, edited by Yong Chun Shin, 9–44. Kyunggi-do: Kimpo College Press.
Kim, Ŭn-jŏng. 2004. *Han'guk ŭi Mubok* [Shamanic Outfits of Korea]. Seoul: Minsogŏn.
Kim, Youna, ed. 2013. *The Korean Wave: Korean Media Go Global*. London: Routledge.
Kister, Daniel. 1996. "A Korean Shaman Folktale and Ritual Skits in Honor of the Grandmother Spirit of Childbirth." *Shaman* 4 (1–2): 115–130.
Kirshenblatt-Gimblett, Barbara. 1998. *Destination Culture: Tourism, Museums, and Heritage*. Berkeley: University of California Press.
Klein, Uri. 2013. "Cinema Is a Potent Generator of Change, Says Iranian Filmmaker during Israel Visit." *Haaretz*, July 11, 2013. https://www.haaretz.com/israel-news/culture/.premium-film-director-who-earned-his-vision-under-iranian-torture-1.5294018.
Koehler, Robert. 2007. "A Woodstock Mudang in a 21st Century World: Talking about Korean Shamanism with Shaman Lee Hae-kyung." *Seoul* 7 (2007): 36–44.
Korean Film Biz Zone. 2013. "Lee Chang-Jae." Korean Film Council. http://www.koreanfilm.or.kr/jsp/films/index/peopleView.jsp?peopleCd=10057682.
Korean Overseas Information Service. 1995. *Folk Paintings*. Korean Heritage Series. Seoul: Korean Overseas Information Service.
Korean Shaman. 2012. "Shamanism in Modern Korea." *Korean Shaman* (blog), May 3, 2012. https://www.tumblr.com/search/korean%20shaman.
Koreanfilm.org. 2011a. "1945–1959." Updated November 15, 2014. http://koreanfilm.org/kfilm45-59.html.
———. 2011b. "1970–1979." Updated November 14, 2012. http://www.koreanfilm.org/kfilm70s.html.
———. 2019. "Documentaries." http://koreanfilm.org/docs.html.
Kraut, R., M. Patterson, V. Lundmark, S. Kiesler, T. Mukopadhyay, and W. Scherlis. 1998. "Internet Paradox: A Social Technology That Reduces Social Involvement and Psychological Well-being?" *American Psychologist* 53 (9): 1017–1031. https://doi.org/10.1037//0003-066X.53.9.1017.
Kunihiko, Nakagawa, director. 1988. *JVC Video Anthology of World Music and Dance*, Vol. 2. Tokyo: JVC. Videotape, 00:50:00.
Kurin, Richard. 1997. *Reflection of a Culture Broker: A View from the Smithsonian*. Washington, DC: Smithsonian Institution Press.
Kwŏn, O-ch'ang. 1998. *Chosŏn Sidae Uriot* [Korean Costumes of the Chosŏn Period]. Seoul: Hyŏnamsa.
Ladner, Mimsie. 2011. "Sunshine and Shamanism." *Seoul Searching* (blog), March, 2011. http://www.myseoulsearching.com/2011/03/sunshine-and-shamanism.html.
Latour, Bruno. 2005. *Reassembling the Social: An Introduction to Actor-Network-Theory*. Oxford: Oxford University Press.

Laufer, Berthold. 1917. "Origin of the Word Shaman." *American Anthropologist* 19 (3): 361–371.
Leakage of the Sky's Mysteries [Ch'ŏn'gi nusŏl]. 2013–present. Television Program. Seoul: MBN.
Lee, Duh-yun (Yi Tu-hyŏn). 1990. "Korean Shamans: Role Playing through Trance Possession." In *By Means of Performance: Intercultural Studies of Theatre and Ritual*, edited by Schechner Richard, and Willa Appel, 149–166. New York: Cambridge University Press.
Lee, Haekyung. 2006. "Hwanghae-do Mansin Yi Hae-gyŏng." *Mansin* (blog). http://www.mansin.co.kr/.
Lee, Jung-young. 1981. *Korean Shamanistic Rituals*. Berlin: Walter de Gruyter.
Lee, Kwang-kyu. 2003. *Korean Traditional Culture*. Seoul: Jimoodang.
Lee, Maggie. 2018. "Film Review: 'The Shaman Sorceress.'" *Variety*. https://variety .com/2018/film/reviews/the-shaman-sorceress-review-1202971164/.
Lee, Namhee. 2007. *The Making of Minjung: Democracy and the Politics of Representation in South Korea*. Ithaca, NY: Cornell University Press.
Lemish, Dafna. 2006. "The Message Is the Message." *Human Development* 49 (1): 54–57. doi:10.1159/000090305.
Lewis, I. M. 1971. *Ecstatic Religion: A Study of Shamanism and Spirit Possession*. London: Routledge.
Lim, In-sook. 2008. "The Trend of Creating Atypical Male Images in Heterosexist Korean Society." *Korea Journal* 48 (4): 115–146.
Lowie, Robert H. 1924. *Primitive Religion*. New York: Boni & Liveright.
Lull, James. 1990. *Inside Family Viewing: Ethnographic Research on Television's Audiences*. London: Routledge.
Maier, Carmen Daniel. 2009. "Visual Evaluation in Film Trailers." *Visual Communication* 8 (2): 159–180. https://doi.org/10.1177/1470357209102112.
Maliangkaij, Roald. 2013. "There Is No Amen in Shaman: Traditional Music Preservation and Christianity in South Korea." *Asian Music* 45 (1): 77–97.
McBride, Richard D. II. 2006. "What Is the Ancient Korean Religion?" *Acta Koreana* 9 (2) 1–30.
———. 2008. *Domesticating the Dharma: Buddhist Cults and the Hwaŏm Synthesis in Silla Korea*. Honolulu: University of Hawaii Press.
McLuhan, Marshall, 1964. *Understanding Media: The Extensions of Man*. New York: McGraw-Hill.
Meyrowitz, Joshua. 1998. "Multiple Media Literacies." *Journal of Communication* 48 (1): 96–108. https://doi.org/10.1111/j.1460-2466.1998.tb02740.x.
———. 1994. "Medium Theory." In *Communication Theory Today*, edited by David Crowley and David Mitchell, 50–77. Palo Alto, CA: Stanford University.
Mickler, Michael L. 2009. "Jumong: A Window into Korean and Unification Culture." *Journal of Unification Studies* 10:51–72.

Miller, Daniel. 2003. "Could the Internet Defetishise Commodity?" *Environment and Planning D: Society and Space* 21 (3): 359–372. https://doi.org/10.1068/d275t.

Miller, Daniel, and Don Slater. 2000. *The Internet: An Ethnographic Approach.* Oxford: Berg.

Mills, Simon. 2007. *Healing Rhythms: The World of South Korea's East Coast Hereditary Shamans.* Aldershot: Ashgate.

Min, Eungjun, Jinsook Joo, and Han Ju Kwak. 2003. *Korean Film: History, Resistance, and Democratic Imagination.* London: Greenwood.

Mitchell, W. J. T. 2005. *What Do Pictures Want? The Lives and Loves of Images.* Chicago: Chicago University Press.

Mittell, Jason. 2003. "Audiences Talking Genre: Television Talk Shows and Cultural Hierarchies." *Journal of Popular Film and Television* 31 (1): 36–46. https://doi.org/10.1080/01956050309602867

Morgan, David. 2012. *The Embodied Eye: Religious Visual Culture and the Social Life of Feeling.* Berkeley: University of California Press.

Morgan, Robert C. 2010. "Thoughts on Re-performance, Experience, and Archivism." *PAJ: A Journal of Performance and Art* 32 (3): 1–15. https://doi.org/10.1162/PAJJ_a_00002.

Morley, David. 1986. *Family Television: Cultural Power and Domestic Leisure.* London: Comedia.

Mun, Ok-p'yo, ed. 1997. *Han'guk'in ŭi Sobi wa Yŏga Saengwhal* [Consumption and Leisure among Koreans]. Sŏngnam: Academy of Korean Studies

Mystery Reportage: Black Hole 2 [Misŭt'eri rŭp'o pŭllaekhol]. 2012. Television Program. Seoul: tvN.

Na, Misu. 2001. "The Home Computer in Korea, Gender Technology, and the Family." *Feminist Media Studies* 1 (3): 291–306. https://doi.org/10.1080/14680770120088909.

Nason, James. 2000. "'Our Indians': The Unidimensional Indian in the Disembodied Local Past." In *The Changing Presentation of the American Indian: Museums and Native Cultures*, edited by Richard W. West, 29–46. Seattle: University of Washington Press.

Neomudang. 2014. *"Mudang task'ŏm."* http://www.neomudang.com (now discontinued).

Nguyen, Van Huy, and Lan Huong Phan. 2008. "The One-Eyed God at the Vietnam Museum of Ethnology: The Story of a Village Conflict." *Asian Ethnology* 67 (2): 201–218.

Nie, Norman H. 2001. "Sociability, Interpersonal Relations, and the Internet: Reconciling Conflicting Findings." *American Behavioral Science* 45(3): 420–435.

ODE. 2008. "Shaman Ritual at South Korea Burnt Down South Gate." *ITN News.* YouTube video, 0:1:57. http://www.youtube.com/watch?v=ofyRS8RZhJ4.

Ogedei. 2008. "An Authentic Korean Shaman Ritual." *Teach English in Asia* (blog). http://www.teachenglishinasia.net/blogs/ogedei/authentic-korean-shaman-ritual (now discontinued).

O'Neill, Mark. 1996. "Making Histories of Religion." In *Making Histories in Museums*, edited by Gaynor Kavanagh, 188–199. London: Leicester University Press.

Oppenheim, Robert. 2007. "Actor-Network Theory and Anthropology after Science, Technology, and Society." *Anthropological Theory* 7 (4): 471–493. https://doi.org/10.1177/1463499607083430

———. 2008. *Kyongju Things: Assembling Place*. Michigan: University of Michigan Press.

Pai, Hyung-il. 2000. *Constructing "Korean" Origins: A Critical Review of Archeology, Historiography, and Racial Myth in Korea State Formation Theories*. Cambridge, MA: Harvard University Press.

———. 2013. *Heritage Management in Korea and Japan: The Politics of Antiquity and Identity*. Seattle: University of Washington Press.

Paine, Crispin, ed. 2000. *Godly Things: Museums, Objects, and Religion*. London: Leicester University Press.

Pak, Ch'an-gyŏng (Park Chan-kyong). 2011. "P'aranmanjang [Night Fishing]." Vimeo video. https://vimeo.com/11548084.

———. 2014. *Mansin: Ten Thousand Spirits*. Seoul: Ollait P'ikch'yŏsŭ. DVD.

Pak, Ki-bok. 2003. *Yŏngmae: sanja wa chugŭnja ŭi hwahae* [Mudang: Reconciliation between the Living and the Dead]. Korea: KOFIC. DVD.

Pak, Mig-yŏng. 1996. *Han'guk ŭi Musok kwa Ŭmak* [Korea's Shamanism and Music]. Seoul: Sejong Ch'ulp'ansa.

Park, Hiha (Pak Hŭi-a). 2004. "Global Shamanic Healing Arts." http://www.hiahpark.com/.

Pearce, Susan M. 1994. "Objects as Meanings: Or Narrating the Past." In *Interpreting Objects and Collections*, edited by Susan M. Pearce, 19–29. London: Routledge.

Philo, Greg. 1990. *Seeing and Believing: The Influence of Television*. New York: Routledge.

———. 1996. *Media and Mental Distress*. London: Longman.

———. 2001. "Media Effects and the Active Audience." *Sociology Review* 10 (3): 26–29.

Philo, Greg, and David Miller. 2001. *Market Killing: What the Free Market Does and What Social Scientists Can Do about It*. New York: Pearson.

Poole, Janet. 2014. "Late Colonial Modernism and the Desire for Renewal." *Journal of Korean Studies* 19 (1): 179–203.

Robinson, Michael E. 1993. "Enduring Anxieties: Cultural Nationalism and Modern East Asian." In *Cultural Nationalism in East Asia: Representation and*

Identity, edited by Harumi Befu, 167–186. Berkley, CA: Institute of East Asian Studies.

Rosaldo, Renato. 1993. *Culture and Truth: The Making of Social Analysis*. Boston: Beacon Press.

Ruah-Midbar, Mariana. 2006. "The New Age Culture in Israel: A Methodological Introduction and the 'Conceptual Network.'" PhD diss., Bar Ilan University, Ramat Gan, Israel.

Saeji, Cedarbough. 2014. "Creating Regimes of Value through Curation at the National Museum of Korea." *Acta Koreana* 17 (2): 609–637.

Sarfati, Liora. 2010. "Objects of Worship: Material Culture in the Production of Shamanic Rituals in South Korea." PhD diss., Indiana University, Bloomington Indiana.

———. 2014. "New Technologies in Korean Shamanism: Cultural Innovation and Preservation of Tradition." In *Performance Studies in Motion*, edited by Atay Citron, David Zerbib and Sharon Aronson-Lehavi, 233– 245. London: Bloomsbury.

———. 2017. "Urban Development and Vernacular Religious Landscapes in Seoul." In *The Palgrave Handbook of Urban Anthropology*, edited by Italo Pardo, and Giuliana B. Prato, 499–518. Cham: Palgrave Macmillan.

Sarfati, Liora, and Shai Sarfati. 2007. "Korean Shaman—Possession by the Spirit of Changun." YouTube video, 0:5:49. https://www.youtube.com/watch?v=R1Sdc9_mqps.

Satlow, Michael L. 2006. "Defining Judaism: Accounting for 'Religions' in the Study of Religion." *Journal of the American Academy of Religion* 74 (4): 837–860. https://doi.org/10.1093/jaarel/lfl003.

Schechner, Richard. 1981. "Restoration of Behavior." *Studies in Visual Communication* 7 (3): 2–45.

———. 1985. *Between Theatre and Anthropology*. Philadelphia: University of Pennsylvania Press.

Schmid, Andre. 2002. *Korea between Empires, 1895–1919*. New York: Columbia University Press.

Seo, Maria. 2002. *Hanyang Kut: Korean Shaman Ritual Music from Seoul*. New York: Routledge.

Shamanic Journeys in Life [Musok kihaeng salm]. 2011. Television Documentary Series. Seoul: ETN.

Shea, Ann Marie, and Atay Citron. 1982. "The Powwow of the Thunderbird American Indian Dancers." *Drama Review* 26 (2): 73–88.

Shelton, Anthony Alan. 2000. "Museum Ethnography: An Imperial Science." In *Cultural Encounters: Representing "Otherness,"* edited by Elizabeth Hallam, and Brian V. Street, 155– 174. New York: Routledge.

Shields, Rob. 1996. *Cultures of Internet: Virtual Spaces, Real Histories, Living Bodies.* London: Sage.
Shin, Chi-yun, and Julian Stringer, eds. 2005. *New Korean Cinema.* Edinburgh: Edinburgh University Press.
Shin, Jeongsoo. 2012. "The Making of King Peony in Korean Literature: A Reading of 'Admonition for the Flower King.'" *Journal of Korean Studies* 17 (1): 125–152.
Simbirtseva, Tatiana M. 1996. "Queen Min of Korea: Coming to Power." *Transactions of the Royal Asiatic Society* 71:41–57.
Sin, Myŏng-gi. 2001. *Mudang Naeryŏk* [A Shaman's Life Story]. Seoul: Minsogŏn.
———. 2010. *Myŏngsŏng Hwanghu Sinp'il pujok* (Magical Talismans of the Empress). Seoul: Taesŏn.
Sin, Sang-ok. 1963. *Ssal* [Rice]. Korea: Shin Films. DVD.
Šmidchens, Guntis. 1999. "Folklorism Revisited." *Journal of Folklore Research* 36 (1): 51–70.
Smithsonian Institute. 2007. "Korean Film Festival DC 2007 Program." http://www.asia.si.edu/KoreanFilm2007/koreanfilms.htm (now discontinued).
Song, Jesook. 2014. *Living on Your Own: Single Women, Rental Housing, and Postrevolutionary Affect in Contemporary South Korea.* Albany, NY: SUNY Press.
Song, Sun-hee. 1974. "The Koguryo Foundation Myth: An Integrated Analysis." *Asian Folklore Studies* 33 (2): 37–92. doi:10.2307/1177549.
Sorensen, Clark W. 1995. "The Political Message of Folklore in South Korea's Student Demonstrations of the Eighties: An Approach to the Analysis of Political Theatre." Paper presented at the "Fifty Years of Korean Independence" Conference, Seoul. http://faculty.washington.edu/sangok/folklore.pdf.
Sorensen, Henrik Hjort. 1993. "The Attitude of the Japanese Colonial Government Towards Religion in Korea (1910–1919)." *Copenhagen Journal of Asian Studies* 8:49–69.
Sparks, Richard. 1992. *Television and the Drama of Crime: Moral Tales and the Place of Crime in Public Life.* Bristol, PA: Open University Press.
Sponsler, Claire. 2004. *Ritual Imports: Performing Medieval Drama in America.* Ithaca, NY: Cornell University Press.
Stoeltje, Beverly J., and Richard Bauman. 1988. "The Semiotics of Folklore Performances." In *The Semiotic Web 1987*, edited by Thomas A. Sebeok, and Jean Umiker-Sebeok, 586–599. Berlin: Mouton de Gruyter.
Suh, Hye-rim. 2013. "Folk Museum Exhibition Offers Deeper Understanding of Shamanism." *Herald Times*, July 17, 2013. http://www.koreaherald.com/view.php?ud=20130717000631.
Tangherlini, Timothy. 1994. "A Review of the Documentary Film: *An Initiation Kut of a Korean Shaman* by Diana Lee and Laurel Kendall." *Journal of American Folklore* 107 (425): 433–435.

———. 1998. "Shamans, Students, and the State: Politics and the Enactment of Culture in South Korea, 1987–1988." In *Nationalism and the Construction of Korean Identity*, edited by Hyung-il Pai and Timothy Tangherlini, 126–147. Berkeley: University of California Press.

Taylor, Chris. 2006. "The Future Is in South Korea." *CNN Business 2.0 Magazine*, June 14, 2006. http://money.cnn.com/2006/06/08/technology/business2 _futureboy0608/index.htm.

Taylor, Diana. 2016. "Saving the 'Live'? Re-performance and Intangible Cultural Heritage." *Études Anglaises* 69 (2): 149–161.

Thacker, Todd. 2004. "Korea through the Looking Glass: An Exhibition of Japanese Colonial Photographs Reveals Details of Korean Lives, Menacing Biases." *Ohmy News*, April 21, 2004. http://english.ohmynews.com/articleview /article_view.asp?no=163679&rel_no=1 (now discontinued).

Thompson, Kevin J., and Leslie J. Heinberg. 1999. "The Media's Influence on Body Image Disturbance and Eating Disorders: We've Reviled Them, Now Can We Rehabilitate Them?" *Journal of Social Issues* 55 (2): 339–354. https://doi .org/10.1111/0022-4537.00119.

TNmS Media. 2011. "Rating of the Drama *49 Days*." http://www.tnms.tv/rating /default.asp (now discontinued).

TNmS Media. 2012. "Rating for *The Moon Embracing the Sun*." http://www.tnms .tv/report/report_view.asp?g_idx=4043&gotopage=1 (now discontinued).

Traditional Performing Arts Festival. 2007. "Festival Program." Seoul: Ministry of Culture and Tourism.

Turkle, Sherry. 1995. *Life on the Screen: Identity in the Age of the Internet*. London: Simon & Schuster.

Turner, Victor. (1967) 1972. *The Forest of Symbols: Aspects of Ndembu Ritual*. Ithaca, NY: Cornell University Press.

———. (1969) 1977. *The Ritual Process: Structure and Anti-structure*. Ithaca, NY: Cornell University Press.

———. (1982) 1992. *From Ritual to Theatre: The Human Seriousness of Play*. New York: Paj.

US Department of State. 2008. "International Religious Freedom Report 2008." https://2001-2009.state.gov/g/drl/rls/irf/2008/108411.htm.

Van Deusen, Kira. 2004. *Singing Story, Healing Drum: Shamans and Storytellers of Turkic Siberia*. Montreal: McGill-Queen's University Press.

Van Zile, Judy. 1998. "Movement in Shamanic Context: An Inquiry." In *Korean Shamanism Revivals, Survivals, and Change*, edited by Keith Howard, 153–186. Seoul: Seoul Press.

Vlastos, Stephen, ed. 1998. *Mirror of Modernity: Invented Traditions in Modern Japan*. Berkeley: University of California.

Vogel, Ezra F. 1991. *The Four Little Dragons: The Spread of Industrialization in East Asia*. Cambridge, MA: Harvard University Press.

Walraven, Boudewijn. 1994. *Songs of the Shaman: The Ritual Chants of the Korean Mudang*. London: Kegan Paul International.

———. 1998. "Interpretations and Reinterpretations of Popular Religion in the Last Decades of the Chosŏn Dynasty." In *Korean Shamanism Revivals, Survivals, and Change*, edited by Keith Howard, 55–72. Seoul: Seoul Press.

Why? [Wai kunggŭmhan iyagi]. 2009–present. Television Program. Seoul: SBS.

Yang, Jongsung (Chong-sŭng). 1994. "Folklore and Cultural Politics in Korea: Intangible Cultural Properties and Living National Treasures." PhD diss., Indiana University, Bloomington Indiana.

———. 2001. "Mudang Kwimul Yŏn'gu: 'Samgukyusa' ŭi Sam Puinkwa Mudang ŭi Kŏul, K'al, Pangul ŭl Chungsimŭro" [A Study of Shamanic Spiritual Objects Focused on the Shaman's Mirror, Sword, Bell, and Shambuin in "Samgukyusa"]. *Senghwal Munmul Yŏn'gu* [Research of Daily Life Objects] 2:54–67.

———. 2003. "Hwanghae-do Kut" [Shamanic Ritual of Hwanghe Region]. In *Han'guk ŭi Kut* [Shamanic Rituals of Korea], edited by Hyo-gil Ha, 31–95. Seoul: Minsogŏn.

———. 2004a. "Kangsinmu Sesŭpmu Yuhyŏngrone Ttarŭn Musokyŏngu Kŏmt'o" [A Discourse of Korean Shamanism Studies Examining Possessed Shamans and Hereditary Shamans]. *Hamguk Musokhak* [Korean Shamanism] 8:9–34.

———. 2004b. "Korean Cultural Property Protection Law with Regard to Korean Intangible Heritage." *Museum International* 56 (1–2): 180–188. https://doi.org/10.1111/j.1350-0775.2004.00473.x.

———. 2005. *Gut (kut)* [Shamanic Ritual]. Seoul: Preservation Society of Shamanic Ritual of General Choi Young (Ch'oe Yŏng).

Yecies, Brian, and Aegyung Shim. 2015. *The Changing Face of Korean Cinema: 1960 to 2015*. New York: Routledge.

Yi, Bu-yŏng (Rhi, Bou-yong). 1986. "Han'guk Sŏlhwae Nat'anan Ch'iryoja Wonhyŏngsang: Son'nimkut Mugarul Chungsimŭro" [Some Aspects of the Healer Archetype in Korean Shaman'S Songs of Sonnim, Gods of Smallpox]. *Sinsŏng Yŏngu* [Research of Spirits and Gods] 1 (1): 5–27.

Yi, Ch'ang-jae. 2006. *Sai-esŏ* [Between]. Korea: EnterOne. DVD.

Yi, Cheong-yeong. 1983. "Shamanistic Thought and Traditional Korean Homes." In *Korean Folklore: the Korean National Commission for UNESCO*, 193–210. Seoul: Sisayongsa.

Yi, Chin-yŏng, dir. 2004–2005. *Wangkkot sŏnnyŏnim* [Lotus Flower Fairy (also called Heaven's Fate)]. Television Series. Written by Im Sŏng-han and Kim Na-hyon. Seoul: MBC.

Yi, Chu-hwan, and Kim Kŭn-hong. 2006-2007. *Chumong* (also called *Prince of Legend*) Television Series. Written by Ch'oi hwan-gyu and Sŏng Hyŏng-su. Seoul: MBC.

Yi, Myong-suk. 2004. "Sŏulchiyŏk Muguwi Sinhwa Wiryechŏk Kinŭng Yŏn'gu: Puchae, Pangul, Taesin K'al ŭl Chungsimŭro" [A Study of Mythological and Ritual Functions of Shamanic Equipment Focusing on the Fan, Tiny Bells, and the Sword). *Han'guk Musokhak* [Korean Shamanism) 8:89–110.

Yi, Po-hyŏng. 1982. "Han'guk Musokŭmak" [Korean Shamanic Music). In *Han'guk Musokŭi Chonghapchŏk Koch'al* [A Comprehensive Investigation into Korea's Shamanism), edited by In-hŭi Kim, 208–230. Seoul: Kodae Minjok Munhwa Yŏngusu Ch'ulp'anbu.

Yi Sŭng-yŏn with a Hundred Women [Yi Sŭng-yŏn kwa 100 inŭi yŏja]. 2011–2013. Television Program. Seoul: StoryonTV.

Yi, Tu-hyŏn. 1996. *Han'guk Musok kwa Yŏnhui* [Korean Shamanism and Theatricality]. Seoul: Seoul Taehakkyo Ch'ulp'anbu.

Yi, Tu-yong. 1981. *Pimak* [The Hut]. Korea: Se-kyeong Productions. DVD.

Yi, Yun-t'aek. 2003. *Ogu: A Hilarious Morning*. Korea: Mao Films. DVD.

Yim, Suk-jay (Im Sŏk-jae). 2005. *Muga: The Ritual Songs of Korean Mudangs*, translated by Alan C. Heyman. Fremont, CA: Asian Humanities Press.

Yim, Suk-jay (Im Sŏk-jae), Roger Janelli, and Dawnhee Yim Janelli. 1987. "Korean Religion." In *The Encyclopedia of Religion*, edited by Mircea Eliade, 8:367–376. New York: Macmillan.

Young, Bae. 2004. "Diffusion and Usage Patterns of the Internet in Korea and Japan: A Comparison of Policy and Cultural Factors." *Development and Society* 33 (2): 229–250.

Yun, Kyoim. 2006. "The 2002 World Cup and a Local Festival in Cheju: Global Dreams and the Commodification of Shamanism." *Journal of Korean Studies* 11 (1): 7–39.

———. 2007. "Performing the Sacred: Political Economy and Shamanic Ritual on Cheju Island, South Korea." PhD diss., Indiana University.

———. 2013. "A Rite of Modernization: Money and Morality in Korean National and Local Discourse of Shamanism." Paper presented at "Modernities" seminar, University of Kansas, Lawrence, March 26, 2013.

Yun, Yŏl-su, and Cho Tae-sup. 2004. *Won Hyŏngŭl Ch'atasŏ T'osok Sinang ŭi: Musokhwa* [Searching for the Origins of Folk Religion: Shamanic Paintings]. Seoul: Kahoe Minhwa Pangmulgwan [Gahoe Museum of Folk Paintings].

Zo, Zayong (Cho Cha-yong). 1973. "Shamanism in Korean Painting." *Korea Journal* 13 (6): 48–51.

———. 1978. *Han'guk ŭi Minhwa* [Korean Folk Paintings]. Seoul: Emile Pangmulgwan [Emile Museum].

———. 1980. "Shamanic Art: Cult or Craft?" *Korean Culture* 1 (3): 13–18.

INDEX

Page numbers in italics refer to figures.

Abelmann, Nancy, 137
actor-network theory (ANT theory), 29, 56
Adorno, Theodor, theory of, 156, 157
aesthetics and artistry in musok: film depictions of, 15, 79–80; film directors' appreciation of, 80–81; of mudang performances, 6, 8, 25, 31, 53, 56; qualities comprising, 173. *See also* film, depiction of musok in; museums; television
agency: of female mansin, 18, 91, 160, 164, 178, 179–80; of objects, 22–23, 29, 98. *See also* documentary films; internet; Sin Myŏng-gi; websites, personal
Akamatsu, Chijo, 9
Akiba Takashi, 9
altars: in kut ritual, *3f, 35f,* 41–42; museum displays of, 104; offerings on, 30; preparation of, 32–33
Andong Folk Museum: diorama of kut ritual in, 106–7, *107f;* physical layout and musok exhibit in, 106–8; religious practice in, 124; ritual artifacts in, 108–9
animal sacrifice, 13, 97
Appadurai, Arjun, 4, 97, 108, 178
apprentices, 44, 57n5, 83–84, 86, 89
Association for Study of Korean Spirit Worship, 121

audiences: donations offered by, 45; importance of, 58n8; maintaining interest of, 45; perceived reality through film, 91; ritual set and communication with audiences, 30–31; sources of information about rituals, 53–54. *See also* film, depiction of musok in; internet; staged rituals; television
authenticity of musok traditions: context and assessment of, 27; in mediated representations, 7, 13; mediation and criteria for, 24; public visibility as proof of, 52–53

Baudrillard, Jean, 173
Bauman, Richard, 56
Berlin International Film Festival, 80
Between. See Sai-esŏ
blogs, 90, 164, 173
Boast, Robin, 97, 125
brochures, 53–54, *54f,* 164, 172
Buddhism: in costuming, 46–47; in Korean religious practice, 96, 100, 101, 126n2; and musok practice, 10, *11f,* 101, 135, 170
Buddhist art, 100, 101, 110–11

Ch'ae Chŏng-nye, 85
chaktu knives: injury from, 49; museum displays of, 104; in ritual's climax, 32, 43, 49–51

Chang Chin-su, 122
Chang Sŏn-u (Jang Sunwoo), 66
Cheju Folk Village, 111, 113–14, 113f
ch'ilsŏng (spirit of seven stars of the great dipper), 46–47
Cho Chin-gyu, 92n8
Ch'oe Kil-sŏng, 9, 100
Ch'oe Nam-sŏn, 9
Ch'oe Sun-sil, 166
Ch'oe Yŏng (spirit of a historic general), 21, 22–23, 26, 37, 43, 48, 49, 170
Ch'ŏngdam Posal (Fortune Saloon, 2009, Kim Chin-yŏng), 69–70, 72, 75–76, 78, 85, 140, 152
Chŏng Un-gwŏl, The Moon Embracing the Sun (Haerŭl p'umŭn tal, Sigongsa, novel), 138
Chosŏn era (Joseon era), 40, 104
Christianity: filmic comparison to musok, 72; in practice of religion in Korea, 96, 126n2
Ch'ukje (Festival, 1996, Im Kwŏn-t'aek), 68
Chumong (also Prince of Legend, 2006, Kim Kŭn-hong and Yi Chu-hwan), 138, 139–40, 154n4
Ch'unch'ŏn musok style, 122
cinematic devices: aestheticism of artifacts to communicate spirituality, 88–89; hybridity of visuals and interviews in documentaries, 89; interviews, 89, 90; use of color in documentaries, 86
clientele of mansin: description of fieldwork participants, 14; effect of the internet on diversity of, 157–58; expectations and perceptions about mansin, 52–53; finding a mansin, 16; and mansin's performance skills, 23, 26; in response to documentaries, 90; of Yi Hae-gyŏng, 86. See also internet
Clifford, James, 99
commercialization of musok, 12, 12f, 34, 55
Compaq, 171
Confucians and Confucianism, 33, 96, 126n2
costumes, legitimacy and representation through, 34–35. See also Sŏ Kyŏng-uk
cultural inclusion and exclusion, 2, 96–97, 116, 133. See also curators; museums

cultural paradoxes, 114–15
cultural preservation, 4, 5–6, 17, 79, 82, 176, 177. See also Ministry of Culture and Tourism; National Folk Museum; national heritage; television
cultural processes: dynamism of, 158; and technological innovation, 60–61
Cultural Properties Preservation Office, 173
curators: on artifacts in displays, 108–9; bias of, 95, 96, 106, 112; as mediators between mansin and the public, 125; as teachers, 105; values of artifacts compared to practitioner values, 110

dances in kut, descriptions of: spinning dances, 37–38, 40–41, 44, 48; warrior dances, 45, 46
Daoism, 96
democratization movement, 66, 177
devination: in Cheju Folk Village, 114; in film, 69–70; Koreans' experience with, 150; televised session of, 151
docudrama genre, 86
documentary films: about mansin, 81–82, 83–86; as intentional interpretations, 90–91; musok as cultural heritage in, 82; narrating reality and spirituality in, 87–92; popularity of, 60; rendered in black and white for museums, 106
documentary series (television), 137, 138, 140–43, 150–51
documentation of kut, 55
drumming and music in kut, 37–38, 48
DVDs, technological features of, 91

Eliade, Mircea, 9
empathy, cultivation of, 134, 141, 143, 151
European Union Chamber of Commerce convention, 143
Exorcist (Eksosisŭt'ŭ, 2008–2009, tvN), 2, 138, 142–43, 148–49
experimental films, 80

Facebook, 164, 165, 168, 169
Fasken Martineau Best Feature Film, 83

INDEX

film, depiction of musok in: and audiovisual qualities of kut, 15–16; as beautiful and efficacious, 72; beginnings of, 176; as dark and scary, 71–72; historical perspective of, 57, 62, 177; as important but threatened tradition, 66–68; juxtapositions in, 63; Korean audiences' experience with, 152; nature of reperformances, 18; as obstacle to modernization, 63–66; producers' interest in kut, 15–16; as prosperous tradition, 68–71; shifting images of mansin, 179; and shift in musok's image, 60–63; and social acceptance of mudang, 62, 74–77, 178; and survival of musok, 62, 77–79; as thrilling and funny, 73–74, 79; visual textures in, 62. *See also* documentary films; experimental films

film, medium of: and depiction of reality, 90, 91; growth of industry in South Korea, 59; as rich medium for musok, 59–60; as vehicle of cultural processes, 79–81

film industry: and added features of DVDs, 91; censorship and control in, 62; growth of, 62–63; melodrama in, 137; popularity of, 59, 62, 83, 92n3; ticket sales for musok films, 69, 83

flag divinations, 38–39, 58n8

Fortune Saloon. See *Ch'ŏngdam Posal*

49 Days (*49 il*, 2011, Cho Yŏnggwang and Pak Yong-sun), 137, 145–46

Gangster Shaman. See *Paksu Kŏndal*

gender roles: female dominance in musok, 60, 64–66; in Korean folklore, 147; male dominance of technology domain, 164; as mansin, 76, 124, 137, 180; in premodern Korea, 101; reversal in musok, 76–77, 137, 142

Gerbner, George, 134, 153

Glassie, Henry, 16, 29, 101

Global Shamanic Healing Arts website, 167, 167f

god paintings *(musindo)*: attitudes of practitioners toward, 109; catalog of, *12f*; communication of musok knowledge through, 30; description of use in kut, 21, 22, 22f; increased appreciation of, 115; in museums, 101–2, 108–9, 115, 116, 122

Goffman, Erving, 36

Golden Bear Award, 80

Gum (1986, Chang Sŏn-u), 67

Hallyu. See Korean Wave

hanbok (traditional clothing), ritual use of, 33, 34

historical dramas, 138–40

Hobsbawm, Eric, *Invented Tradition*, 27–28

Hwanghae-do ritual style, 23, 30, 34, 86, 87, 116, 122

I Am All for Life (*Taech'an insaeng*, 2013, TV Chosŏn), 138, 147, 155n9

identification through television, 132, 144–48

identity, construction of, 6, 134, 136–37, 168

identity politics: and legitimization of musok, 99; of museums, 98; in musok practices, 21–22; and musok's endurance, 83

Im Chang-jung, 69

initiation kut *(sin-naerim)*, 1–2, 19n3, 128, 141, 142–43

Initiation of a Korean Shaman (1991, Diane Lee and Laurel Kendall), 93n13

Insight People (*Insait'ŭ p'ip'ŭl*, 2011, Insite TV), 138

intangible cultural management, 5, 76, 165, 176

internet: anonymity of audiences and musok community in, 157–58, 172; ethnography of, 157; fears about, 174; and global reach of mansin, 167–68; interactivity of, 156–57; as mediator of culture and status, 179; as medium of empowerment, 166; shifting agency in evolving social order, 171–75; virtual musok community on, 169–70

internet representations: exoticism in, 169; and face-to-face interactions, 172, 173; mainstreaming by, 153–54; of musok in nonreligious contexts, 170–71; professionalism of musok in, 163–65; social awareness of musok through, 165–69, 178; as tool to promote musok, 174, 177; viewer interaction in, 18

Interview Documentary (*Int'ŏpyu tak'yument'ari inyongwi kkŭn*, 2011, Living TV), 138
Iŏdo (*Iŏ Island*, 1977, Kim Ki-yŏng), 65–66, 71, 74

James, William, 145
Janelli, Roger, 59, 162, 176
Japanese colonialism, musok under, 24, 102
Japanese Government-General, 8
Japanese scholars and Korean folklore, 5, 102–3, 176
Job Stories (*Sŭt'ori chapsŭ*, 2011–2013, TV Chosŏn), 138, 149–50, 151–52, 155n10

Kalff, Andrea, 89, 144
kangsin-mu (god-chosen practitioners), 83, 84, 87, 89, 107
Kendall, Laurel, 19n3, 27, 105, 162
Kim Chin-yŏng, 92n6
Kim Chongho, 27, 81, 114–15
Kim Chŏng-jung, 154n6
Kim Chong-min, 24, 25
Kim Ki-yŏng, 92n4
Kim Kŭm-hwa (mansin), 74, 81, 84–85, 89, 144, 165, 167
Kim Nam-sun (mansin), 3f, 57n6, 129, 139, 168
Kim Seong-nae, 177
Kim Tŏk-su (Kim Duk-soo), 36–37, 38, 39–40
Kim Tong-ni, 64–65, 80–81
Kim Un-a, 169
Kim Un-sun (mansin), 118
Koguryŏ, 100
Kŏndŭlbawi Museum, 102
Korean Air feature film, 70
Korean Christians, 10, 135
Korean culture, globalization of, 177
Korean folklore: and democratization movement, 66; folk art in, 101; and folklore museums, 126n1, 176; gender roles in, 147; kut and, 25; preservation as national heritage, 4; religious folklore in museums, 100–103; scholarship in, 82

Korean Motion Picture Promotion Corporation, 64
Koreans: consultation with mansin, 3; interest in musok, 177; knowledge about musok and mansin, 4, 129–30, 131–32, 133, 144; progression toward becoming clientele of mansin, 16; view of musok, 128
Korean scholars: attitudes toward mansin, 119, 161–62; attitudes toward private museums, 124; calligraphy and, 162; and online musok activity, 174; research on musok, 176. *See also* scholar-interpreters for kut
Korean Wave (*Hallyu*), 137, 153, 155n11
Korea Traditional Performing Arts Festival: bridging the gap between rituals and audience in, 37; brochures for, 53; government goals for, 24–26; kut as spectacle in, 36; kut rituals as general blessings in, 33; selection of mansin for, 26–27; staging of kut rituals for, 25–26, 27, 29. *See also* World Cup Stadium Park, 2007 staged ritual in
Kŭmsŏngdang, shrine of, 122, 127n14
kut: about, 3–4; adaptations for mediated performances, 13; for business problems, 26; Chinogi kut, 144; *Ch'oe Yŏng changgun tang* kut ritual (*see* Ch'oe Yŏng; World Cup Stadium Park, 2007 staged ritual in); commemoration kut, 170; costs associated with, 45–46; dangerous acts in, 49; healing rituals, 26, 67, 104, 105f; importance of audiences to, 57n8; importance of face-to-face rituals, 179; inclusion of Western elements in, 167; initiation kut, 93n13, 128, 141, 142–43; multiplicity of interpretations of, 25; offerings of donations, 45; Ogu kut ritual, 68; paintings, banners, and decorations for, 21; performances in museums, 111; sensuality of experience of, 15; Ssitkim kut, 144; success and material aspects of, 30, 49; Tari kut, 144. *See also* documentary films; film, depiction of musok in; mansin; museums; private museums; ritual objects; staged rituals; television

Kwisini Sanda (*Ghost House*, 2004, Kim Sang-jin), 78
Kyŏngsan Museum, 127n6
Kyŏngsin yŏnhap (the Federation of Associations for the Respect of Beliefs), 160, 164, 175n1

labeling in museums, 107–8, 114, 125
Latour, Bruno, 12, 29, 56
Leakage of the Sky's Mysteries (*Ch'ŏn'gi nusŏl*, 2013–present, MBN), 138
Lee Jung Young, 100
Lemish, Dafna, 60–61
LG Electronics, 171
Lotte World Folk Museum (Seoul), 111–12, 112f
Lotus Flower Fairy (*Wangkkot sŏnnyŏnim*, 2004–2005, Yi Chin-yŏng): about, 137–38, 146; compared to other kut rituals, 130; cultivation of audience empathy through, 132; description of reperformance in, 128

madang (outdoor performance space), preparation of, 32–33. *See also* World Cup Stadium Park, 2007 staged ritual in
madanggŭk, 66
Makhmalbaf, Mohsen, 79
Man on the Edge. *See Paksu Kŏndal*
mansin: assumptions about, 146, 162; as authoritative figures, 32; core mission of, 16–17, 68, 135; education and sophistication of, 159–60, 161–63; factors in selecting, 6; increased agency of, 18, 91, 178, 179–80; international reach of, 167–68; meaning and use of term, 1, 7, 8, 9, 19n1, 90; as mediators between foreigners and Korean culture, 169; overview of activities of, 2; performance of dangerous acts, 48–49; personal lives of, 85, 147, 149; relationships with scholars, 119–20, 121, 162, 163–64; relationships with technology providers, 164; and religious efficacy of rituals, 24, 25, 28; reputation and popularity of, 27, 36, 39–40, 163; role in kut ritual, 20; shared norms of, 169–70; supernatural protection of, 46; use of costumes in rituals, 35. *See also* clientele of mansin; documentary films; Kim Kŭmhwa; Kim Nam-sun; kut; marginalization of mudang; Pak Min-jung; Park Hiah; professionalism; public image and visibility; Sin Myŏng-gi; Sŏ Kyŏng-uk; spirits and the supernatural; websites, personal; Yi Hae-gyŏng
Mansin (*Mansin: Ten Thousand Spirits*, 2014, Pak Ch'an-gyŏng), 80, 83, 84–85, 86, 89, 91
marginalization of mudang: contemporary disdain for mansin, 119; liminality and social standing of, 74–77; marriageability of, 146; persecution of, 67, 176; stigma against, 28, 85, 119, 150, 151, 166, 171; through history, 6, 18, 84, 101, 124. *See also* public image and visibility of mansin
materiality of rituals, 22, 56, 178. *See also* ritual objects
McBride, Richard, 100–101, 154n5
McHugh, Kathleen, 137
McLuhan, Marshall, 60–61, 131
media: the medium as the message, 60–62, 174; power of, 152; research on, 15
media celebrity, culture of, 69
mediated representations of musok: agency, gender, and objects in, 179; and audience interaction, 16–17; audiences' reception of, 157; compared to actual rituals, 156; modes of, 5; scholarship on, 7, 10. *See also* film, depiction of musok in; internet representations; museums; staged rituals; television
mediation: of contemporary life, 156; definition of, 4; in museums, 97; and social processes, 178–79; spiritual mediation in musok, 52–53; use of term, 63. *See also* ritual objects
mediation assemblage theory, 4
melodramas, scripted, 137–38, 150–51
Mickler, Michael, 154n4
Miller, Daniel, 134, 136
Min (Queen), 25, 163

Ministry of Culture and Tourism: sponsorship of staged rituals, 21–22, 27; support for staged rituals, 24–26
minjung (people's) movement, 5, 6, 62, 63, 66, 102, 176–77
minsok (folklore), 103. *See also* Korean folklore
Mittell, Jason, 151
modernization: and education of mansin, 161–63; filmic depictions of tension with tradition, 64–66, 71
The Moon Embracing the Sun (*Haerŭl p'umŭn tal*, 2012, Kim To-hun and Yi Song-jun), 138, 140
Morley, David, 152
Motion Picture Law, 64
mudang (folk religion practitioners): hereditary traditions of, 8; as symbols of antimodernization in films, 64–66; term of, 90; types of, 7, 107–8. *See also* mansin; paksu
Mudang Dat Com (portal), 169
muga (kut chants), 37, 57n3
Munyŏdo (*A Shaman's Story*, 1972, Ch'oi Ha-won), 64, 71
Munyŏdo (*The Shaman Sorceress*, 2018, An Chae-hun), 80
Museum of Shamanism, 122–23, 123f
museums: beginnings of musok displays in, 176; conflict in planning musok exhibits, 95; culture mediated through, 91; cultures' participation in exhibits, 125; diverse messages about musok in, 124–26; educational purposes of, 95; exhibits of musok art, 101–2; fusion of styles in, 109; images of musok created by, 98–99; impact of staff changes on exhibits in, 106; labeling in, 105, 107–8, 114; musok as extinct tradition in, 101, 102, 104–6; musok as living tradition in, 111–15; recontextualizaton of musok in exhibit planning, 103–11; and religious traditions in, 96–97, 100–103; representation of musok in, 18; role of musok in society established by, 178; sacred objects in,

109; social power of, 98; staged kut rituals at, 56; value of objects to, 109–10. *See also* Andong Folk Museum; Cheju Folk Village; curators; Lotte World Folk Museum; National Folk Museum; private museums
music and drumming: as characteristic of kut, 3, 15, 33, 106–7, 107f, 112, 129, 178, 186; folk music, 85, 86, 147, 176; samulnori, 37, 57n2; and sensual, emotional impact on audiences, 30; spiritual mediation through, 16, 33, 52. *See also* World Cup Stadium Park, 2007 staged ritual in
musindo. *See* god paintings
musogin (people who practice musok professionally), 8, 149
musok: as acceptable practice, 144, 154n8, 179; communities for practitioners of, 169–70; contemporary knowledge about, 163; continuity in tradition of, 29; contribution to society, 80; definition, origin, and use of term, 6–7, 8, 9; diversity of reactions to, 16; forbidden practices in, 139; form and décor in, 42; interest in during the 1950s and 1960s, 59; internationalization of, 144, 153; as living tradition, 101, 102, 108; media and Koreans' exposure to, 55; mediation in, 51–57; power of supernatural entities in, 42; reconciliation through, 67–68; shift in image of, 60–63, 69, 71, 74, 177; socio-cultural changes and, 17; success and the supernatural in, 90; survival of, 77–79; traditions in, 8, 83–84; as vernacular religion, 4, 13, 18–19, 96, 126n2. *See also* film, depiction of musok in; internet representations; kut; mansin; museums; national heritage; staged rituals; television
musok artisans, 110
musok goods stores, 34, 162, 163, 179
musok portals, 164, 169–70, 174
Mystery Reportage: Black Hole 2 (*Misŭt'eri rŭp'o pŭllaekhol*, 2012, tvN), 138

INDEX

Namdaemun gate, ritual at, 138, 144, 154n7
Nason, James, 106
National Folk Museum (Seoul): curator at, 121; donations to, 122; musok collections of, 127n8; performance at, 118; physical layout and musok exhibits in, 104, 105f, 126n5; preservation work in, 110; recontextualization of artifacts in, 103–6; religious practice in, 124
national heritage: education about, 94–95; musok and shamanic rituals as, 5–6, 176; patriotic meanings in, 25; preservation through television, 133; South Korean promotion of, 27, 173–74; staged ritual as performance of, 25–27, 56. See also cultural preservation; Korea Traditional Performing Arts Festival
national identity: kut shrine ritual as event of, 41–42; longing for, 83; musok as part of, 79, 125; objects and creation of, 98; staged ritual and, 21–22
National Museum of Korea, 24, 94, 100, 101
national shamans (narat mudang), 25
New Community Movement, 5, 64, 77–78, 176
New Korean Cinema, 62
news (televised), 137, 143–44
New York Asian Film Festival, 83
Night Fishing. See P'aranmanjang

objects: affective power of, 97; interaction with observers, 97–98. See also actor-network theory; ritual objects
Ogu: A Hilarious Morning (2003, Yi Yun-t'aek), 68, 72, 73, 74–75, 78, 85
Olympic Games in 1988, 6
O'Neill, Mark, 96
Onyang Folk Museum, 101
Oppenheim, Robert, 30, 98

Paekche, 100
Paek Chong-hak, 148
Paine, Crispin, 95, 96
Pak Ch'an-gyŏng, 92n10
Pak Ch'an-uk, 92n10

Pak Chi-yun, 155n10
Pak Chŏng-hŭi (Park Chung-hee), 62, 64
Pak Min-jung, 86
paksu: definition of, 19n1; description of performance of, 1; documentary TV show on, 141–42; in film (see Paksu Kŏndal); representation of, 18–19; use of nicknames by, 172; use of term in book, 9. See also Yi Sŏng-jae; Yi To-ryŏng
Paksu Kŏndal (Man on the Edge, 2013, Cho Chin-gyu), 70, 73–74, 75f, 76–77, 78, 85, 140, 152
Pak Ye-jin, 69
Pang Su-dŏk (mansin), 118
Pang Ŭn-mi, 147
P'aranmanjang (Night Fishing, 2011, Pak Ch'an-uk and Pak Ch'an-gyŏng), 80
Park Gun-hye, 166
Park Hiah (Pak Hŭi-a, mansin), 167
Philo, Greg, 133, 134, 136
photographers, 39, 40
Pimak (The Hut, 1981, Yi Tu-yong), 67
posal (bodhisattva), 10
possession: connotations of, 19n3; mansin's feelings during, 145; performance of, 40; signs of true possession, 50; spirit possession sickness, 7, 19n3. See also sinbyŏng
premodern Korea: experience of rituals in, 3–4; folklore museums and nostalgia for, 102; gender roles in, 101, 126n3; historical film and dramas about, 163; kut rituals in the home in, 159; practice of religion in, 33, 96; promotion of musok and mansin in, 40; spiritual practitioners in, 15, 23, 163; spiritual role of women in, 52; television program about, 138
private museums: about, 115; access to, 115–16; of Dr. Yang, 120–23; government investment in, 124; kut rituals at, 122, 123; of Mansin Sin, 116–20
private rituals: characteristics of, 26; flag divinations in, 39; learning about practices in, 53; preponderance of, 52; problem focus of, 33; settings for, 30

professionalism: in internet representations, 163–65; of kut teams, 34, 54–55; of mansin, 151; of mudang, 90; in museum representations, 94; in musok, 52–54, 160; national organizations and, 177; use of internet as marker of, 163; in websites, 170–71

public image and visibility of mansin: advertising and, 16; as celebrities, 9–10, 69, 131; government support and, 12; internet presence and, 157–58, 159, 164; and legitimization of authenticity, 52–53; mansin's agency in, 91; mansin's control of, 90, 158, 173; as people, 179; shift in, 69, 71, 82, 153, 177; television and improvement of, 129, 131, 132; through musok portals, 169–70. See also Kim Kŭm-hwa; Sŏ Kyŏng-uk; television; Yi Hae-gyŏng

Pul-ŭi ttal (*Daughter of the Flames* 1983, Im Kwŏn-t'aek), 67, 72, 74, 78

Ranger, Terence, *Invented Tradition*, 27–28
reality shows, 137
recontextualization in museums, 98–99, 103–11
religious messages: in contemporary film, 74; in museums, 95–96, 123–24; ritual efficacy and, 24, 25, 28
reperformances: as distinguished from face-to-face practice, 13; legitimacy of, 26; in television and film, 2, 128, 152; World Cup Stadium 2007 staged ritual as, 25
ritual objects: affective presence of, 12; as art, 101–2; artistic *versus* religious collections, 110–11; brass bells, 30, 89–90, 145; braziers, 47; in the context of ANT theory, 56; cymbals, 43–44, 47; flowers and other offerings, 33; food and drink, 32, 33, 42; importance of, 42, 103; to mediate presence of spirits, 20, 29–33; oscillation in holiness of, 108; portrayal in documentaries, 88; power and agency revealed by, 22; role in spiritual mediation, 52; silk flags, 32–33; and success of the rituals, 30; talismans (pujŏk), 161–62, 171; transference to museums, 122–23; use of knives in trances, 40, 45; wands, 44. See also *chaktu* knives; god paintings
romantic dramas, 138–39
Rosaldo, Renato, 130

Sai-esŏ (*Between*, 2006, Yi Ch'ang-jae), 81, 83–89, 91, 92n11, 143, 164
samulnori (song of four instruments), 37, 57n2. See also Kim Tŏk-su
sansin (mountain god), 34, 34f, 43
Schechner, Richard, 6
scholar-interpreters for kut, 41–48, 53. See also Yang Chong-sŭng
Seoul, musok practice in, 14
Seoul magazine on Yi Hae-gyŏng, 86
sesŭp-mu (hereditary shamans), 7–8, 83–84, 85–86, 107
shaman, origin of term, 8–9
shamanic initiation, 1–2, 28. See also initiation kut
Shamanic Journeys in Life (*Musok kihaeng salm*, 2011, ETN), 138
shamanism: Korean history of, 100–103; practices in, 9; Siberian shamanism, 9, 122, 127n13; use of term, 8. See also mudang (folk religion practitioners); musok
Shiamanijum Myujium, 8
Shields, Rob, 173
shrines: home shrines, 11f, 64, 117, 118; Kŭmsŏngdang, 122, 127n14; musok rental shrines, 179
Silla, 100–101
sinbyŏng: depiction in film, 67; use of term, 19n3. See also spirit possession sickness
Sin'gung (*The Divine Bow*, 1979, Im Kwŏn-t'aek), 72
Sin Myŏng-gi (mansin): as collector, curator, and informant, 124; education of, 161–62; on Facebook page, 169, 179; home shrine and kut rituals of, 118; on museum displays, 109; museum of, 116–18, 116–17f, 120; reputation of, 118–20; use of internet to counter bias, 161, 165, 166; website of, 167–68

social media, 55, 129, 164. *See also* blogs; Facebook; Twitter
social mobility, 162
Sŏ Kyŏng-uk (mansin): brochure of, 54f; connections with generals' spirits, 46; costume collection of, 34–35, 34f, 42, 46–47; in film, 80; initiation as a mansin, 28–29; internet presence of, 165; Kim Tŏk-su and, 39, 57n4; musok goods and agency of, 22–23; official recognition for, 21–22; Performing Arts Festival's selection of, 26–27; personal charm and performative abilities of, 23, 37–38; preparation for the staged ritual, 31–32; professional appearance of, 23, 32, 35; on religious importance of kut rituals, 25; reputation and success of, 23; shrine of, 11f; as traditional art performer, 170; website of, 166, 172. *See also* Ch'oe Yŏng; World Cup Stadium Park, 2007 staged ritual in
Sŏndŏk (Queen), 101
South Korea: celebrity culture in, 9, 174; description of fieldwork in, 13–14; digital technologies in, 159, 160; divination services in, 39; educational system in, 161–62; generational differences in perceptions of musok and mansin, 82–83, 177–78; globalization of cultural identity, 6; governmental support of the arts and culture, 24, 25–26, 124; government support of the arts and culture, 114; history told through story of a mansin, 86; mainstreaming of musok in, 153; mass media in, 59; melodrama in, 137; museum visiting in, 99; nation building and modernization in, 2, 63–64; nostalgia for idealized past, 102; political and cultural changes in, 162; practice and influence of musok in, 9–10; prosperity of, 68–69; religious tolerance in, 96, 126n2; symbols of longevity and peace in, 46; technological mediation of human interaction in, 52, 157; television depictions of, 146. *See also* cultural preservation; gender roles; Korean folklore; national heritage; premodern Korea

Sparks, Richard, 134
spatiality, audience response and, 30
spirit possession sickness, 7, 19n3, 172. *See also* possession; sinbyŏng
spirits and the supernatural: beliefs about, 28–29; communication with, 29–30, 90, 101, 135–36, 142; in films, 76; importance of satisfying desires of, 49–50; modern culture and interventions with, 137; representation and communication in rituals, 20; rituals attending to, 42; signs of generosity toward, 44; supernatural affliction, 67. *See also* kut; mansin; musok; possession
spiritual consultations: cost of, 164; as face-to-face events, 173; focus on client in, 147; Koreans participating in, 14, 16; in mansin practice, 23; portrayal on television, 141; virtual, 173. *See also* clientele of mansin
spiritual healing, 31, 67, 166
Sponsler, Clair, 28
Ssal (*Rice*, 1963, Sin Sang-ok), 64, 74
staged rituals: audience size for, 86; authenticity and care of appearances in, 33–36; communication with audiences in, 36–41, 48; humor and enjoyment in, 41; and the Korea Traditional Performing Arts Festival, 24–29; mediating agents for, 20; nature of, 17–18; preparation and appearances in, 33–36; professionals contributing to, 23; religious efficacy in, 56; the ritual set in, 29–33; scholar-interpreters for, 41–48; separation between performers and audience in, 54–55; spatiality and, 30; success through mediation, 51–56; technological mediation in, 52; use of dangerous practices in, 48–51. *See also* ritual objects; World Cup Stadium Park, 2007 staged ritual in
The Story of Ch'unhyang, 147

talk shows, 137, 138, 147, 151, 152
Tangherlini, Timothy, 82

technological determinism, 60–62
technology: change in documentary films from, 91; for mass audiences, 24, 55; as requirement for mansin's practice, 159
technology of the self, 36
televised reperformances: and audiovisual qualities of kut, 15–16; description of, 1–2; and musok's religious message, 135; of rituals, 153
television: construction of culture through, 130; creating bridges between mansin and audiences through, 150–54; depiction of musok on, 178; early documentaries aired on, 82, 177; effect on society, 133–37; genres of musok representation on, 130, 137–38; intertextuality with film and folk performances, 152; juxtaposition of the ancient and modern in, 132–33; mansin as professionals on, 148–50; and mansin's effect on society, 132; options in representation of musok, 125; portrayal of mansin's internal experience on, 131–32, 144–48; portrayal of what mansin do, 131, 138–44; shifting image of mansin through, 179
Toronto Reel Asian International Film Festival, 83
tradition: as interpretive process, 16, 28, 29; as living tradition, 27, 59, 174; objects signifying, 33
trance: possession trance, 38, 43–48; state of consciousness in, 140; use of term, 9
24-Hour Observation Camera (*Kwanch'al k'amera 24 sigan*, 2012–2017, Channel A), 138, 141–42, 154n6
Twitter, 165

websites, personal: compared to institutional websites, 174; for educational purposes, 166–67; first mansin websites, 177; links to TV programs on, 129; mansin's widespread use of, 165; nonreligious representations on, 170–71; promotion through, 164–65; selection for analysis, 159

Why? (*Wai kunggŭmhan iyagi*, 2009–present, SBS), 138, 140–41
World Cup Stadium Park, 2007 staged ritual in: altar preparation, 32–33; blessings in, 37, 41, 44, 45, 46, 48, 50–51; chaktu blade dance in, 49–50; costuming and makeup, 34–36; effect of the weather on, 32, 50–51; kut shrine ritual, 41–43; music and dancing in, 37–38, 40–45, 46, 47–48, 49–51; opening and flag divination, 36–40; possession trances in, 40–41, 43–48; preparing the stage for, 20–22, 23; sharing charms and talismans with audience in, 50–51; sound technology and rehearsal, 31–32; video footage of, 57n6. *See also* Korea Traditional Performing Arts Festival

Yang Chong-sŭng (Jongsung), 26; articles by, 170; on availability of musindo, 102; as collector, curator, and informant, 124; costume collection of, 127n12; efforts to save shrine, 127n14; interpretation and promotion of kut, 41, 42–43, 47, 49; private museum of, 8, 121–22, 123f; as scholar and performer, 120–21; selection of mansin for staged rituals, 26–27
Yi Ch'ang-jae, 86, 93n15
Yi Chŏng-jun, 65
Yi Hae-gyŏng (mansin), 81, 84, 86, 88, 90, 164–65, 168, 173
Yim Chi-yong, 144
Yim Song-hun, 155n10
Yi Sŏng-jae (paksu), 145
Yi Sŭng-man (Syngman Rhee), 59
Yi Sŭng-yŏn with a Hundred Women (*Yi Sŭng-yŏn kwa 100 inŭi yŏja*, 2011–2013, StoryonTV), 138, 151
Yi To-ryŏng, 151
Yi Ŭn-jŏng, 1
Yŏngmae: sanja wa chugŭnja ŭi hwahae (*Mudang: Reconciliation between the Living and the Dead*, 2003, Pak Ki-bok), 83–84, 85–86, 91

LIORA SARFATI is Senior Lecturer (Associate Professor) in the Department of East Asian Studies at the University of Tel Aviv.

www.ingramcontent.com/pod-product-compliance
Lightning Source LLC
Chambersburg PA
CBHW031812220426
43662CB00007B/617